CALLING THE SHOTS

Calling the Shots

THE PRESIDENT,

EXECUTIVE ORDERS,

AND

PUBLIC POLICY

DANIEL P. GITTERMAN

BROOKINGS INSTITUTION PRESS
Washington, D.C.

The Brookings Institution is a private nonprofit organization devoted to research, education, and publication on important issues of domestic and foreign policy. Its principal purpose is to bring the highest quality independent research and analysis to bear on current and emerging policy problems. Interpretations or conclusions in Brookings publications should be understood to be solely those of the authors.

Library of Congress Cataloging-in-Publication data
Names: Gitterman, Daniel Paul, author.
Title: Calling the shots : the president, executive orders, and public policy / Daniel P. Gitterman.
Description: Washington, D.C. : Brookings Institution Press, [2017] | Includes bibliographical references and index.
Identifiers: LCCN 2016045228 (print) | LCCN 2016055740 (ebook) | ISBN 9780815729020 (pbk. : alk. paper) | ISBN 9780815729037 (ebook)
Subjects: LCSH: Executive orders—United States. | Executive power—United States. | Political planning—United States.
Classification: LCC KF5053 .G58 2017 (print) | LCC KF5053 (ebook) | DDC 320.60973—dc23
LC record available at https://lccn.loc.gov/2016045228

9 8 7 6 5 4 3 2 1

Typeset in Sabon
Composition by Westchester Publishing Services

Contents

Acknowledgments

It takes a small village to write a book. I wish to acknowledge and express my gratitude to many people who supported *Calling the Shots*. I must begin where it began, with Professor Terry Moe of Stanford University who encouraged me to write about the power of the purchaser and whose own research has proved invaluable in shaping this book. I am also delighted to share my sincere thanks to Robert Flaherty, Valentina Kalk, William Finan, Janet Walker, and Elliott Beard, and Carrie Engel at Brookings Institution Press for all their support during the publication process. This is my second book with Brookings Press, and they are a wonderful group of collaborative professionals. I wish I could acknowledge more directly the unsung heroes of this work—in this case, the two anonymous reviewers who provided very helpful comments during the peer review process. Let me also acknowledge Melody Negron, from Westchester Publishing Services, and Katherine Scott for letting no detail go unaddressed. I would also like to express my gratitude to John Wiley and Sons for granting permission for me to use parts of Gitterman, D. P. (2013), "The American Presidency and the Power of the Purchaser." *Pres Stud Q*, 43: 225–51, doi:10.1111/psq.12022. I want to extend thanks to my North Carolina–based team—Nora Augustine, Lucie House, and J. Peder Zane for their first-rate copyedit, research, and editorial assistance. Peder, a journalist by training, has a special gift for helping an academic communicate to a general audience. I would not have been able to complete this book without the professional and financial support of Senior Associate Dean Jonathan Hartlyn and Professor Ashu Handa of the UNC College of Arts and Sciences, the Robert Watson Winston Faculty Development Fund, and the Thomas Willis Lambeth Distinguished Chair Fund. I wish to express my appreciation to my parents, Alex and Naomi Gitterman, for their support and encouragement. Most important, my deepest appreciation to my wife, Amy, and our children, Max and Claire, who tolerated that long stretch where my laptop was my companion and now have welcomed me back into our wonderful family. It is your time to call the shots.

ONE

The President, Executive Orders and Memos, and Public Policy

President Barack Obama faced another year of fiercely divided government as he convened his first cabinet meeting of 2014, on January 14. Republicans in Congress, who had a very different ideological vision for the nation, were publicly committed to blocking his agenda at every turn. His public support a year after his landslide reelection was shaky; Democrats would go on to lose nine seats and control of the Senate in the November 2014 election. Obama was frustrated but unbowed on that January morning. The prospects for major legislation may have been beyond dim, but the president told his cabinet he had plenty of authority to act, stating: "We are not just going to be waiting for legislation in order to make sure that we're providing Americans the kind of help that they need . . . I've got a pen . . . and I can use that pen to sign executive orders and take executive actions and administrative actions."[1]

Obama delivered on that promise, using the unilateral authority of the chief executive to advance his policy priorities.[2] For example, after Congress refused to raise the nation's $7.25-per-hour federal minimum wage, Obama issued an executive order to increase it to $10.10 an hour for all employees of federal contractors and subcontractors.[3] Through this lever of power, Obama pressured Congress to act.

Although executive powers are rooted in the United States Constitution ratified in 1788 and have long been a source of presidential authority and controversy, the Obama presidency can be seen as a coming-out party for them. The concept of unilateral executive power has gained far wider traction in recent years, as Obama has touted its use to achieve political and policy goals that faced dim prospects in Congress and Republicans have used his exercise of such power to attack him.[4] For the first time in history, executive authority was a major campaign issue in 2016. Despite their many disagreements, almost all of the seventeen Republicans who sought their party's presidential nomination repeatedly pledged to undo Obama's executive actions. It is telling that the candidates trusted that their voters cared about this issue. The irony is that the partisan and gridlocked state of contemporary politics makes it almost certain that Obama's very different successor, Donald J. Trump, will overturn many of his "illegal" and "unilateral" orders while issuing a slew of his own.

Presidents are central actors in our politics, and one cannot understand the making of American public policy without taking their executive power into account. The United States Constitution lays out three hypothetically equal branches of government—the executive, the legislative, and the judicial—but over the years, the president, the chief executive, has emerged as the dominant political and administrative force at the federal level. The president is advantaged by his position as the chief executive, which gives him the right to make unilateral decisions about the federal bureaucracy and policy.[5] In response to this increasing use of unilateral executive power, we need to think more deeply about the historical patterns that have informed the use of this authority and its implications for contemporary public policy.

Calling the Shots documents a fundamental phenomenon of modern American politics and policy: the rapid increase in the size and scope of the federal government and the ways it has transformed—and been transformed by—the presidency. This study broadens our understanding of presidential power in two ways. First, it focuses on the president's role as a chief executive officer (CEO) of the federal government and his or her motivations to achieve political goals. The president is, in fact, the CEO of the largest and most powerful enterprise in the United States: the federal bureaucracy. Although Trump is the first actual CEO elected in modern times, his new job is exponentially larger than the one that made him a billionaire.

The president stands at the apex of a hierarchy of executive departments and independent agencies, boards, commissions, and committees that purchase billions of dollars' worth of goods and services. In 2015 the health-care domain included almost 500 agencies and subagencies, $447 billion in federal purchases of goods and services, and at least 2.8 million federal employees—plus millions more who work for private companies that contract or subcontract with the federal government. Moreover, the federal government expends almost $1.03 trillion on health programs. Second, *Calling the Shots* broadens our understanding of presidential power by exploring specific ways presidents use their authority as CEO to achieve their political and policy goals. Specifically, it identifies and conceptualizes three vast but underappreciated forms of executive power: the power of the purchaser, the power of the employer, and the power of the payer.

The president deploys the "power of the purchaser" to exercise direct political control over federal procurement rules and to influence policy in a range of areas somewhat related to the "economical and efficient" purchase of goods and services.[6] Since the depression of the 1930s, presidents with increasing frequency attempted to use the economic leverage provided by its purchasing power to achieve social and economic policy objectives. As the CEO of the federal bureaucracy (and the largest purchaser of goods and services) in the United States, the president can dictate additional contractual terms and conditions on which the federal government will do business with the private sector.[7]

The president uses the "power of the employer" to exert political control over federal personnel (civil services) rules and to advance human resource policies. As the CEO of the largest employer in the country, presidents can dictate additional terms and conditions of employment between the federal government and its civilian employees. As just one example, when Obama was facing congressional opposition to paid family and medical leave reform, he granted all federal employees six weeks of paid leave after the birth or adoption of a child, plus the right to six additional weeks of unpaid leave. His memo also applied to federal employees caring for ailing family members.[8]

Exercising the related "power of the ethical employer," the president can also delimit additional principles of ethical conduct and dictate how federal (executive branch) civilian employees and high-ranking political appointees should conduct themselves. Executive orders and memos on ethics rules are shaped by both electoral and partisan politics. Historically, ethics reforms have been associated with a pattern of rare—but highly visible—scandals that have ignited public appeals for new laws or rules from the incoming chief executive. According to a recent work on ethics laws, ethics policies are shaped by politics. "There are the cumulative responses to decades of political position and calculations of political opportunity and advantage: presidents who participated in the construction of ethics policies always did so with an eye on their public appearance—often more than on their practical impacts."[9] For example, Obama issued an executive order requiring every appointee in each federal agency to sign an ethics pledge. Obama's pledge attempted to fulfill a campaign promise to reform politics and create a more ethical federal government.[10] Although the executive order laid out tough rules on how executive branch appointees are to conduct themselves, it also allowed the president to grant waivers.

Finally, the president uses the "power of the payer" to exercise political control over federal health payment rules and to influence the coverage, cost, and quality of health-care services in the United States. As the CEO of the largest payer of bills for health care in the United States, presidents can amend federal health-related program rules and dictate additional terms and conditions of payment to private sector health insurers and providers. For example, in an effort to shape private health market reform, George W. Bush required federal agencies that oversee large health-care programs to gather information about the quality and price of health care and to share that information with one another and with federal program beneficiaries.

Presidents use their executive power in all three areas to accomplish many of the same goals they seek through legislation: to obtain political (electoral) advantage, to deliver benefits to key political constituencies and organized groups, and to influence the behavior and policies of private sector actors. Unlike legislation, which usually involves compromise and coalition building, by using executive orders and memos presidents can act on their own. In simple terms, the president calls the shots. The authority to issue executive orders and memos and impose rules without legislative approval in order to control and influence this vast public organization is more important for presidential power, for the administrative presidency, and for policymaking than political scientists and policy scholars have previously recognized.

THE PRESIDENT AS CEO OF THE FEDERAL BUREAUCRACY

"Chief executives are distinct principals of power," Tom C. W. Lin argues, "and thus, should be understood distinctly." This is true of corporate leaders as well as presidents, who, as the CEOs of the federal bureaucracy, manage a very large political organization that influences the lives of everyday Americans. Indeed, the president is held politically accountable for the functioning of the federal government as is no other type of official or elected representative. As a result, says Lin, "Almost uniquely in government, presidents act on a vision, purpose, and power to shape governance." This framework can help decipher "a long-standing paradigm of power and offer[s] an understanding of executive governance." In comparing presidents and private sector CEOs, Lin concludes that all CEOs operate within larger organizations "that are susceptible to being perilously captured by powerful chief executives."[11]

Throughout history, says Lin, "Presidents of both parties have acted like unitary executives, accumulating power (or attempting to do so), term after term, administration after administration—a constant practice in the winds of political and policy change." As Justice Robert Jackson observed in 1952, "Executive power has the advantage of concentration in a single head in whose choice the whole nation has a part, making him the focus of public hopes and expectations." This unitary vision of the presidency has persisted since the founding of our republic; as the presidency has changed hands and parties over two centuries, it has frequently grown in power. In terms of the politics and policy, says Lin, "Unitary presidents can, in theory, efficiently and effectively execute a national objective without dilutions and distractions from other governing stakeholders." Unilateral action is a vital tool because it can serve as a "bulwark" against political actors with "disparate, competing, and conflicting interests."[12]

Kevin Stack explains that in contrast to legislation or agency rulemaking, for the president there are almost no legally enforceable procedural requirements that he or she must satisfy before issuing (or repealing) an executive order or other presidential directive. In sum, executive orders "rid the president of the need to assemble majorities in both houses of Congress, or to wait through administrative processes, such as notice-and-comment rulemaking, to initiate policy."[13] This explains both their political appeal to the president and the resentment they fuel in the president's rivals.

Presidents are motivated to seek power: to exercise political control over the federal bureaucracy and to exert political influence over public policy. Unilateral action allows them accomplish this, and to act as first movers on a wide array of issues. Indeed, presidents hope that Congress will follow their lead by affirming their executive orders and memos through formal statutes and extending the rules to cover the private sector. Presidents also attempt to expand (or add additional terms and conditions) after prior congressional action, a strategy of "Now that you gave me some, I'll ask for more." Even though executive actions bypass the procedural restraints imposed on other forms of lawmaking, they have a direct public policy impact by implicating individual rights and the structure of the federal government, thereby affecting millions of people.[14] Regardless of partisan affiliation and across time, presidents use these executive powers—of the purchaser, of the employer, and payer—to shape the policy agenda, to secure political control over agency rulemaking, and to exercise political influence over public policy.

Political scientists have shown interest in unilateral action by presidents, creating a growing body of scholarship on the subject.[15] Much of this work occurred during and after Bill Clinton's second term, as the Democratic president turned to executive orders in areas where he couldn't find common ground with a Republican Congress. This work includes three books that focused on the president's unilateral powers as well as a number of articles on executive orders.[16] More recently, and for the first time, edited volumes on the topic of the presidency are devoting chapters to unilateral powers.[17]

Calling the Shots draws upon and contributes to multiple streams of recent scholarship to help illuminate a narrative of the modern president as CEO of the federal bureaucracy.

First, in terms of theory, it affirms that the president is advantaged by his position as the chief executive, which gives him the right to make unilateral decisions about structure and policy.[18] Terry M. Moe and William G. Howell argue that an important aspect of presidential power derives its strength and resilience from the ambiguity of the formal structure. Presidents have "strong incentives to push this ambiguity relentlessly—yet strategically and with moderation—to expand their own powers," and "for reasons rooted in the nature of their institutions, neither Congress nor the courts are likely to stop them."[19]

The president is a unitary political actor in the electoral context. The one individual chosen by a national electorate, he serves as the singular epitome of political vision and electoral mandate.[20] Moe and Howell highlight a key institutional basis for presidential power: the president's formal capacity to take unilateral action and thus make law on his own. As a result, presidents can make policy, shifting the existing status quo without the explicit consent of Congress. Presidents' powers of unilateral action are a force in American politics because they are not specified in the formal structure of government.[21] The struggle is most apparent in the making of public policy, say Moe and Howell, "where elected officials from both institutions wrangle endlessly over the goals and details of public policy."[22] *Calling the Shots* shows how presidents have long used these particular unilateral powers to shape the national agenda, secure control over agencies, influence policy, and shift the prevailing status quo.

Second, in terms of the powers illuminated here, *Calling the Shots* affirms that the president uses executive orders and presidential memoranda as strategic political and policy tools.[23] Historically, presidents issue executive orders in an effort to "plant a flag in a particular policy sphere, to reorganize the structure of the executive branch, or to provide policy leadership when Congress is stuck in the mud." Executive orders vary greatly in their forms, sources of authority, purposes, and interactions with congressional statute—to name just a few variables. Modern presidents have often been criticized for overstepping their authority, yet executive policy actions stemming from presidential executive orders and memorandum are rarely illegal. Each executive order, like every act of governance, is part of the larger narrative of a particular presidency.[24]

Formally, presidential power is derived from Article II of the U.S. Constitution, which states that "the executive power shall be vested in a President of the United States," that "the President shall be Commander in Chief of the Army and Navy of the United States," and that the president "shall take Care that the Laws be faithfully executed." Informally, and in addition, the power to issue policy-related executive orders and presidential memorandum has been recognized by the courts and Congress as an implied constitutional and statutory authority.[25]

Indeed, political scientists recognize executive orders as an important policy tool, despite the constraints of legal and political considerations.[26] Executive orders are not defined in the Constitution, and there are no specific provisions in the Constitution authorizing the president to issue them.[27] They are, instead, directives that draw on the president's unique legal authority to require or authorize some action within the federal government, based on the statutory authority to enforce it, an act of Congress, or the Constitution.[28] These executive orders are used to direct federal agencies and officials in their execution of congressionally established policies. In many instances they have been used to guide federal agencies in directions contrary to legislative intent.[29] In fact, Phillip Cooper calls presidential memoranda "executive orders by another name," and a court ruling has implied that memoranda are legally interchangeable with executive orders. There is no public policy area in which the president operates that has not been shaped by the use of executive orders and memorandums.[30]

Executive orders are accepted by Congress, the courts, and the public as an inherent element of presidential power.[31] Presidents use them to act boldly and unilaterally to effect changes in public policy. They also use them for political ends, as they are "effective devices for paying political debts, demonstrating action for a constituency, responding to adversaries, or sending political signals—real [and] symbolic."[32]

In recent years there has been renewed interest in the opportunities and constraints of executive power and the proper use and possible abuse of executive orders and other presidential directives.[33] Recent evidence suggests a president's use of executive orders increases when he is facing a hostile Congress.[34] New evidence also confirms that the use of presidential memoranda has surged as the issuance of executive orders has decreased, indicating that unilateralism is not declining but rather that the means of such executive action may be shifting.[35]

Third, *Calling the Shots* affirms insights from the literature on the administrative presidency: presidents' efforts to gain political control over administrative agencies and exercise political influence over the implementation of policy. In "The Politicized Presidency," Terry Moe claims that modern presidents politicize administrative arrangements and centralize policy-related concerns in the White House.[36] This regularized and predictable behavior is "driven by institutional incentives and opportunities shared by nearly all presidents and rationally acted upon in their pursuit of strong leadership and bureaucratic control."[37] Moe argues that the "heightening of politicization and centralization during the Reagan White House was the more recent expression of this historical process." Ronald Reagan, more than any modern president before him, moved to take hold of the federal government, especially after his landslide reelection in 1984: "At the heart of his approach was the politicization of administrative arrangements and centralization of policy-related concerns in the White House."[38]

Elena Kagan—a former Harvard law professor, deputy assistant to the president for domestic policy under Clinton, and an Obama appointee to the U.S. Supreme Court—has argued:

The history of the American administrative state is the history of competition among different entities for control of its policies. All three branches of government—the President, Congress, and Judiciary— have participated in this competition, but at different times one or another has come to the fore. In this time, that (political) institution is the Presidency. We live today in an era of presidential administration.[39]

Subsequently, Kagan argued that presidential control of administration expanded dramatically under Clinton, transforming the regulatory activity of federal agencies into an extension of the president's own policy and political agenda. Faced with a Republican Congress after the 1994 midterm election and eager to make progress on policy issues, Clinton "turned to the [federal] bureaucracy to achieve, to the extent it could, the full panoply of his domestic policy goals." Whether the policy area was health care, welfare reform, tobacco or gun control, Kagan notes that a "self-conscious and central object of the White House was to devise, direct, and/or finally announce administrative actions (regulations, guidance, enforcement strategies, and reports) to showcase and advance presidential policies." With this executive action strategy, Clinton "in large measure set the administrative agenda for key agencies, heavily influencing what they would (or would not) spend time on and what they would (or would not) generate as regulatory product."[40] Administrative agencies, through the rulemaking process, in turn make important policy decisions that have broader electoral and political relevance. Thus, presidents have a unique ability to gain political control over administrative agencies and secure political influence over policy.[41]

Calling the Shots argues that exercise of these executive powers is a regular and predictable behavior across time. Throughout American political history, as new presidents came to the White House, they learned from their predecessors how effective, and tenuous, these orders can be. The paradox is that the authority to take unilateral action also makes each president "free to revoke, modify, or supersede his own executive orders or those issued by any predecessor." This occurs most commonly when orders are issued to assert political control over the agency rulemaking process. In the decades of increasing political polarization, *Calling the Shots* illuminates how presidents have issued these executive orders and memos on an ever widening range of controversial and contested policy areas.[42]

THE SIZE AND SCOPE OF EXECUTIVE POWER

The rapid increase in the size and scope of the federal government has transformed the presidency, and been transformed by it. The president, as the CEO of a very large organization, the federal bureaucracy, relies by need and instinct on the three types of authority explored in this book to make the federal government succeed as a tool of policy and politics. First, presidents

FIGURE 1-1. **Federal Procurement Spending by Fiscal Year, 1984–2014**

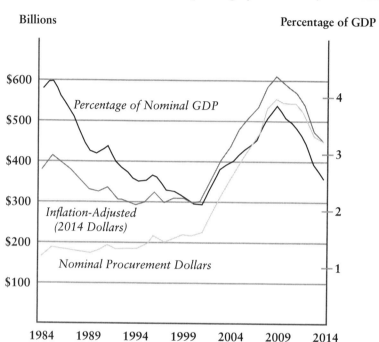

Source: National Contract Management Association and Bloomberg Government, *Annual Review of Government Contracting, 2015 Edition* (http://www.ncmahq.org/docs/default-source/default-document-library /pdfs/exec15---ncma-annual-review-of-government-contracting-2015 -edition).

rely on the power of the purchaser to exercise political control over federal procurement rules and to influence policy in a range of areas often unrelated to the efficient purchase of goods and services. Presidents use this executive power to shape the federal government's procurement policies and to influence Congress to extend the same policies or protections to all private sector workers and workplaces. Presidents exercise this extraordinary power of the purchaser because the federal government is the world's largest buyer of goods and services.[43] This power has grown since the dawn of the twentieth century, when the federal government's expenditures for goods and services were still relatively small. However, as figure 1-1 shows, by fiscal year (FY) 1984, federal procurement spending had reached $168.1 billion annually and a high of 4.2 percent of gross domestic product (GDP). Total federal procurement spending continued to grow to $218.2 billion in FY 2000, and then to a high of $555 billion by FY 2009, before falling to $447 billion in FY 2013. Although spending on federal procurement declined as a percentage of GDP between 1984 and 2014, from 4.2 to 2.6 percent of GDP, the president's purchasing power remains unrivaled.[44]

The president enjoys further power as purchaser-in-chief because approximately one-quarter of all U.S. workers are employed by federally funded contractors and subcontractors.[45] Thus, the president influences substantial segments of the U.S. private sector workforce.

The private sector companies that contract with the federal government and must conform to its rules are not small players: the top fifty federal contractors in 2014 accounted for nearly half of all federal procurement dollars in 2014, the top twenty-five contractors accounted for nearly 37 percent, and the top ten contractors accounted for over 25 percent (see table 1-1). The top five contractors in terms of dollar value of their contracts were Lockheed Martin, Boeing, General Dynamics, Raytheon, and Northrop Grumman. Moreover, as a result of "flow down" requirements commonly written into contracts between the federal government and a prime contractor, a subcontractor may be bound by provisions identical to those of the principal contractor. Unlike a negotiated agreement between two private individuals, the president's contract provisions are an executive order with the force of law.[46] For more than half a century, presidents have exercised political control over procurement and exerted influence on private sector behavior, affirming executive power to set terms and conditions beyond a traditional proprietary contractual relationship.

Second, as the chief executive officer of the largest employer in the county, the president can dictate terms of the employment relationship between the federal government and its civilian employees and conditions of the workplace. Presidents have signed orders and memos to demonstrate their political support for federal benefits and workplace rights that are popular among federal and private sector employees. Presidents use executive power to shape the federal government's human resource policies and to influence Congress to extend these same or similar protections to private sector workers and workplaces.

With approximately 2.7 million civilian employees, the U.S. government is the largest employer in the country. For reference, Wal-Mart has 2.2 million employees worldwide.[47] Thus, the president is the employer-in-chief. Federal government jobs are located in every state and large metropolitan area; the federal government also has employees in 140 foreign countries.

TABLE 1-1. Top Fifty U.S. Federal Contractors: Actions, Dollar Value
of Contracts, and Percent of Total Federal Procurement Spending, 2014

Rank	Contractor	Actions*	Value of contracts	Percentage of all federal procurement spending
1	Lockheed Martin Corporation	20,846	$32,229,878,000	7.26
2	Boeing Company	13,232	$19,610,963,000	4.41
3	General Dynamics Corporation	17,490	$15,350,243,000	3.46
4	Raytheon Company	10,945	$12,619,848,000	2.84
5	Northrop Grumman Corporation	11,575	$10,262,979,000	2.31
6	McKesson Corporation	82,969	$6,210,505,000	1.40
7	United Technologies Corporation	9,251	$5,976,712,000	1.35
8	L-3 Communications HOLDINGS Inc.	9,432	$5,789,742,000	1.30
9	BAE Systems PLC	9,868	$4,988,057,000	1.12
10	Huntington Ingalls Industries Inc.	3,230	$4,660,530,000	1.05
11	SAIC Inc.	15,820	$4,582,006,000	1.03
12	Bechtel Group Inc.	186	$4,100,624,000	0.92
13	Humana Inc.	395	$3,585,484,000	0.81
14	Booz Allen Hamilton Holding	7,683	$3,473,952,000	0.78
15	URS Corporation	4,052	$3,382,566,000	0.76
16	Unitedhealth Group Inc.	413	$3,251,012,000	0.73
17	Health Net Inc.	40,544	$3,225,829,000	0.73
18	Computer Sciences Corporation	3,887	$2,946,646,000	0.66
19	United Launch Alliance L.L.C.	134	$2,883,772,000	0.65
20	Hewlett-Packard Company	43,583	$2,850,849,000	0.64
21	Exelis Inc.	2,894	$2,480,824,000	0.56
22	General Electric Company	7,405	$2,453,989,000	0.55
23	Los Alamos National Security LLC	45	$2,294,192,000	0.52
24	Battelle Memorial Institute Inc.	2,052	$2,132,000,000	0.48
25	CACI International Inc.	4,054	$2,126,134,000	0.48
26	Bell Boeing Joint Project Office	2,859	$2,018,972,000	0.45
27	Honeywell International Inc.	6,928	$1,947,245,000	0.44
28	Harris Corporation	3,637	$1,915,631,000	0.43
29	California Institute of Technology	2,074	$1,726,581,000	0.39
30	General Atomic Technologies	779	$1,633,991,000	0.37
31	Royal Dutch Shell PLC	528	$1,615,435,000	0.36
32	Textron Inc.	3,839	$1,598,600,000	0.36
33	Jacobs Engineering Group Inc.	3,763	$1,531,014,000	0.34
34	Amerisourcebergen Corporation	69,045	$1,509,492,000	0.34

Rank	Contractor	Actions*	Value of contracts	Percentage of all federal procurement spending
35	Lawrence Livermore National Security LLC	95	$1,458,140,000	0.33
36	Merck & Co. Inc.	127	$1,386,416,000	0.31
37	Alliant Techsystems Inc.	2,265	$1,383,319,000	0.31
38	UT-Battelle LLC	55	$1,347,424,000	0.30
39	International Business Machines	2,034	$1,343,253,000	0.30
40	Mitre Corporation	834	$1,309,499,000	0.29
41	Cardinal Health Inc.	95,253	$1,269,944,000	0.29
42	Consolidated Nuclear Security LLC	17	$1,265,644,000	0.28
43	Fluor Corporation	584	$1,222,204,000	0.28
44	State of California	1,882	$1,215,695,000	0.27
45	Accenture Public Limited Company	1,153	$1,141,656,000	0.26
46	CH2M Hill Companies Ltd.	1,765	$1,122,790,000	0.25
47	Deloitte LLP	2,083	$1,122,449,000	0.25
48	Babcock & Wilcox Company	269	$1,114,307,000	0.25
49	Sterling Parent Inc.	2,261	$1,109,090,000	0.25
50	B. L. Harbert Holdings LLC	117	$1,087,701,000	0.24
TOTAL		526,231	$198,865,828,000	44.8

Source: Federal Procurement Data System, fpds.gov (https://www.fpds.gov/fpdsng_cms /index.php/en/reports/62-top-100-contractors-report3.html).
*Actions means any oral or written action that results in the purchase, rent, or lease of supplies or equipment, services, or construction using appropriated dollars over the micro-purchase threshold, or modifications to these actions regardless of dollar value.

The federal government employs approximately 2.7 million civilian government employees plus 1.5 million uniform military employees (see figure 1-2a). These employees constitute almost 3 percent of the employed workforce in the United States (see figure 1-2b).[48]

The executive branch of the federal government is also the largest employer of veterans in the United States—one of every four federal employees is a veteran.[49]

The president can influence the ethical behavior of a large number of federal employees.[50] The president also uses the power of the employer-in-chief

FIGURE I-2A. **Total Federal Personnel, 1981–2014**

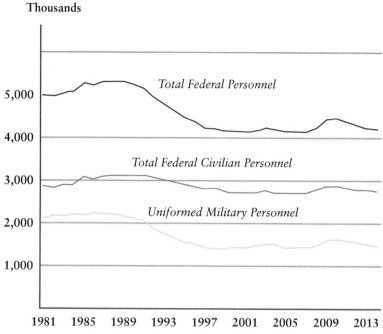

Thousands

Total Federal Personnel

Total Federal Civilian Personnel

Uniformed Military Personnel

5,000

4,000

3,000

2,000

1,000

1981   1985   1989   1993   1997   2001   2005   2009   2013

Sources: Federal employment data from U.S. Office of Personnel Management, "Historical Federal Workforce Tables: Executive Branch Civilian Employment since 1940" (https://www.opm.gov/policy-data -oversight/data-analysis-documentation/federal-employment-reports /historical-tables/executive-branch-civilian-employment-since-1940/); U.S. Office of Personnel Management, "Historical Federal Workforce Tables: Total Government Employment since 1962" (https://www.opm.gov/policy -data-oversight/data-analysis-documentation/federal-employment-reports /historical-tables/total-government-employment-since-1962/).

Note: Total federal personnel is the sum of all civilian personnel and uniformed military personnel.

to exert political control over federal ethics rules and dictate how executive branch employees should conduct themselves ethically—that is, the president can formulate additional ethics rules and standards of ethical conduct that all employees should know and follow. Overall, approximately 3,000 Obama appointees were required to comply with new ethics

FIGURE I-2B. **Total Federal Civilian Employees and Uniform Military Employees, 1981–2014**

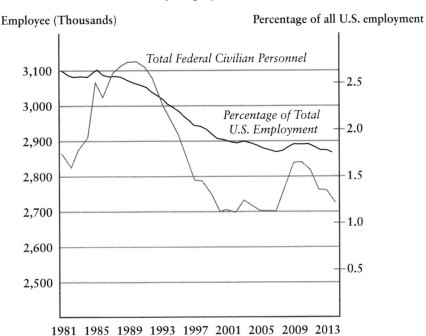

Employee (Thousands)   Percentage of all U.S. employment

Sources: Federal employment data from U.S. Office of Personnel Management, "Historical Federal Workforce Tables: Total Government Employment since 1962" (https://www.opm.gov/policy-data-oversight/data-analysis-documentation/federal-employment-reports/historical-tables/total-government-employment-since-1962); civilian employment data from the Bureau of Labor Statistics, "Occupational Employment Statistics" (http://www.bls.gov/oes).

Note: Federal civilian personnel include all federal (full-time permanent, temporary, part-time, and intermittent) employees of the legislative, judicial, and executive branches, including postal employees. Percentage of total refers to federal civilian personnel as a percentage of total U.S. employment.

FIGURE 1-3. **Number of Obama Appointees Required to Sign an Ethics Pledge and Types of Appointment, 2009–14**

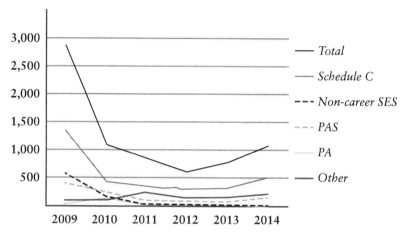

Number of appointments

— *Total*

— *Schedule C*

--- *Non-career SES*

--- *PAS*

— *PA*

— *Other*

Source: U.S. Office of Government Ethics, "Annual Report on Executive Order 13490 (Ethics Pledge)," May 26, 2016 (https://www.oge.gov/web /oge.nsf/Annual+Report+on+Executive%20Order%2013490%20 (Ethics%20Pledge)).

Note: Schedule C refers to noncompetitive appointments to accepted service positions graded GS-15 and below; non-career SES refers to political appointees at the senior executive level; PAS refers to presidentially appointed, Senate-confirmed employees; PA refers to presidentially appointed employees (without Senate confirmation requirement); other refers to all other categories of non-career position appointments.

requirements. Figure 1-3 shows the number of full-time, non-career appointees who were required to sign the ethics pledge between 2009 and 2015.[51]

Third, as the CEO of the largest payer for health care services in the United States, presidents exercise political control over federal health program rules to influence the coverage, cost, and quality of health care in the United States. Three programs—Medicare, Medicaid, and the Child Health Insurance Program—currently account for almost one-third of U.S. health expenditures.[52] The Department of Defense and Department of Veterans Affairs also make up a significant part of federal health program outlays.

FIGURE 1-4A. **Federal Health Program Outlays, 1962–2017**

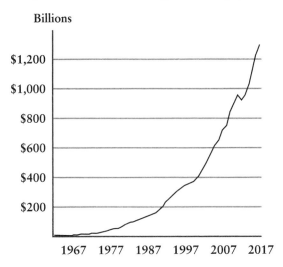

Source: Office of Management and Budget, Table 15.1—Total Outlays for Health Programs: 1962–2021 (https://www.whitehouse.gov/omb/budget /Historicals).

Other significant outlays are made for the largest employer-based group payer of health insurance, the Federal Employees Health Benefits Plan, which contracts with health insurance companies that offer a complete line of medical services.

Figure 1-4a shows the growth in federal health program outlays and figure 1-4b highlights the distribution of the federal government's two largest health program outlays in FY 2015: $630 billion for Medicare, $350 billion for Medicaid, and $159 billion for all other federal health expenditures.[53]

Medicare has consistently accounted for a large portion of total federal health spending, representing 45 percent of total health-care outlays in 1967 and 55 percent of total health-care outlays in 2015. The share of total outlays for Medicaid has been smaller than for Medicare, but Medicaid spending has roughly doubled as a share of total health outlays from 16 percent in 1968 and to 31 percent in 2015.

Figure 1-4c shows the distribution of non-Medicare and non-Medicaid federal health outlays in FY 2015: $48 billion on the Defense Health Program, $61 billion on Veterans Health Care, $48 billion on FEHBP, and $29 billion on health insurance assistance.

FIGURE I-4B. **Federal Outlays for Health Care,
by Program, 1962–2017**

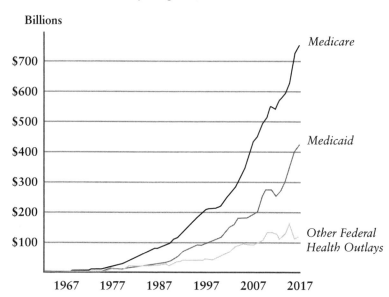

Source: Office of Management and Budget, Table 15.1—Total Outlays for Health Programs: 1962–2021 (https://www.whitehouse.gov/omb/budget /Historicals).

Note: Other federal health outlays include Veterans Health Care, health insurance assistance, Federal Employees Health Benefits Program, and other health expenditures.

Total federal health outlays have increased substantially since the 1960s, from approximately 0.4 percent of GDP in 1962 to 6.7 percent of GDP in 2017, most of it due to increased spending on Medicaid and Medicare (see figure 1-4d).[54]

Approximately 19.1 million additional people are expected to enroll in Medicare over the next eleven years as more baby boomers, those born between 1946 and 1964, become eligible for Medicare. For the period from 2014 to 2024, health spending is projected to rise at an average rate of 5.8 percent per year.[55] As these numbers grow, the president will accrue increased power in the health-care market as the payer-in-chief.

FIGURE I-4C. **Other Federal Health Outlays,
by Program, 1962–2017**

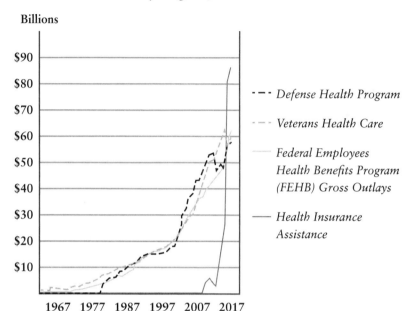

Source: Office of Management and Budget, Table 15.1—Total Outlays for Health Programs: 1962–2021 (https://www.whitehouse.gov/omb/budget /Historicals).

Note: Health insurance assistance includes health insurance tax credit and programs like the Pre-Existing Condition Insurance Plan Program.

CALLING THE SHOTS AND THE CHAPTERS TO COME

The chapters that follow identify how presidents use the power of the purchaser, employer, and payer to gain control over federal agency rulemaking and to influence a wide range of public policy in the United States. Chapter 2 focuses on how presidents from Franklin D. Roosevelt to George W. Bush have used the power of the purchaser-in-chief to influence policy in a range of areas. Chapter 3 examines how Obama used the power of the purchaser-in-chief to influence policy in a range of old and new areas.

Chapter 4 analyzes how presidents use the power of the employer-in-chief to exert political influence over the federal employment system—the

FIGURE 1-4D. **Outlays by the Federal Government for Health Programs, as Percentage of GDP, 1962–2017**

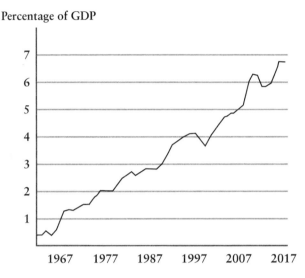

Percentage of GDP

Source: Office of Management and Budget, Table 15.1—Total Outlays for Health Programs: 1962–2021 (https://www.whitehouse.gov/omb/budget /Historicals).

federal civil service—in a range of policy areas. Chapter 5 explains how presidents use the power of the employer-in-chief to dictate the federal government's equal employment opportunity policy and to create a diverse and inclusive federal workplace. Chapter 6 illuminates how Obama used executive power to dictate the employment relationship between the federal government and its employees in a range of existing and new areas.

Chapter 7 describes how modern presidents, particularly since the Watergate scandal, have used the power of the ethical employer to delimit the basic principles of ethical conduct for federal employees and political appointees. Typically, new ethical guidelines introduced by a president have stayed in effect unless they were lifted or modified by a subsequent president. The chapter also highlights Obama's recent efforts to shape the principles of ethical conduct for federal employees and political appointees.

Chapter 8 explores how presidents have used the power of the payer-in-chief to exercise political control over federal health program payment rules and to influence the coverage, cost, and quality of health care, not just for federal health program beneficiaries and enrollees but also for the broader privately insured population. This chapter also explains how presidents, as the largest premium payer of employer-sponsored health insurance, have used the power of the payer to dictate the terms and conditions of private sector health plan options available for federal employees.

Chapter 9 concludes *Calling the Shots* by offering an assessment both of how other political actors respond to these unilateral actions and of the impact of these executive orders and presidential memos on public policy. Presidents rely on these executive powers to shift the policy status quo, and the final chapter assesses how voters, Congress, the courts, presidential successors, and the private sector or market respond to such shifts. Although executive orders and memos bypass the procedural restraints imposed on other forms of lawmaking, they implicate individual rights and the structure of the federal government, thereby affecting millions of people.[56]

Many citizens will almost certainly continue to measure and remember presidents on the basis of their major domestic legislative accomplishments and foreign policy challenges. But, given the deep differences between the parties and the continuing expansion in the size and scope of government, executive power will increasingly define the institutional presidency as presidents continue to use executive authority to further their agendas. In contrast to legislation or agency regulation, there are almost no legally enforceable procedural requirements that the president must satisfy before issuing or repealing an executive order or memo. That, no doubt, is central to their appeal to presidents.[57]

It is ironic that the gridlocked nature of current hyper-partisan American politics has created the context in which the next president, whether Republican or Democrat, will be obliged to uncap the presidential pen—whether to undo some of Obama's efforts or to build and expand on them, and to further her or his own policy objectives. As the political scientist Phillip J. Cooper has observed, "Executive orders can be used to do an end-run around Congress. They are quick and easy ways to take action. They can convey a sense of purpose, rally supporters and address dire problems, and they are not easy to challenge—at least while the president who signed them is in office."[58] In sum, the next president can, and will, call the shots.

TWO

The President and the Power of the Purchaser

A s CEO of the federal bureaucracy and the largest purchaser of goods and services in the United States, presidents dictate rules that define how the federal government will conduct business with the private sector—contractors and subcontractors. This rather dry statement obscures the dynamic and transformative role this authority—the power of the purchaser—has played in reshaping the presidency and America.

Presidents have always had a unique managerial role, one that has enabled them to control and influence procurement policymaking.[1] The great growth in the federal government, especially since the beginning of the twentieth century, has made this power of the purchaser one of the most potent weapons presidents have to expand their power and shape policy in areas where Congress has—and has not—acted. Across time and across party, presidents have strategically used this authority to change the behavior of private sector actors, federal contractors and subcontractors, and to channel benefits to key political constituencies.

In this chapter we will look at how presidents have exercised the power of the purchaser through executive orders and memos to shape and further a wide range of issues, including labor-management relations; unemployment, inflation, and poverty reduction; small-business opportunities; compliance with federal tax, labor and employment, environment, antitrust, and consumer protection laws; immigration enforcement; international child labor standards; gun control; and faith-based contracting. The unilateral power of the purchaser also has been the force behind antidiscrimination efforts and equal employment opportunity in all federal purchasing.

Today, these unilateral terms and conditions apply to significant sectors of the U.S. economy and impact approximately 22 percent of all U.S. workers.

We all also see how the courts, in all but one case, and Congress have acceded to this accretion of authority. While presidential procurement orders are affirmed as consistent with the separation of powers by federal courts, presidents have used unilateral authority to set terms and conditions beyond a traditional proprietary contractual relationship, acting in highly contested policy areas only somewhat related to the efficient purchase of goods and services.

THE POLITICIZATION AND CENTRALIZATION OF PROCUREMENT WITHIN THE CHIEF EXECUTIVE

The federal government buys many of the products and services it needs from suppliers who meet certain qualifications. In theory, the procurement process allows the federal government to draw on a wide range of private sector expertise and thereby to perform core functions more effectively and efficiently.[2] In practice, procurement has long been used—by both Congress and presidents—to achieve political and policy goals unrelated to economic efficiency.

To exercise the power of the purchaser, presidents claim powers under Article II of the Constitution. They also act under the 1949 Federal Property and Administrative Services Act (FPASA), through which Congress delegated statutory authority to the president to act as the "principal and uniform purchaser" in contracting with any private sector actor doing business with the federal government.[3] Congress set forth its goal of an "economical and efficient system" for procurement, directing the president to "procure supplies in a manner advantageous to the government in terms of economy, efficiency, or service."[4] In addition, Congress also declared that "price was not the sole consideration; instead, the contract most advantageous to the federal government, price and other factors considered, should be the guide for purchasing decisions."[5] "Other factors" are two extremely powerful words. They have allowed presidents to employ "a strategy of seeking the greatest advantage to the federal government, short- and long-term," as they understand it with the chief constraint being the maintenance of the public's trust.[6]

To oversee federal procurement, in 1949 Congress created the General Services Administration (GSA), with an administrator appointed by the president and confirmed by the Senate, to manage procurement of federal government property.[7] In 1984 Congress established a single set of Federal Acquisition Regulations (FAR) to codify uniform policies for the acquisition of supplies and services and to govern the federal procurement of property and services by all agencies.[8]

Over time, Congress affirmed the centralization of federal procurement policy in the chief executive: the 1974 Federal Procurement Policy Act created the Office of Federal Procurement Policy (OFPP) as part of the Office of Management and Budget (OMB) and recommended that the OFPP be placed within the Executive Office of the President to "give it prestige and leverage in dealing effectively with all agencies."[9]

This has created some tension in the system. Generally, federal procurement officials have opposed the president's special contracting provisions because they increased costs to the public.[10] The OFPP has recognized that its charge, to improve government performance, can conflict with the incentives of presidents to exercise political influence over additional terms and conditions on federal contract and subcontracts.[11] In fact, OFPP bureaucratic concerns have merit. Presidents have often been motivated by short-term political advantage and policy aims rather than longer-term benefits of economic efficiency in exercising the power of the purchaser.

THE POWER OF THE PURCHASER AND
LABOR-MANAGEMENT RELATIONS

In recent decades, one of the key areas where presidents have used the power of the purchaser for partisan political advantage is labor-management issues. For example, to improve his electoral prospects in the 1992 election, George H. W. Bush issued an order to decrease the influence of union money in presidential elections. Most significant, it informed employees of federal contractors that they were not required to pay for the political activities of unions representing them. Citing a symbolic need to ensure the "economical and efficient administration and completion of government contracts," it required contractors to post notices declaring that their employees could not "be required to join a union or maintain membership in a union in order to retain their jobs."[12] If a private sector actor did not comply, the contract could be "cancelled, terminated, or suspended and the contractor declared ineligible for further contracts."[13]

Organized labor groups did not legally challenge this and Bush's other pro-management orders. Instead they hoped that Bill Clinton, a political ally, would win the race and revoke them. Their strategy paid off as a triumphant Clinton delivered immediate political and economic benefits to organized labor by repealing the Bush orders and directing federal agencies to revoke any rules implementing them. In addition, Clinton required contractors that took over as successors from other service-related contractors to offer employment on a right-of-first-refusal basis to qualified employees who otherwise would lose their jobs. Clinton claimed that a "carryover workforce reduces disruption to the delivery of services and provides the federal government the benefits of an experienced and trained workforce."[14]

After failing to persuade Congress to adopt the 1994 Workplace Fairness Act, which would have prohibited companies from permanently replacing striking workers, Clinton prohibited the federal government from contracting with employers who permanently replaced striking workers. Clinton's order affected some of the largest federal contractors, including Bridgestone/ Firestone, Pirelli Armstrong Tire, Caterpillar, and Diamond Walnuts.[15] Clinton aimed to limit the Supreme Court's rulings related to *National Labor Relations Board v. Mackay Radio & Telegraph,* which allowed private sector employers to hire permanent strike replacements.[16]

Clinton's logic for issuing this order illustrates how presidents use language and precedent to expand their power and reward their allies. Citing his authority under the Federal Property and Administrative Services Act, he claimed he was acting to protect "the government as a contracting party from harms related to a labor dispute" rather than to regulate an employer's use of permanent replacements.[17] Thus, he tied his political effort to deliver benefits to labor to traditional federal government policy aims by asserting that the federal government's interests in "economy and efficiency" are best secured by contracting with businesses that have "stable relationships with their employees."[18]

However, the U.S. Court of Appeals for the District of Columbia Circuit overturned Clinton's executive order in *Chamber of Commerce v. Reich.* The court determined that Clinton's executive order, although issued pursuant to broad authority delegated to him under FPASA, was invalid because it conflicted with a provision of the National Labor Relations Act, which guarantees the right to hire permanent replacements during strikes. It is significant that this is the *only* case in which the courts have placed a limit on the president's use of the power of the executive order (EO).[19]

George W. Bush, in a predictable shift to deliver benefits to business, repealed Clinton's EOs and reissued George H. W. Bush's, including the order that employees could only be required to pay the share of union costs relating to collective bargaining, contract administration, and grievance adjustment and not political efforts.[20] Bush also reinstated the "preservation of open competition and government neutrality," revoked the right of first refusal, and allowed for the displacement of qualified workers under service contracts.[21]

THE POWER OF THE PURCHASER AND THE PROBLEMS OF UNEMPLOYMENT, POVERTY, AND INFLATION

Presidents have used the power of the purchaser to address the political and economic problem of unemployment, urban and rural poverty, and inflation. In 1952, Dwight Eisenhower pledged to use federal defense spending to alleviate unemployment. In response, the Office of Defense Mobilization issued the defense manpower policy number 4 (DMP-4), which gave preference to companies in areas of labor surplus or high unemployment.[22] Lyndon Johnson amended the DMP-4 to offer incentives for companies to locate in "high-poverty" neighborhoods, establishing preferences for contractors who perform "substantial portions of their contracts in or near sections of concentrated unemployment or underemployment."[23] Jimmy Carter implemented a procurement set-aside in labor surplus areas.[24] Clinton relied on "empowerment contracting" "to expand the pool of contractors in economically distressed communities."[25] These areas were defined as all urban and rural communities with federal poverty rates of at least 20 percent.[26] Signaling how presidential power had broadened the concept of "economic efficiency," Clinton asserted that "fostering growth of federal contractors in economically distressed communities and ensuring that those contractors become viable businesses for the long term will promote economy and efficiency in Federal procurement and help to empower those communities."[27]

Richard Nixon and Carter relied on the power of the purchaser to combat inflation, a complex problem with political challenges.[28] In response to escalating construction costs, Nixon prohibited unions from negotiating wages and benefits without government intervention.[29] He also imposed general wage and price controls, freezing salaries for ninety days and authorizing a presidential council to order employers to maintain wage records.[30] Carter's efforts were also expansive. He directed the Council on Wage and Price Stability to establish noninflationary wage and price standards for the entire economy.[31] He encouraged noninflationary pay and price behavior by the private sector and labor unions, prohibited contractors from raising prices and wages beyond prescribed "non-inflationary limits,"[32] and denied federal contracts to firms that refused to follow his wage guidelines.

Although debarment for noncompliance was authorized by Congress and was not uncommon, Carter's prohibition against inflationary procurement practices was the first time it was used to enforce noninflationary pay and price behavior.[33] Later, Ronald Reagan opposed wage and price controls to combat inflation and issued an order to "terminate the regulatory burdens of the wage and price program."[34] No successor chief executive officer has used the power of the purchaser to address inflation, in large part because the rate of inflation has been low since the 1980s.

THE POWER OF THE PURCHASER AND OPPORTUNITIES
FOR SMALL BUSINESS

Modern presidents and the Congress have largely agreed that the federal government should use the federal procurement system to aid small business. Congress in 1979 required federal agencies to "maximize the use of small socially and economically disadvantaged businesses."[35] This largely echoed Nixon's 1969 executive order calling on federal agencies "to foster and promote minority business enterprises."[36] Reagan reaffirmed the federal government's commitment to the goal of encouraging opportunity for minority entrepreneurs, directing all agencies "to develop a minority business development plan and to develop incentives to encourage greater minority business subcontracting by prime contractors."[37] Clinton required increased access for socially (those who have been subjected to racial or ethnic prejudice or cultural bias) and economically disadvantaged businesses (socially disadvantaged individuals whose ability to compete has been impaired due to diminished capital and credit opportunities) to contracting opportunities, directing agencies "to take all necessary steps to increase [such] contracting."[38] Clinton also established "mechanisms that ensure that small businesses owned and

controlled by socially and economically disadvantaged individuals," historically black colleges and universities, and minority institutions have a "fair
opportunity to participate in procurement."[39]

Just as Franklin Roosevelt used executive orders in response to growing
calls for civil rights, more recent presidents have issued small-business procurement rules to benefit rising constituencies.[40] Carter, for example, created the National Women's Business Enterprise Policy, and directed each
"agency to take an action to facilitate, preserve and strengthen women's
business enterprise by ensuring their participation in all business related
activities including procurement."[41] Clinton affirmed his commitment to
small, disadvantaged, and women-owned businesses in federal procurement
by encouraging "the use of various tools, including set-asides [and] price
preferences as necessary to achieve the policy objective."[42] In a specific effort to help Vice President Al Gore's electoral prospects with women in the
2000 election, Clinton also promised to "ensure maximum participation of
women-owned small businesses in the procurement process."[43]

To reach out to potential new political constituencies as he faced reelection in 2004, George W. Bush expanded federal contracting opportunities to
businesses owned by Asian Americans and Pacific Islanders.[44]

Presidents have also used the power of the purchaser to help veterans con-
fronting the challenge of rejoining the civilian workplace. Nixon facilitated
the employment of Vietnam War veterans by requiring all agencies, contractors, and subcontractors to list employment openings with employment
service systems.[45] George W. Bush, who was leading wars in Iraq and Afghanistan, strengthened opportunities in contracting for businesses owned by
service-disabled veterans and declared that a minimum of 3 percent of all federal government contracts must go to service-disabled veterans.[46] Bush also
required federal agencies to "significantly increase the federal contracting and
subcontracting of businesses run by service-disabled veterans."[47]

THE POWER OF THE PURCHASER AND COMPLIANCE
WITH FEDERAL REGULATIONS

Clinton, in response to core political constituencies, used the power of the
purchaser to influence private sector compliance with federal tax, labor and
employment, environmental, antitrust, and consumer protection laws. Al
Gore, the Democrats' 2000 presidential nominee, announced the Clinton
order requiring all federal agencies to consider contractor compliance with

labor laws when making "responsibility determinations."[48] Clinton issued rules clarifying how federal contracting officers were to make these "responsibility" determinations.[49]

The procurement rules, which were to take effect on the last day of the Clinton presidency, specified that private sector actors must have a record of integrity and business ethics, including "satisfactory compliance with the law including tax, labor and employment, environment, antitrust and consumer protection laws."[50] Companies that had committed these violations could be disqualified from obtaining contracts.

THE POWER OF THE PURCHASER AND
IMMIGRATION ENFORCEMENT

Since the passage of the 1986 Immigration Reform and Control Act (IRCA), Congress has struggled to deal with employment issues involving foreign nationals who are in the country illegally or who are in the country legally but are not authorized to work. Efforts to verify a person's right to work in the United States were unknown before the passage of the IRCA, which set up a paper-based system (non-web based) whereby employers were required to review employees' documents, complete I-9 forms, and maintain these records or face fines and penalties.[51] For the first decade, enforcement of employers' obligations under the IRCA was sporadic and ineffective, leading Congress to make changes with the 1996 Illegal Immigration Reform and Immigrant Responsibility Act. This act required the Department of Justice to create programs that would more "efficiently and accurately" verify employees' work status.

Beginning in 1997, the Immigration and Naturalization Service allowed but did not require private sector employers to use an electronic system, called E-Verify, to check new employees' social security numbers against a database maintained by the Social Security Administration.[52] The system also checked the Department of Homeland Security (DHS) databases for immigration information. For a variety of reasons, many private sectors employers chose not to use the system.

Clinton, in an effort to appear politically tough on illegal immigration and to prohibit unfair employment practices, prohibited the federal government from contracting with companies that "knowingly employ unauthorized alien workers."[53] After the failure of immigration reform, George W. Bush required federal contractors to verify their employees' work eligibility using E-Verify.[54]

THE POWER OF THE PURCHASER:
INTERNATIONAL CHILD LABOR AND GUN CONTROL

Clinton, in an effort to respond to political demands, used the power of the purchaser to address child labor abuses, directing federal agencies to "take actions to enforce the laws prohibiting the manufacture or importation of goods, wares, articles, and merchandise mined, produced, or manufactured wholly or in part by forced or indentured child labor."[55] Clinton required contractors to certify that they have made "a good faith effort to determine whether forced or indentured child labor was used to produce the items listed."[56] Clinton, a supporter of free-trade policies, exempted those countries that were part of the North American Free Trade Agreement (NAFTA) and signatories to the World Trade Organization's (WTO) agreement on procurement from his executive procurement order.

Clinton, facing a Republican Congress that refused to act on his Anti-Gang and Youth Violence Act, called on gun manufacturers to install voluntary trigger locks and issued a memo to mandate child-safety locks on all federally issued firearms. The president's directive was significant because the federal government procures many firearms—for the armed forces, FBI agents, DEA agents, IRS agents, postal inspectors, immigration agents, and park rangers.[57] Clinton did not mandate use of a particular brand or one specific type of safety-lock device.[58]

Clinton also required agencies to ensure that a safety-lock device be provided with each handgun issued to federal law enforcement officers; to inform all federal law enforcement officers of the policy, and to provide instructions for the proper use of devices when issued. Clinton also issued a memorandum clarifying that the directive covered all firearms, not just handguns, issued to federal law enforcement officers.[59]

THE POWER OF THE PURCHASER AND
EQUAL EMPLOYMENT OPPORTUNITY

Historically, presidents have used the power of the purchaser to prohibit discrimination and encourage equal opportunity in doing business with the federal government. During the 1930s, several forces came together as civil rights groups faced a more politically responsive president in Franklin Delano Roosevelt. These historical forces included the Great Migration of blacks from the Jim Crow South to the North, which increased their electoral impact and the dramatic shift of African American voters in the North from the Republican to the Democratic Party. Through the 1930s it became clear that Democratic presidents needed to reach out to these minority voters, who were increasingly important to their getting elected.[60] The war effort in particular, which expanded the needs and reach of federal government, gave them particular latitude in this sphere. In response, Franklin Roosevelt and Harry Truman used the executive power of the purchaser to impose antidiscrimination rules on all defense and civilian contracts.

When civil rights groups protested that African American workers were excluded from segregated war production factories, Roosevelt used the broad "authority vested in the presidency by the Constitution and statutes" to require all industries engaged in defense production "to refrain from discriminating on the basis of race, creed, color or national origin" and to engage in fair employment practices.[61] The president's executive orders, derived from the chief executive's war powers (Article I, Section 8, Clause 11 of the U.S. Constitution), were not challenged by Congress or the courts.[62]

Roosevelt's order was historic: it was the first time a chief executive had used the procurement power to prohibit employment discrimination by private sector contractors. He also issued a similar order that broadened the scope of the order to all federal government contractors.[63] Throughout World War II, Roosevelt, aware of the need to acknowledge statutory authority and political realities, claimed these actions were based not only on the civil rights issue per se but also on an "overall war effort and need to maximize the pool of workers available for defense production."[64] No president, Democrat or Republican, could afford to alienate the South by pushing too hard on civil rights reform or antidiscrimination measures, and the chief executive mirrored the dominant racial attitudes of the time.[65]

Following Roosevelt, presidents built upon these wartime precedents to use the federal procurement systems as a tool for advancing civil rights. Truman ordered nondiscrimination in all industries engaged in "work contributing to the production of military supplies or to the effective transition to a peacetime economy."[66]

He also created the Committee on Government Contract Compliance to see that federal contractors met the nondiscrimination provisions of Roosevelt's order. Eisenhower not only affirmed earlier antidiscrimination orders but also created the President's Committee on Government Contracts and established an additional obligation of the federal government to promote "equal employment opportunity" in all federal contracts.[67]

Despite that activity, John F. Kennedy still marks a turning point in the chief executive's use of the power of the purchaser. During the 1960 campaign he argued that the president "must above all be the Chief Executive in every sense of the word. He must be prepared to exercise the fullest powers of his office—all that are specified and some that are not." Active political opposition from southern Democrats in Congress for Kennedy's antidiscrimination agenda obliged him to follow through with the robust use of executive orders.[68] Declaring "an urgent need for expansion and strengthening of efforts to promote full equality of employment opportunity," Kennedy issued an order during his first hundred days to "promote the economy, security, and national defense of the United States through the most efficient and effective utilization of all available manpower."[69] Kennedy subsequently defined what he meant by "all available manpower" through a series of executive orders that required federal government contractors to "take affirmative action to ensure that applicants are employed, and that employees are treated during employment, without regard to their race, creed, color or national origin." He empowered federal contracting agencies to punish contractors who violated their equal employment obligations. President Lyndon Johnson extended the antidiscrimination prohibition to federally assisted construction contractors. In a "federally assisted contract," the construction project receives federal funding, but neither the federal government nor its agencies are parties to the contract. Typically, a federally assisted construction contract involves funds received by way of a federal grant, loan, insurance, or guarantee.

Kennedy also extended antidiscrimination to all federally assisted housing—specifically, the sale, lease, or use of future housing constructed by the federal government or guaranteed under the Federal Housing Administration or Veterans Administration programs. The order had a very limited initial reach, applying in the end to less than 1 percent of the nation's housing units.

Kennedy also used executive orders to create new structures for enforcing civil rights. He created the President's Committee on Equal Opportunity in Housing.[70] He replaced the Committee on Government Employment Policy and the Government Contract Committee with a more vigorous President's Committee on Equal Employment Opportunity, which, upon congressional adoption of the 1964 Civil Rights Act, became the Equal Employment Opportunity Commission.[71]

As he did in so many areas, Johnson expanded upon Kennedy's use of executive orders regarding federal procurement. He required all federal contractors and subcontractors (and entities working on federally assisted construction contracts) to offer equal employment opportunity, regardless of race, creed, color or national origin.[72] Moreover, Johnson banned discrimination on the basis of sex, race, color, religion, or national origin in hiring and employment by federal government contractors.[73] In sum, Johnson demanded that any private sector actor doing business with the federal government go beyond nondiscrimination and "affirmatively act" to ensure that employment opportunities were open to women and minorities.[74] Johnson also prohibited federal contractors and subcontractors from taking adverse employment actions against applicants and employees for asking about, discussing, or sharing information about their pay or the pay of their coworkers.[75]

Carter consolidated all contract compliance functions relating to equal employment opportunity into the Department of Labor (DOL) in 1978.[76]

The power of the purchaser is not immune to shifts in partisan presidential preferences and interest group pressures. But, as the conservative Ronald Reagan learned, politics can constrain presidents from the political use of executive orders. Reagan considered signing an order to clarify that the "federal government does not require, authorize or permit the use of goals, or any other form of race or gender-specific preferential treatment by contractors." But he never issued it for fear that Democrats in Congress would adopt a statute that entrenched in actual legislation the order he sought to overturn.[77] Indeed, in those instances where the power of the purchaser might spark congressional or judicial response, presidents have often proceeded with caution. Knowing that their orders will promptly be overturned, presidents have determined that discretion is the better part of valor. This explains why Reagan and George H. W. Bush (1981–92) did not amend any of the Kennedy-Johnson-Carter equal employment opportunity orders.[78]

THE POWER OF THE PURCHASER
AND FAITH-BASED CONTRACTING

George W. Bush, serving as governor of Texas, issued a gubernatorial executive order that required Texas state agencies to encourage faith-based contracting.[79] When he sought the presidency in 2000, faith-based initiatives became a part of Bush's compassionate conservativism agenda, "allowing him to appeal not only to his electoral base of religious conservatives and evangelicals, but also to reach out to potential supporters among urban

Latinos and African Americans, who tend to vote Democratic while also being religious."[80] In 2001, Bush proposed faith-based reforms, under the 2001 Charitable Choice Expansion Act, that would permit religious groups to receive federal funds for social services.[81] After these efforts failed in Congress, Bush relied on the power of the purchaser.[82] Bush—intending to "ensure the economical and efficient administration and completion of government contracts"—allowed religious organizations contracting with the federal government to discriminate in their hiring practices.[83] Bush's justification for the constitutionality of the order was that it would "further the strong federal interest in ensuring that the cost and progress of federal procurement contracts are not adversely affected by an artificial restriction of the labor pool caused by the exclusion of faith-based organizations."[84]

Bush also established federal guidelines for ensuring what he termed "equal protection" for religious organizations seeking partnerships with the federal government.[85] Bush's order allowed religiously affiliated employers to consider applicants' religion while making some employment decisions. Specifically, employers were permitted to favor candidates of the same faith as theirs. Thus, Bush reversed Johnson's EO 11246, which excluded providers with discriminatory hiring practices from receiving federal funding.[86]

Bush also mandated that no organization could be discriminated against by the federal government on the basis of religion or religious belief within federal contracting, grant making, and other areas where federal money would be distributed.[87]

CONCLUSION

The complex and dynamic evolution of the federal bureaucracy during the twentieth century might be boiled down to this: the president became more powerful. This was especially apparent in the tremendous authority the president accrued as chief executive officer of the federal procurement system. The simple fact of managing the largest purchaser of goods and services in the nation afforded the president vast and growing power. As Congress recognized that a larger federal government required a strong chief executive officer to manage the bureaucracy, the power of the purchaser became central to the modern presidency. Presidents issued orders or memos to make profound changes in a broad range of public policy areas.

Where Roosevelt and Truman used World War II exigencies to expand the power of the purchaser, Congress directly delegated this authority through the 1949 Federal Property and Administrative Services Act. In retrospect, this nondescript-sounding measure was important as it empowered the president to act as the "principal and uniform purchaser" in contracting with any private sector actor doing business with the federal government. Congress declared that "price was not the sole consideration; instead, the contract most advantageous to the federal government, price and other factors considered, should be the guide for purchasing decisions."[88] One of the great lessons of government is that vague language is open to interpretation. In this case, "other factors" have afforded presidents a dizzying amount of latitude to set additional terms and conditions. Courts have upheld the power of the purchaser as long as the "requisite nexus exists between the president's actions and goals of economy and efficiency in procurement."[89]

Economy and efficiency, as we have seen, are often in the eye of the president. Hence, some former presidents have seen their orders reversed by their successors—and then, happily, seen them restored by their successor's successor. The power of the purchaser reflects two dynamics: presidents have almost uniformly sought to expand their authority, but in addition have used their power to pursue a diverse range of policy goals that reflect their own particular electoral incentives and political motivations.

As we have seen, presidents have tilted the balance of power in their direction by issuing executive orders and memos when Congress acted or refused to act either to support or to work around presidents' preferences. For decades, Congress did not endorse any of the presidents' equal employment opportunity orders, nor could they overturn them. However, electoral changes in the mid- to late 1960s led Congress to enshrine a range of prior orders in federal law in the 1964 Civil Rights Act, which made express reference to the earlier procurement orders, and again in 1972 amendments to the Civil Rights Act as approved by Nixon.[90] Congress affirmed a national policy prohibiting discrimination on the basis of race, color, religion, sex, or national origin.[91]

Even knowing that their orders might be overturned in more controversial policy domains such as labor-management relations, presidents still act and strike out on their own. To deliver benefits to labor, Clinton repealed all of George H. W. Bush's orders and directed agencies to revoke rules implementing them. In 2001, in a predictable shift to deliver benefits to business, George W. Bush repealed Clinton's orders and reissued George H. W. Bush's orders. Democrats and Republicans each sought short-term political advantage for their favored groups, labor or business, and to shape and reshape the enduring labor-management battle. Indeed, the polarization of parties appears only to have increased the willingness of presidents to exercise their unilateral power of the purchaser in the area of labor-management relations.

With few exceptions, each president has used the power of the purchaser more aggressively than his predecessor. Indeed, the presidency is an institution where each actor learns from those who came before and tries to push the boundaries a bit further. Kennedy marked a turning point in the bold use of the power of the purchaser, especially in the areas of equal employment opportunity. Johnson, Nixon, Carter, Reagan, Clinton, and Bush learned from him and each other, finding broad new areas in which to exercise this authority.

As we will see in the next chapter, between 2009 and 2016 Obama used the power of the purchaser perhaps more than any prior chief executive to influence policy in a very wide range of new areas only somewhat related to the federal government's efficient purchase of goods and services.

THREE

Barack Obama and the Power of the Purchaser

Near the end of Bill Clinton's second term and facing Republicans in control of Congress, White House chief of staff, John Podesta, proposed a series of executive orders that would achieve political and policy goals. This became known as Project Podesta.[1] A decade later, in 2008, Podesta returned to a position of power, heading Barack Obama's presidential transition team. Even before Obama was sworn in, executive power became a central element of his strategy as Podesta devised plans to use unilateral orders to achieve political and policy goals.[2] To secure early victories, the president "needs to take advantage of the power of the executive branch to make change happen on its own."[3] With the strong support of a Democratic Congress during his first two years, Obama's unilateral actions were relatively limited. That soon changed. "When the Republican victory in the 2010 midterm election raised the prospect of political gridlock, Podesta, as a counselor to the President, was ready with an answer: Obama should bypass Congress and wield the executive powers of his office. Less than two weeks after the mid-term election, Podesta compiled 47 pages of proposals for unilateral action on issues from immigration to solar energy."[4] Reflecting that presidents had accrued authority in ways not fully understood even by those who worked in and around the federal government, Podesta asserted, "Pundits and politicians across the ideological spectrum are focusing on how difficult it will be for Obama to advance his policy priorities through Congress. The U.S. Constitution and the laws of our nation grant the president significant authority to make and to implement policy."[5] Obama, with the power of the purchaser, did just that.

As Republicans increasingly saw their political interest in rejecting almost anything he favored, President Obama explicitly pursued a range of strategies that did not require their approval. In his 2014 State of the Union address, after Democrats had lost nine seats and control of the Senate, Obama defiantly outlined plans for a "year of action" that would restore public confidence in his presidency. Vowing to use executive authority to advance his agenda, Obama took on "a more pragmatic tone, acknowledging that getting his agenda past House Republicans was unlikely and therefore he would use his power to do what he can on his own."[6] Obama pledged to take unilateral action because "America does not stand still. Wherever and whenever I can take steps without legislation to expand opportunity for more American families, that's what I'm going to do." Obama issued several executive orders and memos to reward key Democratic constituencies on policy initiatives stalled by partisan gridlock in Congress.[7]

Like his predecessors, Obama affirmed, modified, or reversed some existing executive orders in accordance with his own electoral incentives and political motivations. And, like his predecessors, he expanded their use and reach—perhaps more than any prior chief executive. Obama used the power of the purchaser to influence policy in both traditional areas, such as labor-management relations and issues involving small-business contracting, and a wide range of new areas only tangentially related to the federal government's "efficient" purchase of goods and services. These included transparency and accountability in federal procurement, human trafficking, workplace safety and fair pay, minimum wage and overtime pay, equal pay for equal work, nonretaliation for disclosure of compensation, and equal employment opportunity in federal contracting regardless of sexual orientation and gender identity. In one area of public policy, however, Obama did not exercise the power of the purchaser: he decided not to act on a draft "dark money" order, which would have required companies doing business with the federal government to disclose their political contributions.

LABOR-MANAGEMENT RELATIONS

After Obama's election, it was widely expected that organized labor would push for the reintroduction of the Employee Free Choice Act, whose purpose was to make it easier for all workers to join unions. But Obama indicated a reluctance to engage in that controversial battle so early into his presidency, especially as it might pit him against private sector employers during a recession.[8] In order to appease organized labor, Obama backed other labor-related measures that, he said, would "reverse many of the policies towards organized labor that we've seen these last 8 years . . . to level the playing field for workers and the unions that represent their interests, because we know that you cannot have a strong middle class without a strong labor movement."[9]

In the ping-pong of presidential power, Obama issued several executive orders in 2009 to reverse George W. Bush's orders against organized labor, thereby reinstating many of Bill Clinton's orders. First, Obama made it difficult for federal contractors to discourage employees from forming or joining labor unions. Second, Obama allowed employees working under old federal contracts the right to continue their employment when the federal government signed a new contract. Third, Obama reversed a George W. Bush order that had required federal contractors holding contracts worth more than $100,000 to post notices informing employees of their right to not pay union fees for activities unrelated to collective bargaining. Obama also required contracts to contain language that informed employees of their right to unionize. Fourth, Obama required federal contractors to hire union workers for federal construction projects, and reinstated a Clinton order that created labor-management forums in every federal agency.[10] One observer concluded, "Obama's orders change how the federal government will conduct contracting—demonstrating a pendulum swing away from business and toward labor." Organized labor supported all the orders, calling Obama a "champion in the White House."[11]

SMALL-BUSINESS CONTRACTING

Obama campaigned to help small firms compete for more federal contracts and ensure that agencies take their annual small-business-contracting goals more seriously.[12] In particular, Obama reaffirmed the government's commitments to assist minority-owned and small businesses. Instead of just issuing orders to the existing agency system, Obama created the Interagency Task Force on Federal Contracting Opportunities for Small Businesses, "committed to ensuring that small businesses—firms owned by women, minorities, socially and economically disadvantaged individuals, and service-disabled veterans— have fair access to federal government contracting."[13] This new entity reflected both the vastness of federal bureaucracy—a new entity was required to coordinate the work of other federal agencies—and the way presidents can centralize and entrench their control of the federal procurement process.[14] Obama also launched a QuickPay initiative, which helped accelerate payments to large federal subcontractors and required them in turn to pay their small-business subcontractors faster. In addition, he expanded the Supplier Pay initiative, a partnership with the private sector to strengthen small businesses by increasing their working capital, so they could grow and hire more workers.

TRANSPARENCY AND ACCOUNTABILITY

Transparency is politically popular, and Obama attempted to secure political benefits by contrasting his approach with that of the George W. Bush administration, whose wartime footing engendered a reputation for secrecy. To many observers, the Bush presidency operated "too much in the dark, begetting a general mistrust of Bush's motives and actions."[15] In the 2008 campaign, Obama sought to present himself as a new and different leader when he promised to "restore honesty, openness, and common sense to federal contracting and procurement."[16] During the transition, Obama pledged to confront the issue of the growing number of no-bid contracts and to create a contracts and influence database that would disclose how much federal contractors spent on lobbying, what contracts they were receiving, and how well they completed their contracts.[17] In his first inaugural address, he claimed that "those of us who manage the public's dollars will do our business in the light of day, because only then can we restore the vital trust between a people and their government."[18]

One of Obama's first executive actions committed the federal government "to creating an unprecedented level of openness in government."[19] The power of the purchaser afforded him the opportunity to demonstrate this as he focused on procurement reform as well as transparency and accountability in procurement spending. First, Obama required a federal-government-wide review of federal contracting to ensure more "full and open competition in the often-overwhelmed procurement system." Obama also enhanced federal contractor accountability for improper payments through a "do-not pay" list which agencies were required to check before paying a federal contractor.[20]

IMMIGRATION ENFORCEMENT

As the number of legal and illegal immigrants in the United States increased sharply following the 1965 Immigration and Naturalization Act, the president's authority also expanded because of his obligation to enforce such laws. This inherently political issue became even more complicated when global competition and free trade deals seemed to hasten the decline of industries, especially in manufacturing, that had offered relatively well-paying jobs to semi-skilled workers. This led to interest group and electoral pressure on presidents to clamp down on the employment of illegal immigrants. George W. Bush tried to harness new technologies to strengthen immigration enforcement. He required all federal agencies to use E-Verify, an Internet-based system that compares information from an employee's I-9 form (Employment Eligibility Verification) with data from U.S. Department of Homeland Security and Social Security Administration records to confirm employment eligibility.[21] Bush also mandated that certain public and private businesses contracting with the federal government use E-Verify to verify their employees' employment eligibility.[22] These rules were scheduled to take effect in January 2009—less than a week before Obama was to enter the White House. Obama postponed implementation of Bush's order four times.[23]

Obama agreed to start enforcing the E-Verify rule in September 2009.[24] The Obama rules required certain employers that contract with the federal government to check the employment eligibility of all newly hired employees and the eligibility of all existing employees "assigned by the contractor to perform work on the federal contract."[25] Obama, however, rescinded a "no match" rule in Bush's initial order, which would have required the Department of Homeland Security to send guidance letters to employers who were already receiving "no-match" letters from the Social Security Administration. Under Bush's order, if the employer did not resolve a "no match" within ninety days, it was required to terminate the worker or face sanctions. Obama concluded that Bush's rule—which already had been blocked by court order and had never taken effect—was flawed because of inaccuracies in the E-Verify address databases.

HUMAN TRAFFICKING

It has been customary for presidents to use the power of the purchaser to influence labor conditions at home; Obama expanded his reach to distant shores to respond to human trafficking (the use of force, fraud, or coercion to obtain some type of labor or commercial sex act), including labor trafficking (individuals perform labor or services through the use of force, fraud, or coercion). His efforts in this area also suggested the increasingly global cast of U.S. interests and interest groups. Since 2004, Department of Defense (DOD) contractors have been subject to anti-trafficking provisions aimed at stamping out trafficking-related activities among defense contractors, the military, and federal government employees. In 2006, in response to reports of labor trafficking in Iraq by defense contractors and subcontractors, DOD instituted its Trafficking in Persons program. In 2007, DOD rules required that federal contractors provide anti-trafficking training to all employees and ensure compliance with U.S. law, host-nation law, and "local theater" directives on combating human trafficking.[26] In 2011, Obama called upon Congress to reauthorize the Trafficking Victims Protection Reauthorization Act, which had been reauthorized three times in the past by bipartisan majorities.[27] Efforts to reauthorize the Violence Against Women Act (VAWA), which had expired in 2011, stalled during the 112th Congress when the Senate and House passed different versions.

Obama expanded the DOD's zero-tolerance policy regarding human trafficking to all who provide goods and services to the federal government.[28] According to the new Obama order, federal agencies must take several steps to "strengthen the efficacy of the Government's zero-tolerance" for trafficking by contractors and subcontractors. Obama argued that as the largest purchaser of goods and services in the United States, the federal government has a responsibility to ensure that companies it buys from do not engage in forced sex trafficking or forced servitude. In 2012, Obama issued compliance rules for federal contractors to prevent all human trafficking as part of a wider effort to increase compliance measures in the broader corporate supply chain.

A FLEXIBLE, FAMILY-FRIENDLY WORKPLACE

Obama, in his 2015 State of the Union address, proposed multiple policies to aid the middle class, including paid family and medical leave for American workers. His order on paid leave was another use of executive power designed to change the rules of the workplace and reward his supporters in organized labor. Obama's Council of Economic Advisors had reported that a large fraction of American workers lacked access to paid leave, including for an illness or the birth of a child.[29] Obama called on Congress to pass the Healthy Families Act, which would allow employees to earn an hour of paid sick time for every thirty hours they worked. House Republicans introduced an alternative measure, the Working Families Act, whereby private sector employers could offer paid time off in lieu of cash wages for overtime hours worked.[30]

Obama used the power of the purchaser to resolve the standoff, requiring federal contractors to provide up to seven days of paid sick leave per year. According to Obama, "Providing access to paid sick leave will improve the health and performance of employees of federal contractors and bring benefits packages at federal contractors in line with model employers, ensuring that they remain competitive employers in the search for dedicated and talented employees."[31] Critics claimed that Obama was "piling expensive directives onto companies doing business with the federal government as a sop to his political base without accounting for additional costs."[32] As his predecessors had, most notably regarding civil rights, Obama hoped the order would set a standard that would influence Congress, private employers, and state and local governments to expand their leave policies.

SAFE WORKPLACES AND FAIR PAY

When Obama came to office, he faced both the immediate challenges of the 2008–09 Great Recession as well as long-term economic issues that had led to stagnant or declining wages, especially for the middle-class and working poor. Working with a Democratic Congress, he passed a flurry of major legislation during his first two years, including the stimulus, the bailout of auto manufacturers, and health-care reform. Early in his presidency Obama also explored using the power of the purchaser to push up wages and benefits for federally contracted employees. According to a draft order, Obama proposed that a "positive weight" be assigned to federal contractors based on the compensation offered to their employees.[33]

Obama claimed that 400,000 workers employed under federal contracts—such as cafeteria workers, security guards, and landscaping workers at federal buildings—were earning less than $22,000 a year, the federal poverty line for a family of four, assuming one paycheck in a household.[34] The Obama order would have applied not only to private sector employees working on federal government contracts but also to all the private sector employees working for companies that do some business with the federal government. Large private sector companies, such as Exxon Mobil and General Electric, contract with the federal government but obtain most of their revenue from nonfederal sources.[35]

Obama's political logic was similar to Clinton's "blacklisting" effort, blocked by George W. Bush, which required federal agencies to take into account a firm's compliance with tax, labor and employment, environmental, antitrust, and consumer protection laws before awarding the firm a contract. But, in a reminder that even unilateral power is constrained by political and economic forces, Obama decided not to issue this order because of Republican and corporate opposition as well as stubbornly high rates of unemployment and low rates of labor participation.[36]

However, Obama did issue executive orders on the minimum wage and safe and fair workplaces in 2014.[37] As part of his 2014 "year of action," he also promised to "crack down on federal contractors who put workers' safety and hard-earned pay at risk."[38] Obama issued an order on fair pay and workplace safety to prohibit federal contractors who have violated labor laws from competing for certain types of work.[39] Under the current law, federal agencies could bar awarding contracts to companies that commit serious violations of various laws. Obama issued an additional memorandum to federal agencies regarding the role of the labor compliance adviser and directed them to designate a senior-level official within the agency to serve in this role.[40]

FAITH-BASED CONTRACTS

During the 2008 campaign, candidate Obama promised to expand Bush's executive order regarding federal faith-based contracting. By reaching out to centrist and liberal evangelicals, who had been pushing to broaden their political agenda beyond traditional social issues, Obama was "hoping to chip away at a margin that has favored Republicans." Obama claimed that he would call for "a pre-inauguration review of all executive orders pertaining to the religion-based program, particularly those dealing with hiring." The program would "be central to our White House mission."[41]

But Obama was again walking a political tightrope—competing political pressures often shape actual presidential actions. Some of his staunch Democratic allies were concerned about the mix of religion and politics. In response, he renamed Bush's office the Office of Faith-Based and Neighborhood Partnerships, to make it sound more secular.[42] Obama also pledged that when legal or constitutional issues arise regarding "existing or prospective programs and practices," the office would seek the opinion of the White House counsel and the attorney general.[43]

Obama created the Interagency Working Group on Faith-Based and Other Neighborhood Partnerships to review existing rules, guidance documents, and policies.[44] He also instructed federal agencies to adopt rules and guidance consistent with his 2010 executive order.[45] The final Obama rule barred faith-based organizations that receive federal assistance from discriminating against beneficiaries of their services on the basis of "religion, a religious belief, a refusal to hold a religious belief, or a refusal to attend or participate in a religious practice." Obama required faith-based organizations to notify beneficiaries of these protections.[46]

MINIMUM WAGE AND OVERTIME PAY

Although Obama had promised a federal minimum wage increase from $7.25 to $9 an hour during his 2008 campaign, he did not propose one in his first two years when Democrats controlled Congress. Then Republicans took control of the House in 2011.[47] Obama later expressed support for the 2013 Fair Minimum Wage Act, but Congress refused to act.[48] Democrats and their allies in organized labor pushed Obama to use the power of the purchaser to raise the federal minimum age.[49] In his 2014 State of the Union address Obama stated:

> I will issue an executive order requiring federal contractors to pay their federally funded employees a fair wage of at least ten dollars and ten cents an hour. . . . Of course, to reach millions more, Congress does need to get on board. Today, the federal minimum wage is worth about twenty percent less than it was when Ronald Reagan first stood here.[50]

He followed through by mandating that all workers who earn compensation as part of a federal contract or subcontract be paid $10 per hour.[51] Obama also increased the minimum wage for workers who receive tips to "at least . . . 70 percent" of the $10.10 for workers who don't receive tips.[52]

Obama's final rules raised the minimum wage for workers on federal service and construction contracts to $10.10 per hour and indexed it to inflation in future years. Obama estimated the order would benefit nearly 200,000 American workers.[53]

Obama also expanded overtime protections for millions of workers. Congress, under the Fair Labor Standards Act (FLSA), requires employees to receive overtime pay of at least one and half times their regular pay when they work more than forty hours in a week.[54] Obama updated the rules regarding which white-collar workers are protected by the FLSA's minimum wage and overtime standards. Consistent with the goal of "ensuring workers are paid a fair day's pay for a fair day's work," Obama directed the Department of Labor to "look for ways to modernize and simplify the regulations while ensuring that the FLSA's intended overtime protections are fully implemented." For instance, the rules do not account for inflation, so that over time, what was considered a higher salary became a relatively low salary: "The threshold has been raised only once since 1975, when it covered nearly half of U.S. workers; in 2015, it stood at less than $24,000, or lower than the poverty level for a family of four."[55]

Obama updated the rules governing which executive, administrative, and professional employees (white-collar workers) are entitled to minimum wage and overtime pay protections under the FLSA. These rules had not been updated since 2004, and the salary threshold for exemption was $455 per week, or $23,660 per year. With the proposed rule, Obama updated the salary level required for exemption to ensure that the FLSA's intended overtime protections were fully implemented and to simplify the identification of nonexempt employees. In doing so, Obama aimed to make the executive, administrative, and professional employee exemption easier for employers and workers to understand and apply.[56]

EQUAL PAY AND NONRETALIATION FOR
DISCLOSURE OF COMPENSATION

In his 2013 State of the Union address, Obama called on Congress to pass the Paycheck Fairness Act, which would prohibit all employers from retaliating against workers who ask questions about compensation and would require private sector employers to prove that disparities in pay between women and men are due to differences in skill and background and not to gender.[57] In 2014 Obama claimed that when it came to equal pay issues, "I'm not going to stand still either. So in this year of action I've used my executive authority whenever I could to create opportunity for more Americans. And today I'm going to take action—executive action—to make it easier for working women to earn fair pay.[58] In an attempt to discourage pay discrimination, Obama required federal contractors to allow employees to discuss their compensation with each other, by adhering to a new procurement order known as "Non-Retaliation for Disclosure of Compensation Information."[59]

In 2015, Obama's Office of Federal Contracts Compliance Programs proposed additional changes to its anti-sex-discrimination rules, which had not been updated since 1970.[60] Obama's rules addressed various issues, including pay, sexual harassment, workplace accommodations for pregnancy and for those with nonconforming gender identity, and family caregiving.[61]

PROTECTING VETERANS AND INDIVIDUALS
WITH DISABILITIES

Obama was, essentially, a wartime leader. Service members returning from Iraq and Afghanistan were a key concern and constituency, and Obama pledged his commitment to upholding the "sacred trust with America's veterans and wounded warriors."[62] He fulfilled this pledge by establishing the Interagency Task Force on Veterans Small Business Development "to increase access to capital by veteran-owned firms, to ensure that federal agencies were meeting contracting goals, and to better certify that those contracts were only awarded to small-business concerns owned and controlled by a veteran or service-disabled veteran."[63] The new task force made eighteen recommendations across three priority areas.[64]

Presidents do not have to issue new rules or create task forces to expand their authority. They can also direct the federal bureaucracy to enforce existing rules more vigorously. Without a formal executive order, Obama's Office of Federal Contracts Compliance Programs (OFCCP) imposed several new rules on federal contractors and subcontractors.[65] As noted by one observer, the Department of Labor's "formerly low-profile sub-agency, the Office of Federal Contract Compliance Programs, has been making a name for itself over the past year and a half, increasing its regulatory and enforcement activities to unprecedented levels."[66] Obama's OFCCP issued new rules for veterans under the Vietnam Era Veterans' Readjustment Assistance Act and for individuals with disabilities under the 1973 Rehabilitation Act.[67] Obama provided contractors with a quantifiable metric for their success in recruiting and employing veterans by requiring contractor's to adopt an annual benchmark based on either the national percentage of veterans in the workforce (8 percent as of mid-2016) or their own best available data.[68]

Obama's disability rule provided a hiring goal for federal contractors and subcontractors: 7 percent of the positions in each job group in their workforce must be held by qualified individuals with disabilities.[69]

SEXUAL ORIENTATION AND GENDER IDENTITY

No set of political and social issues evolved more quickly during Obama's presidency than those involving sexual orientation and gender identity. When Obama sought the Democratic nomination, running against Hillary Clinton, both of these leading liberals said they opposed same-sex marriage. During the 2012 election, Obama publicly reversed his position. In 2014, he began to take strong action, making it illegal to fire or harass employees of federal contractors based on their sexual orientation or gender identity.[70] Then, invoking the power of the purchaser, he added sexual orientation and gender identity to the list of prohibited reasons for discrimination.[71]

Obama's decision to explicitly prohibit—in executive order and in legislation—discrimination on the basis of gender identity was truly trailblazing, especially since he issued it at a time when transgender issues were just beginning to register on the radar of American politics. Obama stated, "America's federal contracts should not subsidize discrimination against the American people. This executive order is part of a long, bipartisan tradition. Roosevelt signed an order prohibiting racial discrimination in the national defense industry. Eisenhower strengthened it. Johnson expanded it. Today I'm going to expand it again."[72]

Many religious groups urged Obama to include an exemption to allow certain federal contractors to discriminate against gay, lesbian, bisexual, and transgender individuals.[73] They noted that religious groups with federal contracts had a limited exemption from existing antidiscrimination rules in Bush's 2002 faith-based contracting executive order.[74] Bush had allowed religiously affiliated contractors (religious corporations, associations, educational institutions, and societies) to favor hiring individuals of a particular religion. But Obama did not add exemptions for religious organizations beyond those in Bush's order.[75]

WHERE OBAMA DID NOT USE THE POWER
OF THE PURCHASER-IN-CHIEF

In one area facing congressional challenge Obama chose not to use his power of the purchaser-in-chief: disclosure of political contributions. Like same-sex marriage, money in politics had become a front-burner issue during Obama's presidency because of public pressure and a Supreme Court decision, *Citizens United v. Federal Election Commission* (2010), which struck down the limits on indirect campaign contributions through third-party advocacy nonprofits and deemed such payments free speech.[76] In 2011 Obama floated a draft order, "Disclosure of Political Spending by Government Contractors," mandating that agencies require federal contractors to "disclose certain political contributions and expenditures."[77] Many federal contractors were already required to report certain kinds of political spending—including direct payments to candidates, campaigns, and parties—to the Federal Election Commission. Obama's order would have compelled the disclosure of money given to third-party groups with the "reasonable expectation that parties would use those contributions to make independent expenditures or electioneering communications."[78]

Obama's order would have also required any entity bidding for a federal government contract to disclose political contributions to federal candidates or parties made within the past two years that exceeded $5,000.[79] In a telling nod to political exigencies, his order would not have applied to public sector unions or grantees, which tended to support Democrats. Congressional Republicans opposed Obama's order. "This order is a purely political act offered under the benign label of disclosure," claimed Rep. Darrell Issa (R-Calif.), chairman of the House Oversight and Government Reform Committee."[80] Republicans claimed the order "would not impose the same requirements on labor unions or other organizations that support the President." They also claimed that Obama was unnecessarily "politiciz[ing] the federal procurement process."[81] Democrats also opposed the Obama order. The substance of Obama's proposed order was contained in the Democracy Is Strengthened by Casting Light on Spending in Elections (DISCLOSE) Act, which passed the House in 2010 but did not receive a vote in the Senate. Obama did not issue the order.[82]

In early 2016, Obama again considered a "dark money" executive order to require companies doing business with the federal government to disclose their political contributions.[83] It would mandate that federal government contractors publicly report their contributions to third-party groups that spend money to influence campaigns, and its purpose was to expose the political activity of the largest companies and thereby narrow the flow of corporate contributions. Republicans claimed the real goal was "to harass, intimidate and silence those with whom Obama disagrees."[84]

As of late 2016, federal law prevented federal contractors from making political contributions during the negotiation or execution of a contract, but it leaves open a big loophole by not mentioning political activity before negotiations.[85] In the 2016 campaign, Hillary Clinton made campaign finance reform a major theme. Hillary Clinton stated that if elected president, she would require federal contractors to disclose their contributions.[86]

CONCLUSION

Although each president since Franklin Roosevelt has increased the scope and reach of presidential power through executive orders, Obama ranks with John F. Kennedy and Bill Clinton as a chief executive who expanded the authority into significantly uncharted territory. By means of both orders and presidential memoranda, he made this authority a central aspect of his administration from the very beginning, trumpeting it like no president before to assure his allies that he would and could act despite strong opposition from Republicans. Indeed, if the modern presidency is the story of increasing power resulting from the growth of the administrative state, Obama's presidency marks the point where the relatively obscure power of the president as purchaser took center stage.

FOUR

The President and the Power of the Employer

As the CEO of the largest employer in the United States, the president uses executive power to define the relationship between the federal government and its employees. Much like the power of the purchaser, this authority has expanded dramatically with the growth of the federal government. The increasing complexity of the federal civil service bureaucracy required greater presidential accountability and oversight. This has forced presidents to balance the aspiration for a merit-based bureaucracy with the desire to exert political control and influence over a loyal federal workforce through patronage. It has also provided presidents as the employers-in-chief with new opportunities to shape the political and policy agenda, by adopting "model" federal personnel policies that might be emulated in the private sector, as well as opportunities to reward old political allies and cultivate new political constituencies.[1] By way of executive order or memo and federal civil service rules, presidents have used the power of the employer to shape a range of policies that impact federal employees, including labor-management relations; worker health and safety (the use of seat belts, drugs and tobacco, issues related to AIDS, efforts to encourage health and fitness in the workplace); and the development of a more flexible, family-friendly workplace. The president is often the first mover in this area.

THE PRESIDENT AS CEO OF THE FEDERAL
(CIVIL SERVICE) BUREAUCRACY

Since the federal government was organized in 1789, individuals have served as employees of the executive branch in departments, agencies, and bureaus. However, the Constitution did not provide either the president or Congress with clear authority over the federal bureaucracy's workforce. This was not a pressing issue in the early republic because the federal government was relatively small and most of its employees were hired on the basis of patronage. Patronage workers were expected to be politically active on behalf of their presidential sponsor by engaging in partisan activities and making mandatory campaign contributions, known as political assessments.

This began to change after the Civil War. As the economy expanded and became more urban-based and industrialized, the federal government grew dramatically in response to demands for public services. The federal government was already the nation's largest employer by 1871, with 51,020 civilian employees, but over the next thirty years its workforce increased almost five-fold, to 239,000 civilian employees.[2] In response to the problems of administering a growing workforce that had become increasingly corrupt and ineffective, rules and sanctions were added to limit presidential and congressional access to the federal bureaucracy and to shield federal employees from political manipulation or threats.[3] This shift began with the 1883 Pendleton Act, whereby Congress authorized merit hiring for a small portion of the federal labor force. Merit—not political patronage—was to determine federal employment. Federal employees were to focus on doing their jobs competently and efficiently rather than on meeting the political needs of their patrons and party. The system was gradually extended and modified over the next century, and ultimately patronage as the principal means of hiring and firing most federal employees was displaced by merit hiring.

Some loyalty is, of course, essential for efficient government. Presidential appointees must also be political allies. Recognizing this, the Pendleton Act separated federal employees into two groups: classified (hired on the basis of merit) and unclassified (patronage). The federal civil service covers most federal civilian employees; the classified (or competitive service) employees have job tenure; and classified employees are restricted in the types of political activities in which they may engage.[4] The Pendleton Act affected about 10 percent of the federal government's civilian labor force, and Congress authorized the president to include additional positions through executive order.[5] Congress delegated authority to the president to classify positions within the executive branch through executive orders or revisions of the rules drafted by executive branch department heads.[6]

Nevertheless, a major reform set in motion by the Pendleton Act protected federal employees from removal through executive or legislation action. Congress also created the United States Civil Service Commission (CSC) to administer the merit system. The president was authorized to appoint three persons—not more than two from the same political party—as Civil Service commissioners.[7]

Without challenging the merit system, presidents sought to exert control and influence over the emerging federal civil service bureaucracy. As Terry Moe explains, modern presidents politicize administrative arrangements and centralize policy-related concerns in the White House. Moe argues convincingly that these features of the institutional presidency—politicization and centralization—have nothing to do with presidents as individuals, "but are driven by institutional incentives and opportunities shared by nearly all presidents and rationally acted upon in their pursuit of strong leadership and bureaucratic control."[8]

Franklin D. Roosevelt, as a first mover on federal personnel reform, in 1938 established the Council of Personnel Administration to "advise and assist the President and the [Civil Service] Commission in the protection and improvement of the merit system."[9] Roosevelt reaffirmed the commission's oversight role of federal personnel administration and established a method for ensuring cooperation across federal agencies. Harry S. Truman reorganized federal personnel administration, centralizing it under the Executive Office of the President.[10] Truman charged the new Office of Personnel Management, which he established in 1947, with providing leadership on personnel matters throughout the federal service. Truman reaffirmed the CSC as the federal government's central personnel agency, but also extended presidential authority by asserting that personnel management should be consistent for the federal government as a single employer.[11] Thus, the president would function as a chief executive officer of this single employer.

The struggle over the appropriate role of partisan politics in federal civil service employment resurfaced in the 1970s.[12] The Civil Service Commission had long struggled to balance its dual mission of advising the president on personnel matters and ensuring fair treatment of federal employees—of representing both management and labor. In the Civil Service Reform Act (CSRA) of 1978, Congress helped resolve some of this tension while strengthening presidential political control and influence over the federal civil service system by replacing the Civil Service Commission with three agencies: the Office of Personnel Management, the Merit Systems Protection Board, and the Federal Labor Relations Authority. The OPM would serve the president, advising him directly on federal personnel policy, its director to be appointed by and serve at the pleasure of the president; the Merit Systems Protection Board would safeguard employees from unfair treatment; and the Federal Labor Relations Authority would oversee relations between the federal government and its employees. Each of these entities assumed a portion of the Civil Service Commission's responsibilities, with the OPM responsible for all personnel management in the federal government. The OPM was charged with the administration of civil service laws, including conducting competitive examinations.[13] The director of the Office of Personnel Management, a presidential political appointee, implements all policy created to support federal human resources or personnel policy—including those pertaining to classification and qualifications systems, hiring authorities, and performance management as well as pay, leave, and benefits.

FEDERAL LABOR-MANAGEMENT RELATIONS

American politics is affected by the ongoing battle between organized labor and management of businesses. During the nineteenth century, when patronage ruled the federal bureaucracy, most labor-management disputes involved private sector employees. Presidents generally took the side of management, which they saw as promoting order and stability, a view that would for some time also shape their relations with public sector employees. For example, Andrew Jackson was in effect a strikebreaker when he sent troops to the construction sites of the Chesapeake and Ohio Canal in 1834 to quell a labor riot. In the railway strikes of 1877, Rutherford B. Hayes sent troops to ensure delivery of the mail. In 1894, Grover Cleveland used soldiers to break the Pullman strike.

Theodore Roosevelt softened this tough stance, playing a more neutral mediator role in the struggles between labor and management. For example, during the strike by miners of anthracite coal in Pennsylvania in 1902, employees demanded more pay and shorter hours while management claimed that profits were low and that the union destroyed discipline.[14] Roosevelt believed that both capital and labor had responsibilities to the public and sought to end the strike through compromise. This marked the shift of the employer-in-chief from strikebreaker to peacemaker in labor-management disputes. Truman anticipated a strike by private sector railroad workers in the mid-1950s and issued an executive order in 1950 putting America's railroads under the control of the U.S. Army.[15] Truman, as chief executive officer and commander-in-chief, concluded that the "federal governmental seizure [of the railroads] is imperative" for the protection of American citizens and "essential to the national defense and security" of the United States. In 1953 Dwight D. Eisenhower created a federal board to report on labor disputes affecting the U.S. maritime industry.[16]

The president as employer-in-chief has unique sovereign powers regarding the federal civil service bureaucracy.[17] For example, both Theodore Roosevelt and William Howard Taft embraced the president's managerial prerogatives over federal employees.

Both Roosevelt and Taft issued executive "gag" orders attempting to stop federal employees (postal employees), either individually or as a workers' union, from petitioning Congress for improvements in pay or working conditions. In 1906, Roosevelt issued another executive order that permitted department heads to dismiss employees without notice and—contrary to previous practices—without stating the reasons in writing.

Congressional attention to the problem of politically motivated removals was prompted by the issuance of Executive Orders by Presidents Roosevelt and Taft that forbade federal employees to communicate directly with Congress without the permission of their supervisors. In response to the president's unilateral action, Congress passed the Lloyd–La Follette Act in 1912, which established procedures for the discharge of federal employees and guaranteed the right of federal employees to communicate with members of Congress. Congress did not establish collective bargaining or the right to strike for federal employees, but only the freedom to petition Congress.[18] Thus, Congress protected federal employees from unwarranted or abusive executive removal by codifying "just cause" standards.[19] Congress also protected a postal employee's right to join a federal employee union so long as it was not affiliated with an organization that imposed a duty to strike against the federal government.

It would be a quarter century before the issue of federal employee and management relations was addressed formally by a chief executive. FDR did permit aggressive union action in the private sector by signing into law the 1935 National Labor Relations Act, to protect the rights of employees and employers, to encourage collective bargaining, and to limit certain private-sector labor and management practices. Two years later, however, Roosevelt declared a distinction between federal and private sector employees. He emphasized the responsibility of the federal government to the "citizenry" and the limits on public sector collective bargaining imposed by Congress's authority to set wage and benefits for federal employees.[20] In sum, Roosevelt reaffirmed the federal government as a sovereign employer.[21] However, due to his political support of labor-management relations in the private sector, unions worked to reelect Roosevelt in 1936. Indeed, this election marked the beginning of the still ongoing alliance between organized labor and the Democratic Party. Unions provide votes, money, and volunteer time, and Democrats in Congress and the White House tend to support their initiatives regarding public and private sector employees.[22]

Thus, it was another Democrat, John F. Kennedy, who transformed the relationship between the federal government and its employees by empowering unions. To secure the political support of federal employee and postal unions, a group critical to him in the 1960 presidential election, Kennedy promised to support collective bargaining between federal employees and agencies.[23] He delivered on this promise in his first year in office, issuing a memo asserting "the right of federal employees to participate in employee organizations and to seek to improve working conditions and the resolution of grievances." In his Executive Order 10988 of January 1962, Kennedy was the first chief executive officer to legitimize unions in the federal government, giving employees the right to engage in collective bargaining through labor organizations.[24] As a result, Kennedy institutionalized a new form of labor-management relations within the federal civil service bureaucracy. The order galvanized labor, and union membership of federal employees increased from 12 percent to 48 percent between 1964 and 1970.[25] Kennedy also empowered federal employee unions to represent members' grievances over issues such as transfers, promotions, discharge, safety, and health.[26] The Kennedy order contributed to the growth in state and local unionization, and many states followed the order and adopted collective-bargaining policies for public employees. But Kennedy reaffirmed the long-standing federal government prohibition against strikes by federal employees. Some organized unions, especially postal employee unions, lobbied to reform federal labor relations, as they believed Congress would be more receptive to their political demands and prohibit unilateral action by a future president. But Johnson affirmed Kennedy's EO 10988.[27]

Richard Nixon, elected in 1968, was not expected to expand labor rights for federal employees. He had long supported policies that limited the rights of labor unions in the private sector, and once compared labor union practices to "those of Hitler and Mussolini."[28] Nevertheless, Nixon reached out to labor in significant ways. Like Johnson, Nixon affirmed the accomplishments of Kennedy's order on Employee-Management Cooperation in the Federal Service.[29] He also expanded federal employees' rights by creating the Federal Labor Relations Council and Federal Service Impasses Panel. The Federal Labor Relations Authority would oversee the entire program; make definitive interpretations and rulings on provisions of the executive order; decide major policy issues; hear appeals on unfair labor practice charges and representation claims; resolve appeals from negotiability decisions made by agency heads; and decide exceptions to arbitration awards. The Federal Service Impasses Panel was given discretionary authority to assist parties in resolving bargaining impasses when voluntary arrangements failed.[30] Establishing a framework to govern labor-management relations in the federal government, these entities defined unfair labor practices and authorized the use of binding arbitration for certain disputes.[31]

Nixon's move toward labor reflected electoral concerns. In preparation for his 1972 campaign, he viewed organized labor as an important addition to the "silent majority" whose votes he needed to win reelection. He was right. Throughout his campaign, Nixon appealed to the "Middle Americans" who he claimed were angry at the excesses of antiwar protest and ghetto violence, tired of the Vietnam War, disappointed at the results of the Great Society programs, and discontented with the deteriorating economy. The nation's blue-collar workers—who made up a third of the electorate and had represented the core vote of Democratic presidential candidates since the 1930s— supported Nixon over George McGovern by 57 to 43 percent. In fact, for the first time since the early 1930s, a majority (54 percent) of members of labor union families voted for the Republican president in his landslide win.[32] This augured a new trend in presidential politics. Even though organized labor would continue to be among the Democratic Party's staunchest allies, union members, though still reliably Democratic, would often support Republicans.

Although federal employees were empowered with collective bargaining rights under Kennedy's and Nixon's executive orders, those rights were not necessarily secure, as any executive order is subject to amendment or termination by a successor president.[33] Thus, after Jimmy's Carter's election, federal employee groups lobbied Congress to codify the right of collective bargaining through legislation. Congress, under the 1978 Civil Service Reform Act, "essentially codified Nixon's executive order" but did not introduce any changes to labor-management relations in the federal work-force.[34] Under Title VII of the Civil Service Reform Act, also known as the Federal Service Labor-Management Relations Statute, Congress affirmed prior executive labor-management orders that had given nonpostal federal employees the right to organize, bargain collectively, and participate in de-cisions affecting their working lives through labor organizations of their choice.[35] Congress also established the Federal Labor Relations Authority to resolve impasses between employees and management and outline the scope of collective bargaining, but excluded the right to strike.[36]

That exclusion led to one of pivotal moments in the conservative "Rea-gan revolution." Federal air traffic controllers directly challenged federal labor-management policy when their union, the Professional Air Traffic Controllers' Organization (PATCO), called a strike in 1981. Prior to this ac-tion, there had been thirty-nine illegal work stoppages against the federal government between 1962 and 1981. Reagan warned PATCO that a strike called by a federal employee union would be illegal.[37] When PATCO refused to reverse its action, Reagan fired the striking controllers, and the Federal Aviation Administration (FAA) asked the Federal Labor Relations Author-ity to withdraw formal union recognition from PATCO.[38] Consistent with Reagan's position during the PATCO strike, federal labor-management re-lations became more adversarial and pro-managerial during his presidency. Indeed, the PATCO strike represented an "eruption of a systemic problem of adversarial labor-management relations in the federal government."[39] It also had its limits. Reagan, the only president to have led a union, the Screen Actors Guild, opposed strikes but supported the right of federal workers to unionize and bargain collectively.[40]

Bill Clinton's election marked a return to Democratic pro-labor priori-ties and an expansion of presidential authority as the employer-in-chief. In response to demands from organized labor and the belief that a "hostile climate diminished the quality of federal public service," Clinton worked to transform the adversarial relationship between federal unions and manage-ment.[41] He established the National Partnership Council to support "the creation and promotion of labor-management partnerships and propos-als."[42] Clinton also charged federal agencies with pursuing more joint deci-sionmaking with employees and their union representatives. As a result of Clinton's executive order on labor-management partnerships, the number of partnership agreements between employees and management increased throughout the federal government.[43]

Clinton's executive order on federal labor-management relations did not survive George W. Bush's first term. Like Reagan, the new Republican chief executive officer viewed the federal government as a pro-management employer. Under the mantle of promoting "more efficiency" within the federal bureaucracy, Bush issued executive orders that revoked all of Clinton's actions on labor-management relations in the federal government.[44] As a result, the National Partnership Council was dissolved and federal agencies were no longer required to form labor-management partnerships (the order did not repeal any collective bargaining agreements in effect at the time). After Bush's Executive Order 13203, federal agencies did not know whether the president intended to prohibit, or simply discourage, labor-management partnerships.

After the September 11 attacks, Bush as employer-in-chief established new rules regarding federal labor-management relations in a select number of agencies: the changes by Bush tipped the balance of power in favor of management.[45] Bush took a series of actions: He canceled an executive order issued by his predecessor that directed federal agencies to cooperate with union representatives in addressing common issues, withdrew collective bargaining rights from groups of federal employees based on national security considerations, and narrowed the scope of issues over which unions in two of the largest federal agencies were permitted to bargain.

Specifically, Bush excluded units of the Departments of Energy, Homeland Security, Justice, Transportation, and the Treasury from the existing federal labor-management relations program. Thus, the president acted as an employer-in-chief to introduce greater management flexibility, particularly in agencies concerned with national and homeland security.[46]

FEDERAL EMPLOYEE HEALTH AND SAFETY

Presidents use executive power to respond to interest groups and political allies, including those advocating for change resisted by Congress, entrenched groups and, sometimes, the public at large. This is nowhere more apparent than in the concept of the federal government as a "model employer" that unilaterally sets new standards that could be adopted by the private sector, through choice or by congressional mandate. This dynamic arose after the Civil War when the rapid increase in factory-related employment led to high rates of workplace injuries and deaths. In response to these developments, in 1882 Congress adopted the first workers' compensation protection for federal employees.[47]

Theodore Roosevelt invigorated this effort as he reflected on and responded to progressive demands for change. A critical moment occurred when he introduced the concept of the federal government as a "model employer" in his seventh State of the Union address.[48] While encouraging private sector reforms concerning liability laws, child labor, and the maximum length of the workday, Roosevelt called for the federal government to provide compensation to all employees injured in government service.[49] Recasting the federal workforce as a policy tool, he declared, "The National Government should be a model employer. It should demand the highest quality of service from each of its employees and it should care for all of them properly in return." Roosevelt's premise was that the federal government should lead efforts to change society's ills by addressing the needs and welfare of wage earners.[50] This was part of his larger effort to push executive powers to new limits in response, he argued, to the rise of industrial capitalism, which had rendered a limited federal government obsolete. Roosevelt is widely regarded as the first modern U.S. president, not least because he thought that the president had the right to use any and all powers not specifically denied to him by the Constitution.[51]

Roosevelt's immediate successors were less active than he in advancing efforts concerning federal workplace health and safety issues. When the American entry into World War I created a crisis in the war production industries, it was Congress that acted. Under the 1916 Federal Employees' Compensation Act (FECA), Congress agreed to provide protection for economic losses in the form of compensation to civilian employees of the federal government injured in the line of duty and protect their families in cases of federal employment-related deaths.[52] Woodrow Wilson delegated administration of the FECA program to the Federal Employees' Compensation Commission.[53] It was almost a quarter century before the next important executive action, when FDR acted to increase federal employee health and safety by creating the Federal Interdepartmental Safety Council with Executive Order 8071 in 1939.[54]

As the post–World War II economy boomed, concern for worker health and safety reemerged in regard to the construction and automobile industries. Truman took several steps to "strengthen the arm of the Federal Government for better integration of services in the fields of health, education, and welfare."[55] He abolished the Federal Employees' Compensation Commission, transferring its duties to the Federal Security Agency (1946).[56] Truman also established the Federal Safety Council, whose purpose was to serve in an advisory capacity on matters relating to the safety of civilian employees of the federal government. He charged the council to advise on "the development of adequate and effective safety organizations and programs in federal agencies with respect to criteria, standards, and procedures designed to eliminate work hazards and health risks and to prevent injuries and accidents in federal employment."[57] In 1954 Eisenhower issued a memo on federal employee health and safety in which he requested "the head of each [federal] agency to review their accident experiences and the safety program and to take all necessary steps to reduce accidents."[58]

By the 1960s, organized labor began to put pressure on the federal government to address health and safety in the private sector. Up to that point, individual states had been responsible for health and safety regulation. But organized labor concluded that federal reform was needed to set uniform federal standards—and presidents responded by acting unilaterally as "model employers." Kennedy kick-started the effort by reestablishing the Federal Safety Council. Johnson launched a health and safety policy for the federal government called Mission SAFETY-70.[59] Johnson charged "every administrator in the federal government with personal responsibility to see that the causes of accidents are found and eliminated. We want the federal government to set standards of safety that will be copied by public and private groups."[60] Nixon, building on prior orders, introduced "ZERO IN on Federal Safety" and required each federal agency to identify and remove work hazards. Nixon concluded that quality of life and safety "in the workplaces of the Federal service must be the best—both for the protection of our employees and as an example to the Nation."[61]

Following the lead of several presidents, Congress affirmed prior executive orders on health and safety by adopting the Occupational and Safety Health Act (OSHA) to assure "safe and healthful" working conditions in the private sector in 1970.[62] From its inception, OSHA faced resistance from the private sector. Nixon, seeing an opportunity to shift blue-collar voters away from Democrats, announced his support for federal employee health and safety reform. Consequently, Nixon issued an executive order as a catalyst for federal leadership. Nixon affirmed OSHA by strengthening and reinforcing health and safety rules in the federal government. Echoing Theodore Roosevelt and Johnson, Nixon claimed, "As the Nation's largest employer, the Federal Government has a special obligation to set an example for safe and healthful employment." However, Nixon's mandated only that federal agencies have occupational health and safety plans "of some kind."

Even though Nixon attempted to make the rules for federal employees more specific, they remained unclear and confusing.[63]

As the economy slid into a period of lower growth and higher inflation, dubbed "stagflation" by some, Nixon began expressing concern about the influence of health and safety rules in the private sector of the economy.[64] Ford agreed that the rules had spurred inflation and become excessively burdensome. But he also needed union support in 1976, so he affirmed Nixon's executive order, expanding health and safety standards for federal employees in Executive Order 11807. Ford's order was not very different from Nixon's, but it strengthened reporting mechanisms.[65]

Federal employee unions made new political demands on Jimmy Carter to address the lack of compliance with health and safety standards in the federal workplace as well as the disparity in enforcing standards across the federal and private sector workplace. President-elect Carter named "safe working conditions" as one of his goals as president. Carter subsequently required that health and safety standards for federal employees be on par with those in the private sector.[66] After mandating that federal agencies, including the United States Postal Service, comply with all OSHA rules, Carter also directed all agencies to create Occupation Safety and Health Committees that would monitor the agency's performance. Carter's unilateral action marked a significant expansion of health and safety protections for federal employees. Carter's order applied to all federal employees (except military personnel) and required all federal agencies to ensure that workplaces were "free from hazards that could cause death or physical harm," operate an occupational safety and health program, comply with standards set by the Labor Secretary, establish safety procedures, perform periodic workplace inspections, and respond to employee reports of dangerous or hazardous conditions.

Reagan, with different ideological preferences, exercised the flip side of executive authority—the power not to act. Rather than vigorously enforcing OSHA rules, Reagan sought voluntary compliance from private sector employers on health and safety matters. Reagan did issue a brief policy statement on health and safety for federal employees, but he focused on improving the "efficiency" of the federal government, stating: "Besides our overriding goal of providing a safer and healthier workplace for federal employees, this effort should result in significant cost savings."[67] George H. W. Bush issued an executive order to reduce life-threatening conditions faced by employees in buildings owned by the federal government.[68]

Clinton, a so-called New Democrat attempting to balance labor and business concerns, issued a "New OSHA" order whereby its principal enforcement tools—inspections, citations, and penalties—were replaced with new, more flexible mechanisms such as partnership, compliance assistance, outreach, and training.[69] Despite reforms of worker health and safety rules in the private sector, Clinton undertook only moderate efforts to support health and safety reforms in the federal workplace. For example, Clinton only authorized the continuance of the Federal Advisory Council on Occupational Safety. The Federal Advisory Council was first established by Nixon's Executive Order 11612, and then reestablished by Ford and Carter. Clinton was the first president to reestablish the council since Carter in 1980. Clinton did provide compensation for Department of Energy nuclear weapons workers and established the Energy Employees Occupational Illness Compensation Program.[70]

During the 2000 campaign, George W. Bush, like Reagan, promised to promote greater "efficiency" within the federal government.[71] Bush concentrated on improving federal employee health and safety as a means of reducing the health and financial costs of accidents in the federal workplace and enhancing worker productivity.[72] As a result, Bush established the Safety, Health, and Return-to-Employment initiative for federal agencies. SHARE aimed to improve efficiency by focusing on different aspects of a safety, health, and injury case management program: lower total injury and illness case rates, lower lost-time injury and illness case rates, improved timely reporting of injuries and illnesses, and reduced rates of lost production days due to work-related injuries and illnesses.[73]

In sum, in the case of federal employee health and safety, Congress affirmed Nixon's executive orders and Carter acted to expand upon what Congress did. Congress, affirming prior executive orders, adopted the 1970 Occupational and Safety Health Act to assure "safe and healthful" working conditions. However, Congress created two different statutory frameworks, for federal and private sector employees. The major difference was the lack of policing and enforcement mechanisms for ensuring health and safety in the federal workplace. In the private sector, an Occupational Safety and Health Administration was responsible for conducting inspections and investigations, and OSHA would enforce violations through monetary penalties. This compliance and enforcement process was absent in the federal government, in which Congress placed all authority over health and safety with the federal agencies themselves.[74] Thus, Carter was instrumental in requiring health and safety standards for federal employees to be on a par with those in the private sector.[75]

A BROAD VIEW OF FEDERAL EMPLOYEE HEALTH
AND SAFETY IN THE WORKPLACE

Historically, presidents also have acted on a broad range of other health and safety issues that affect the federal workplace and its employees. These have included requiring the use of seat belts for federal employees whose jobs involve driving, establishing a drug-free and smoke-free workplace, addressing AIDS in the federal workplace, and promoting a healthy workplace. Reagan, once again focusing on improving efficiency and reducing costs, required all federal employees to wear seat belts on the job. Acting as the employer-in-chief, Reagan noted, "On-the-job safety belt use policy for Federal employees will reduce human pain and suffering, set an example for the private sector, and reduce the burden on the taxpayers caused by motor vehicle accidents." Reagan directed all federal agencies to take all appropriate measures within their existing employee health and safety programs. Clinton extended Reagan's order to include military personnel.[76]

As a crack epidemic ravaged many parts of America, Reagan focused on illegal drug use in both the private sector and the federal workplace. Reagan declared a "war on drugs" and subsequently made it a priority of his presidency. Outlining steps to achieve his goal of a drug-free America, Reagan concluded, "Our first goal is to seek a drug-free workplace for all Americans. . . . To accomplish this we propose to create a drug-free workplace for all federal employees." One of his most ambitious proposals, to require mandatory drug testing of federal employees, attracted little political support from the Democrat-controlled Congress. This presented Reagan with a problem faced by other presidents: the possibility that Congress might take action to reject the power of the employer-in-chief.[77]

To preempt Congress, Reagan issued an executive order "to promote a drug-free federal workplace and workforce." Reagan aimed to establish a precedent for the "federal government, as the largest employer in the Nation, to show the way towards achieving drug-free workplaces." Reagan's EO 12564 established a program to offer drug users a "helping hand" while illustrating the federal government's intolerance of drug usage through mandatory drug testing for all federal employees. It required all federal agencies to develop five-point plans for creating a drug-free workplace and all executive agency and department heads to develop plans to promote a drug-free workplace. It also created an Employee Assistance Program for any federal employee with a drug use problem.[78]

In the lead-up to the 1986 midterm election, Reagan's executive order faced resistance from within federal agencies themselves. In addition, federal employee unions challenged the constitutionality of the drug tests. Several federal courts ruled that mandatory drug tests violated a federal employee's Fourth Amendment rights. Indeed, the court placed some limits on the power the employer-in-chief.[79]

The AIDS epidemic, which began in the early 1980s, presented new challenges to the nation and the presidency. Responding to the fear that AIDS could be spread by casual contact in the federal and private sector workforce, in 1987 Reagan created the Presidential Commission on the Human Immunodeficiency Virus Epidemic, which published recommendations for federal agencies.[80] Reagan then ordered federal agencies to adopt guidelines that would prevent discrimination against federal employees carrying the AIDS virus. Reagan stopped short of issuing an executive order, a measure that the commission had recommended.[81] Instead, Reagan directed the attorney general to review the commission's antidiscrimination recommendations and requested federal agencies to adopt a policy based on Office of Personnel Management guidelines on how to treat HIV-infected persons in the workplace.[82] One observer, citing the prevalence of AIDS in the gay community, concluded that Reagan's decision was a "political capitulation to the rising wave of a new, staunchly reactionary and religious Republican constituency that was to reshape not only the party but the state of American politics."[83]

In 1986, Reagan addressed a slightly less controversial issue: calls for smoke-free workplaces following the surgeon general's warnings about the dangers of secondhand smoke. Some federal agencies banned smoking in their buildings, but George H. W. Bush ultimately abandoned plans to prohibit smoking across the federal government in a bow to pressure from Big Tobacco lobby.[84]

Clinton, responding to public health advocacy groups, was more willing to take on the tobacco industry and banned smoking in the White House immediately after taking office in 1993 and eventually banned smoking in federal buildings. Clinton's EO of 1997 established a smoke-free environment for federal employees and members of the public who visited or used federal facilities. Clinton's EO was followed by a series of additional executive actions taken "to curb the tobacco industry." In 2000, he directed all federal agencies to review their current tobacco cessation programs. Clinton also charged the OPM with establishing a Model Smoking Cessation Program. The order also allowed for the establishment of smoking cessations programs in each federal agency but did not affect designated smoking areas, residential accommodation, or federally owned buildings leased or rented in entirety to nonfederal parties.[85]

George W. Bush, building on prior federal workplace orders, issued an executive order to improve the efficiency and coordination of federal policies regarding personal fitness. Bush directed federal agencies to review all policies, programs, and regulations related to physical activity, nutrition, screenings, and making healthy choices.[86] Thus, presidents relied on executive power to address a broad range of health and safety issues in the federal workplace.

A FLEXIBLE, FAMILY-FRIENDLY WORKPLACE

Historically, presidents have used executive orders and memos to be politically responsive to changes in the composition of the electorate and the federal workforce. As far back as 1957, the comptroller general approved the payment of salaries to federal employees for work done at home.[87] Since the 1970s, as the American economy and workplace have been transformed by the rise of technology as well the rise of both two-income and single-parent households, presidents have used the power of the employer to achieve political and policy goals, including support for a flexible, family-friendly federal workplace.[88]

Fulfilling a campaign promise, Carter established the White House Conference on Families. In an effort to accommodate electoral shifts and demographic changes, especially the increase in the number of women who were their families' breadwinners, Carter pledged "to encourage the introduction of more flexible work alternatives to benefit federal employees with children, students, and the older or handicapped worker." Carter directed the Civil Service Commission to establish innovative programs "to expand opportunities for men and women seeking part-time employment" to ensure that the federal government made the best possible use of job candidates' available talents. His memo included redesigning jobs and work schedules to open up permanent part-time opportunities; recruitment efforts to attract capable men and women to part-time work; eliminating artificial barriers to part-time employment; and pilot programs to determine where part-time employees could make the maximum contribution.[89]

However, Reagan's pro-management preferences came into political conflict with Carter's innovative alternative work scheduling procedures. Reagan opposed any efforts to make flextime permanent, and his OPM sought more management and productivity controls over current and future flextime programs across the federal government.[90] George H. W. Bush, in contrast, offered more support for flextime, asserting that "flexible workplace policies will allow you to find and keep the best talent."[91] Bush implemented the Federal Flexible Workplace Pilot Project (Flexiplace) to gain experience and information from work-at-home programs, satellite work center programs, and flexiplace accommodations for disabled workers.[92]

As divorce became more common in the United States beginning in the 1960s, presidents relied on the power of the employer to strengthen child support enforcement in the federal workplace. For example, Carter ordered the garnishment of wages of federal employees owing money for child support or alimony payments. Clinton's support for enforcing child support was also connected to his larger goal to "end welfare as we know it." During the 1992 election campaign, Clinton promised that his plan of increasing compliance with child support orders would shrink welfare rolls. Congress included child support enforcement measures in the 1996 welfare reform legislation. Clinton also affirmed the federal government's position as a "model" employer with respect to the financial support of employees' children.[93]

Clinton established new rules for child support enforcement for employees of the federal government, requiring all federal agencies, including the military, to help establish paternity and child support orders and assist with enforcing and collecting child and medical support where action was required. After Congress passed the 1993 Family and Medical Leave Act (FMLA), Clinton in 1994 issued his Family Friendly Workplace memo to expand opportunities for federal employees to participate in flexible work arrangements.[94] Clinton stated that "in order to recruit and retain a federal work force that will provide the highest quality of service to the American people, the executive branch must implement flexible work arrangements to create a 'family-friendly' workplace." Following up on the memo, Clinton directed all federal agencies to establish a program to encourage and support the expansion of flexible family-friendly work arrangements, including job sharing, career part-time employment, alternative work schedules, and telecommuting and satellite work locations.[95]

Clinton issued an additional memo to address the family and medical needs of federal employees who did not qualify for unpaid leave under the 1993 FMLA or sick leave under the 1994 Federal Employees Family Friendly Leave Act. Without support from Congress, Clinton took immediate action within existing statutory authorities to ensure that federal employees could schedule and be granted up to twenty-four hours of leave without pay each year for a range of activities including school and early childhood educational activities; routine family medical purposes; elderly relatives' health or care needs.[96] Clinton directed the OPM to propose government-wide regulations to enable federal employees to use up to twelve weeks of accrued sick leave each year to care for a spouse, son, daughter, or parent with a "serious health condition." Clinton directed the OPM to establish an Interagency Family Friendly Workplace Working Group to promote, evaluate, and exchange information on federal family-friendly workplace initiatives, and he directed each executive department and agency to appoint a family-friendly work-life coordinator to serve as a member of this working group. Clinton also directed all federal agencies to identify positions that could be relocated to alternate work sites and filled by qualified individuals and to develop an action plan for encouraging the recruitment and employment of qualified individuals with significant disabilities.[97]

As the post-9/11 wars continued, George W. Bush supported efforts to expand the 1993 FMLA to provide unpaid leave to military families when a spouse is seriously wounded in combat.[98] He also created the Commission on Care for America's Returning Wounded Warriors in 2007. The purpose of the commission was to "provide a comprehensive review of the care provided to America's returning Global War on Terror service men and women from the time they leave the battlefield through their return to civilian life."[99] Congress would later affirm Bush's effort.

In sum, affirming Carter's order on a flexible federal workplace, Congress allowed federal agencies to increase part-time opportunities for federal employees.[100] Congress also extended the authority of federal agencies to allow employees more flexibility in scheduling their workweeks.[101] Congress affirmed Clinton's order by passing the Federal Employees Family Friendly Leave Act in 1994, which provided federal employees the same (and some expanded) benefits offered to private employees under the FMLA.[102] It also institutionalized the flextime benefits mandated by Clinton's 1994 memo. In 1996, Congress refused to "allow federal and eligible private sector workers 24 hours of unpaid leave annually to fulfill family obligations."[103] Clinton hoped the employer-in-chief's first-mover advantage, as a model employer, would encourage Congress to follow with new rules for the private sector. Congress also affirmed George W. Bush's order, extending family and medical leave to military families under the National Defense Authorization Act in 2008.[104]

Affirming a Clinton EO on child support enforcement, Republicans in Congress in 1996 passed the Personal Responsibility and Work Opportunity Reconciliation Act, which included provisions to enhance the enforcement of child support. Congress, affirming the Clinton EO, in 1996 also passed the Debt Collection Improvement Act to make it easier for states to collect overdue child support.

CONCLUSION

The complex and dynamic evolution of the federal civil service during the twentieth century boils down to the conclusion that the modern president sought greater political control and influence over federal personnel policy. As Congress recognized that a larger federal government required a chief executive officer to manage the federal civil service, the power of the employer-in-chief became central to the modern presidency. For electoral and political reasons, presidents used their executive power to define the terms and conditions of the employment relationship between the federal government and its employees—in labor-management relations, in employee health and safety, and in a more flexible, family-friendly workplace.

Historically, there were fundamental differences in employer-employee relations in the federal government as compared to the private sector.[105] Because negotiations over wages, benefits, and workplace rules take place in the political arena, private sector and federal employees have been treated differently, although those differences have diminished over time. Federal employees have been organized to lobby since the early twentieth century, and they have been able to secure a political advantage to pressure both Congress and the president for benefits and workplace protections. Since federal employees help elect chief executives, "They are in a position to use their voting power to set the agenda at the bargaining table, and politicians have incentives to be responsive."[106]

Presidents, responding to political demands, relied on the power of the employer-in-chief to transform the federal workplace into one that recognized collective bargaining, protected employees' health and safety, and created a more flexible, family-friendly work environment.

However, the power of the employer has also become a contentious and partisan issue during the past few decades as the relative strength and influence of private sector unions has diminished while that of public sector unions has increased.[107] In 2010, for first time, a majority of union members were government employees rather than private sector employees.[108] Federal employees are four times more likely to be unionized as private sector workers.[109] The political overtones are clear: over the two decades since the mid-nineties, federal employee unions have become more visible and active in American politics, supporting Democrats in a majority of cases. Thus, Republicans are more likely to act in ways to restrict their political influence in elections.[110] In 2015, federal unions added approximately 40,000 members, the largest net number of new members in one year since 2008.[111]

In the century between Reconstruction and the 1960s civil rights era, the president as employer-in-chef was the central mover in establishing the federal government's nondiscrimination policies and efforts to create a diverse and inclusive federal workplace. Both Republican and Democratic presidents successfully used the power of the employer-in-chief to expand equal opportunity in federal employment.

FIVE

The President and the Power of the Equal Opportunity Employer

The history of American politics has often centered on the nation's complicated relationship with its founding ideal that "all men are created equal." This tension was made manifest in the Constitution, with its provision counting each slave as three-fifths of a person for purposes of representation. When the United States was founded, its female citizens did not share all of the same rights as men, including the right to vote. Since then, the United States has made strides to prohibit discrimination based on race, color, religion, sex, or national origin and to ensure equal opportunity, especially with the passage of the Thirteenth, Fourteenth, and Fifteenth Amendments to the Constitution, passed after the Civil War, the Nineteenth Amendment in the 1920s, and the 1964 Civil Rights Act. One of the underappreciated aspects of this political history is the pivotal role that presidents using the executive power of the employer-in-chief have played in this process. Especially during the century between Reconstruction and the civil rights era, the president was often the central mover, creating the nondiscrimination and equal employment opportunity policies that fostered a more diverse and inclusive federal workplace. Often acting in the face of strong public or congressional opposition, presidents ultimately inspired more far-reaching legislation.

There also were some occasions when presidents used the power of the employer-in-chief to increase discrimination and undermine equal opportunity, in ways that affected women during the Great Depression and homosexuals during the McCarthy era. The larger pattern, however, is of presidents moving the federal government from a more exclusive to a more inclusive employer. American society and politics have become more diverse, and as various interest groups have emerged, presidents have responded, and their executive orders have been a key tool for extending opportunity not just to racial minorities but also to veterans, women, those with disabilities, and members of other groups. These EOs often paved the way for broader congressional reform.

THE PRESIDENT AND THE POWER OF THE (EQUAL OPPORTUNITY) EMPLOYER

Racial discrimination has long been one of the most controversial and contentious issues in American politics. Just as presidents have used the power of the purchaser to fight racial discrimination in the private sector, many presidents have used the power of the employer to fight discrimination in the federal civil service. In both cases their executive actions often served as models that helped transform society and pushed Congress to act. This was not true of every twentieth-century president. Woodrow Wilson, in particular, reduced the number of black federal employees and allowed the segregation of workers.[1] But the next Democrat to hold the White House, Franklin D. Roosevelt, was the first chief executive to prohibit employment discrimination within the federal government.[2] As World War II loomed, Roosevelt faced demands from civil rights groups which protested the exclusion of over 75,000 eligible African American workers from industrial defense-related jobs.[3] Their leaders claimed that an antidiscrimination order was the only way to prevent "the largest demonstration in our capital's history."[4]

In response, Roosevelt used his power as employer-in-chief to mandate "that there shall be no discrimination in the employment of workers in defense industries or government because of race, creed, color, or national origin."[5] He also created "a committee for fair employment practice," which became known as the Fair Employment Practices Committee (FEPC).[6] The president directed the FEPC to investigate charges of discrimination, marking an unprecedented reform of antidiscrimination measures in the federal workforce.

For several years the FEPC had limited authority and weak enforcement power, and Congress authorized minimal funding. Once again demands from civil rights groups prompted Roosevelt to act. He strengthened the FEPC by bringing it directly under his political control in the Executive Office of the President (created by Roosevelt in 1939).[7] Roosevelt's order, known as "the second FEPC," broadened the scope of the committee's work and required all federal government contracts to include nondiscrimination-in-employment clauses.[8] Roosevelt also extended the oversight of the FEPC to nongovernment contracts and defense industries.[9]

Roosevelt's order quickly increased the employment of African Americans in defense-related jobs. The number of blacks employed by federal agencies or defense industry contractors doubled between 1942 and 1944, rising from 4.2 to 8.6 percent of all federal employees.[10] In Washington, D.C., itself, where the president had the greatest influence, the number of black federal employees more than doubled, increasing from 8.4 percent of all federal employees in the nation's capital in 1938 to 19.2 percent in 1944.[11] Although Roosevelt opened employment opportunities for minorities in the federal workforce, the FEPC faced political uncertainty. Southern Democrats in Congress ended FEPC funding after Roosevelt's death.[12]

Facing pressure from civil rights groups and needing black support as he faced a tough election in 1948, Harry S. Truman built upon Roosevelt's precedent by prohibiting discrimination in federal employment and noncivilian employment.[13] Like Roosevelt, he relied on executive orders to work around the opposition of southern Democrats in Congress.[14]

Truman created the President's Committee on Civil Rights in 1948 and charged it to recommend action that would "safeguard the civil rights of the people."[15] This committee recommended that Congress adopt the Federal Fair Employment Act to prohibit discrimination in private employment and also urged Truman to ban discrimination in federal employment "by presidential mandate."[16] The committee also recommended that the U.S Civil Service Commission (CSC) be empowered to enforce the mandate so that all federal agencies complied with a "nondiscrimination policy in federal employment."[17]

In one of the boldest uses of executive power in the nation's history, Truman also ordered the desegregation of the armed forces in 1948, requiring that there be "equality of treatment and opportunity for all persons in the armed services without regard to race, color, religion or national origin."[18] America's fighting forces were integrated when the Korean War began in 1950. Still, most of the actual enforcement of the order—including the desegregation of military schools, hospitals, and bases—was accomplished during Dwight D. Eisenhower's administration.[19]

Truman proposed a ten-point plan for civil rights reform, but Congress balked.[20] So Truman took executive action.[21] Truman required each federal

agency to establish an equal employment program for its employees; to ensure that all personnel actions by federal appointing officers be based solely
on merit and fitness; and to take appropriate steps to prevent discrimination due to race, color, religion, or national origin. Truman established the
Fair Employment Board to review cases from federal agencies and issue periodic reports to the president. Additionally, Truman required the desegregation of all federal agency dining rooms.[22] Truman's order initiated change
in the diversity of the federal workforce.[23] Despite the positive effects within
some agencies, Truman faced political resistance from other federal agencies. For example, the Treasury Department resisted hiring blacks in the
Bureau of Engraving and Printing. Truman pushed back, and mandated that
the bureau hire black candidates.[24]

When Eisenhower won the 1952 election, Congress remained resistant
to civil rights reform. Eisenhower was more reluctant than his Democratic
predecessors to issue antidiscrimination orders. Although he supported
equal rights, he "believed equally strongly in limited government."[25] Like
his two immediate predecessors, however, he faced increasing demands
from civil rights groups.[26] Eisenhower abolished Truman's Fair Employment
Board and established the President's Committee on Employment Policy.[27]
Eisenhower claimed it was "the policy of the United States Government that
equal opportunity be afforded all qualified persons, consistent with law,
for employment in the Federal Government" and reaffirmed "with respect to
all personnel actions in the executive branch, that there shall be no discrimination because of race, color, religion, or national origin."[28]

After the 1960 election, John F. Kennedy faced political demands to reward civil rights groups and African American voters, who had given him
70 percent of their vote in a contest that Kennedy won by a razor-thin margin.[29] Kennedy advanced antidiscrimination measures and enforced equal
employment opportunities within federal agencies.[30] He also recognized a
troubling truth: that many executive orders used similar sweeping language
but they did not all have the same sweeping impact. Kennedy concluded that
a "review and analysis of existing executive orders, practices, and government agency procedures relating to government employment and compliance
with existing non-discrimination contract provisions reveal[s] an urgent need
for expansion and strengthening of efforts to promote full equality of employment opportunity."[31] In response to the results of this review, Kennedy
reorganized the federal government's equal employment efforts under a
new committee, the President's Committee on Equal Employment Oppor-

tunity (PCEEO). Kennedy charged the PCEEO with studying employment practices in the federal government and recommending additional affirmative steps that federal agencies could take in order "to realize more fully the national policy of nondiscrimination within the executive branch of the government." Kennedy required federal agencies to comply with nondiscrimination standards, and authorized the PCEEO to sanction agencies that violated nondiscriminatory employment practices.[32] As a result of Kennedy's order, African Americans represented 18 percent of new federal hires in 1962, compared to 2 percent in the prior year.[33] By 1963, 13 percent of all federal workers were African American. But the PCEEO also reported that while African Americans made up 12.6 percent of the federal workforce, they were concentrated in low-skilled jobs.[34]

Following Kennedy's lead, Lyndon B. Johnson also acted unilaterally to enforce equal opportunity policies, adding women and the elderly to the list of groups explicitly protected from discrimination.[35] After Congress followed decades of presidential action by passing the 1964 Civil Rights Act, Johnson issued an executive order to support the enforcement of equal employment opportunities.[36]

Richard Nixon did not share his predecessor's electoral motivations for supporting equal employment—African American voters had supported Hubert Humphrey in the 1968 election. Yet he shared their belief that the federal government was obligated to help minorities achieve economic success through access to jobs.[37] In fact, Nixon criticized his predecessors' efforts, arguing that prior orders prohibiting discrimination had not adequately increased the representation of minorities and women in the federal workforce.[38] Thus, Nixon ordered that "the head of each executive agency establish and maintain an affirmative action program of equal employment opportunity for all civilian employees and applicants for employment."[39] Nixon authorized nondiscrimination in federal employment for all persons regardless of race, color, religion, sex, national origin, handicap, or age, reaffirming (but also superseding) prior orders.[40] Nixon's executive order became the official nondiscrimination statement of the federal government, and future presidents would amend Nixon's order when they added protected groups to the nondiscrimination statement. Rather than simply prohibiting discrimination in the federal workforce, Nixon required affirmative efforts to recruit minority and female employees.[41] Nixon's order was the first to mandate that all federal agencies implement an "affirmative action program" with specific goals and timetables.[42] Nevertheless, Nixon's order was having limited impact on the number of women and minorities in the federal workforce.[43] In response, in 1971 the CSC mandated federal agencies to set goals and timetables for minority employment.

Jimmy Carter issued a series of executive orders designed to improve the "efficiency and effectiveness" of the equal employment opportunity policies established by both prior executive order and legislation.[44] Eliminating discrimination on the basis of age and disability had been part of the equal employment policy, but prior to Carter's order the federal government's official antidiscrimination statement did not include these groups as protected classes.[45] Carter also consolidated all equal employment oversight for both private sector and federal employees (previously under the Civil Service Commission) under the Equal Employment Opportunity Commission (EEOC), created by the 1964 Civil Rights Act, while establishing a single standard for evaluating selection procedures used in hiring for all types of employers. Ronald Reagan, with different ideological preferences, did not support affirmative action and considered reversing prior affirmative action policies.[46] In the end, he took no action.

Bill Clinton became the first chief executive after Nixon to reform the federal government's equal employment opportunity policy. Signaling that he was a "New Democrat" seeking a middle ground between the left and the right, Clinton declared his position on affirmative action as "mend it, don't end it."[47] Clinton also acknowledged changing demographics by pledging to create a cabinet that "looked like America."[48] Indeed, the Hispanic vote was becoming important to Democratic victories in presidential elections.[49] Clinton won over 60 percent of the Hispanic vote in the 1992 and 72 percent of Hispanic vote in 1996.[50] In response to this important political constituency, Clinton argued that the federal government must address the fact that "Hispanics remain underrepresented in the Federal workforce." He not only challenged the federal government to increase the number of Hispanic employees in the federal workforce, but also directed all federal agencies to give preference to Hispanics in federal employment, as long as this could be done while upholding standards of merit.[51]

Clinton reaffirmed federal government policy of nondiscrimination in the federal workforce by instructing each agency to develop a program for recruitment and career development of Hispanics in federal employment.[52] Clinton required plans for assessing barriers to the recruitment and hiring of qualified applicants; appointed Hispanic federal executives to rating, selection, and review panels and boards; promoted the participation of Hispanic employees in management, leadership, and career development; and advanced other outreach efforts.[53] George W. Bush followed suit. According to reports from the Office of Personnel Management, Hispanics represented 7.9 percent of the federal workforce in 2008, the last year of Bush's term.[54]

FROM EXCLUSION TO INCLUSION OF WOMEN IN FEDERAL CIVIL SERVICE EMPLOYMENT

After women secured the right to vote under the Nineteenth Amendment, political calculations changed for the president as employer-in-chief. Women had sought federal employment at an increasing rate since the institution of the merit-based system reforms.[55] By 1920, all classes of civil service examinations were open to women, but those in charge of hiring could decide whether they wanted a man or a woman for the job.[56] In the midst of the Great Depression, in 1932, Congress amended the civil service rules with a "marriage clause" that put women at a deeper disadvantage in regard to federal employment.[57] This marriage clause allowed federal agencies to deny employment to women or fire employees because they were women.

As organized women's groups strengthened in the 1940s, there was increased political demand on the chief executive to provide employment opportunities for women in the federal government.[58] These groups played a key role in helping Truman secure women's votes in the 1948 election, including a "Housewives for Truman" campaign. To reward his electoral supporters, Truman appointed several women to positions in the executive branch.[59] Truman, and later Eisenhower, however, offered limited support to their demands for the appointment of a Commission on the Status of Women.[60]

Eisenhower, in an effort to reach out to women as a political constituency, told women voters, "If it should be my destiny to serve as chief executive, I would utilize the contributions of outstanding women to the greatest extent possible."[61] Like Truman, Eisenhower appointed women to key cabinet positions, but he never issued any order regarding opportunity for women in federal employment.

Kennedy was the first president to advance the status and increase the number of women in the federal civil service workforce beyond political appointments. Kennedy, unlike his predecessors, responded to political demands, as women now made up 50 percent of the electorate and had supported him overwhelmingly in the 1960 election.[62] Kennedy established the

President's Commission on the Status of Women and charged it with reviewing "the employment policies and practices of the federal government and
developing additional affirmative steps to assure nondiscrimination on the
basis of sex and to enhance constructive employment opportunities for
women."[63]

Kennedy relied on the legal opinion of the attorney general—his brother,
Robert F. Kennedy—for the authority to issue a memo on equal opportunity for women in the federal service that opened up greater opportunities
for them in federal employment.[64] Kennedy directed the CSC to review personnel policies affecting the employment of women, and "to assure that selection for any career position is made solely on the basis of individual merit
and fitness."[65]

Johnson initially was less supportive of equal opportunity for women in
federal employment, opposing Title VII of the 1964 Civil Rights Act, which
prohibits employment discrimination based on race, color, religion, sex and
national origin.[66] However, after repeated political demands from women's
groups, Johnson did prohibit discrimination based on sex in federal employment.[67] Johnson also inserted "sex" as a category covered by federal equal
opportunity policy, which would have far-reaching consequences.[68] The Johnson antidiscrimination measures were applicable to those working in administrative, executive, and professional positions.[69] Johnson's order was more
aggressive than other antidiscrimination measures legislation—including the
1963 Equal Pay Act, which prohibits sex-based wage discrimination.[70]

Nixon also advocated for women's issues, including for passage of the
Equal Rights Amendment, in a political effort to secure women's votes.[71]
Nixon directed federal agencies to develop plans for attracting "more qualified women to top appointive positions,"[72] and required federal agencies to
establish Federal Affirmative Employment Programs to foster equal employment opportunity for minorities and women.[73]

In the 1976 election, women emerged as a key political constituency for
Carter. Affirming Johnson's order, Carter directed all agencies "to provide
maximum employment opportunities for women in the Federal career service. This means developing, within merit principles, innovative programs
to recruit and hire qualified women and to be sure they have the opportunity for satisfying career development."[74] Carter demanded that the federal
government "aggressively and creatively" provide employment opportunities for women in the federal workforce.[75] Neither George H. W. Bush nor
Bill Clinton took specific action to advance the employment of women in
the federal workplace.[76]

Although religion has been a powerful force in American politics, it has not been a primary issue in federal employment. Introducing a merit-based system for hiring with the 1883 Pendleton Act, Congress mandated open selection of federal employees and guaranteed the right of citizens to compete for federal appointment without regard to political affiliation, religion, race, or national origin.[77] Subsequently, Grover Cleveland, FDR, and Eisenhower reaffirmed that the religious and political opinions of employees could not be a factor in any part of the federal hiring process.[78]

Evangelical Christians renewed their political engagement, especially during the Reagan years. Subsequently, during the Clinton presidency, religious discrimination became a controversial issue. In response to concerns from religious groups and some members of Congress concerning Equal Employment Opportunity Commission rules on limiting "religious harassment,"[79] Clinton issued a memo "reinforcing the right of religious expression."[80] Clinton also affirmed the 1993 Religious Freedom Restoration Act, which declared that the federal government could enforce a law that "substantially burdened" the free exercise of religion only if it furthered a compelling state interest and was the least restrictive way to achieve it.[81] The law was overturned by the U.S. Supreme Court as an unconstitutional extension of Congress's authority.

Clinton mandated that federal agencies "shall not discriminate against employees on the basis of religion, require religious participation or non-participation as a condition of employment, or permit religious harassment."[82] The Clinton guidelines addressed employees' religious exercise and religious expression when the employees were acting in their personal capacity within the federal workplace and the public did not have regular exposure to the workplace. The Clinton guidelines did not address whether and when the federal government and its employees may engage in religious speech directed at the public. They also did not address religious exercise and religious expression by uniformed military personnel, or the conduct of business by chaplains employed by the federal government.[83]

VETERAN PREFERENCES

Today, affirmative action is associated with policies to combat discrimination based on race or gender. But the precedent for these efforts—which are distinct from hiring preferences associated with patronage—can be traced back to the plight of Civil War veterans and efforts to make sure they got preference in hiring. Because most of these efforts to offer preferences to veterans were uncontroversial, Congress took the lead. Beginning in 1865 it passed a series of measures that gave preference in federal hiring to disabled veterans;[84] prohibited veterans seeking federal employment from being penalized for time spent in military service; and mandated that when reductions in the federal workforce were necessary, the government retain "those persons who may be equally qualified who have been honorably discharged from U.S. military or naval service and the widows and orphans of deceased soldiers and sailors."[85]

When it reformed the civil service by means of the 1883 Pendleton Act, Congress protected preferences previously granted to "those honorably discharged from the military or naval service."[86] An 1888 CSC rule gave absolute preference to disabled veterans over all other eligible candidates.[87] In 1912, Congress, in the Sherwood Act, bestowed upon veterans an absolute preference for their retention—that is, a veteran was preferred for job retention even over nonveteran federal employees with more seniority or higher performance ratings.[88] Later, in the 1919 Census Act Rider on Veteran Discharges, Congress gave special preference to disabled and nondisabled veterans by adding points to their scores on civil service tests.[89]

Historically, presidents' orders to support the preferential hiring of veterans followed a predictable pattern of increasing after a conflict that produced veterans who needed jobs, and were accompanied by political demands on Congress and the president to make it easier for veterans to return to civilian life.[90] Between the Civil War and World War I, presidents began to act within their congressionally delegated authority to reinforce preferential treatment of veterans in federal employment. For example, Benjamin Harrison allowed honorably discharged veterans who had formerly worked as federal employees to be reinstated in their jobs at any time, without a time limit to the length of time after their discharge.[91] This was the first instance of reinstatement eligibility as applied to veterans; reinstatement rights were then extended to the widows and orphans of veterans.[92] Theodore Roosevelt ordered federal departments to adhere to laws "giving preference to veterans."[93]

Between 1919 and 1944, as presidents expanded their use of executive orders, it was often to reform the strong preferences afforded to veterans. At the end of World War I, the nation experienced a recession as it was forced to absorb a large number of veterans of a foreign war for the first time. This helped create tension between those who had fought and those who had remained. Warren G. Harding claimed that existing rules violated notions of fairness and allowed unqualified people to be appointed to government positions. Harding removed absolute preference for veterans, requiring instead that they be given only a weighted preference on civil service examinations.[94]

Herbert Hoover amended civil service rules to change the way the point system on exams was applied to disabled and nondisabled veterans.[95] FDR further dialed back the level of veteran preference by ordering the CSC to grant only five extra points in rating candidates who had served in World War I, the Spanish-American War, or the Philippine Insurrection.[96] In 1938, however, the CSC once again strengthened veteran preferences: a new rule mandated that decisions to hire a nonveteran job candidate over a veteran were subject to additional review.[97]

These early executive orders, between 1919 and 1944, set the precedent for future actions by chief executives on the employment of veterans in the civil service. Roosevelt, for example, directed the CSC to give special preference to World War II veterans in federal employment.[98] In 1944 the Veterans Preferences Act Congress affirmed the thrust of executive orders that had been issued over the previous quarter of a century.[99] The reemployment and retention preferences were not dramatically different from those already in effect under executive order, but Congress, in response to political demands from veterans' groups, considered it important to give legislative sanction to those benefits.

Truman, using authority delegated by Congress under the Veterans Preferences Act, modified civil service rules to make it easier for returning veterans to be hired by the federal government.[100] During World War II and the Korean War, Truman expanded veterans' access to federal employment by making several positions into noncompetitive appointments. Truman also ordered the CSC to give disabled veterans a new competitive classified status.[101]

The Vietnam War presented once again the political challenge of addressing the reemployment of veterans in the federal government. Johnson, while prosecuting an increasingly unpopular war, claimed: "the federal government has long set an example for the rest of the nation as a good employer of veterans. But I am convinced that the Federal Government can be even a better employer."[102] Johnson allowed veterans to enter the federal workforce without taking civil service examinations.[103]

Nixon followed suit, mandating that federal agencies use affirmative action policies—which were also being extended to other groups—in the hiring of veterans.[104] Nixon empowered federal agencies to make an excepted appointment during the hiring process. Nixon called it a "readjustment appointment" because he said it was the federal government's responsibility to help veterans readjust to civilian life by offering job opportunities.[105] Nixon established the first equal employment policy for veterans in the federal government. He also created a "Jobs for Veterans" program that urged private companies and state and local governments to hire veterans.[106] Nixon required federal employment systems to list vacancies specifically for veterans.[107]

Jimmy Carter required all federal agencies to strengthen their efforts and advance federal employment of Vietnam veterans.[108]

George H. W. Bush, like all his predecessors, supported federal government efforts to provide jobs for returning veterans. Bush mandated that federal agencies accommodate veterans returning from Operation Desert Storm.[109] This included restoring veterans (military reservists and members of the Air and Army National Guard) to the federal jobs that they had left and granting extra leave time from their duties.[110] Bush specifically included military reservists, a group that had not been the beneficiaries of veterans' preference under the Veterans Readjustment Act.

FROM VETERANS TO ALL INDIVIDUALS WITH DISABILITIES

In many ways the logic and political advantage of providing preferences to disabled veterans provided the foundation for helping all citizens with disabilities. A prime example of this transference of preferential treatment occurred after World War II, when presidents gradually introduced efforts to extend protections and preferences to disabled job seekers and workers who had not served in the military. Truman, for example, also required federal agencies and the armed forces to provide employment preferences for veterans with a "service-connected disability," which is an injury or illness that was incurred or aggravated during active military service.[111] Truman enlarged the group of those affected when he stated: "One of today's major challenges is the finding of suitable employment for disabled veterans and other handicapped workers. As long as they are not gainfully employed they represent a substantial loss to the productive capacities of our country."[112]

Truman established the President's Committee on National Employ the Physically Handicapped Week, and every subsequent president has reinstated this committee.[113] The President's Committee on Employment of the Handicapped, founded by Eisenhower, ultimately became the Office on Disability Employment Policy when affirmed by Congress in 2001.[114] Kennedy expanded the committee's brief by instructing it to develop employment opportunities for individuals with physical or mental handicaps. Kennedy directed the CSC to "issue a 2-year special authority to make excepted appointments of mentally handicapped persons to federal positions."[115] In a memorandum written by Johnson, the category of "handicapped" was described as "the qualified mentally retarded, who can perform well some of the simpler tasks that must be done in any large organization; the mentally restored, whose only handicap is that they once were ill; the physically impaired, who are not thereby occupationally disabled."[116]

Congress, under Section 501 of the Rehabilitation Act of 1973, eventually codified these actions, prohibiting federal executive branch agencies, including the U.S. Postal Service and the Postal Rate Commission, from discriminating in hiring against qualified individuals with disabilities. It required executive branch agencies to take affirmative action in the hiring, placement, and advancement of individuals with disabilities.[117] Congress also established the Interagency Committee on Employees who are Individuals with Disabilities.[118] As the nation's largest employer, presidents reaffirmed that the federal government has a special responsibility to lead by example in including people with disabilities in the workforce.

After Congress approved the Americans with Disabilities Act in 1990, George H. W. Bush issued a memo urging federal agencies to serve as a model for American businesses in their policies and practices regarding the employment of Americans with disabilities. Bush pushed the federal government to adopt policies and initiatives that "remove barriers that prevented people with disabilities from gaining access to employment opportunities." Bush also called on federal agency heads to "share your experiences and success stories with the private sector so they can benefit from the lessons learned."[119]

In 1998 Clinton created the National Task Force on Employment of People with Disabilities to "create a coordinated and aggressive national policy to bring adults with disabilities into gainful employment at a rate as close to that of the general population" as possible.[120] Clinton, in an effort to "ensure that the Federal Government is a model employer of adults with disabilities," directed the OPM to develop, and all federal agencies to implement, a plan to increase the representation of adults with disabilities in the federal workforce.[121] Clinton established timetables and goals for the federal government to hire an additional 100,000 qualified individuals with disabilities from 2000 to 2005. To meet this benchmark, Clinton also requested that federal agencies expand their outreach efforts to individuals with disabilities.[122] Clinton also required all federal agencies to establish written procedures to facilitate the provision of "reasonable accommodation" for individuals with disabilities.[123]

In response to demands from mental health advocacy groups, in 1999 Clinton mandated that federal agencies give employees with "psychiatric disabilities the same opportunities as employees with physical disabilities or severe mental disabilities."[124] In sum, from Kennedy to Clinton, presidents' executive orders broadened the definition of disablement to include individuals with more types of disability.[125]

SEXUAL ORIENTATION: FROM EXCLUSION TO INCLUSION

As mentioned earlier, presidents sometimes used executive orders to restrict the federal employment of subgroups rather than to protect them from discrimination. This was especially true regarding individuals with nonconforming sexual orientation. Such individuals were often labeled perverts, and especially during the 1940s and 1950s, were linked with policymakers' fears of "political subversives" within the federal government. These policymakers considered political subversives to be not only Communists but also "sexual perverts," or homosexuals.[126] It would be misleading to blame one person for a long and government-wide persecution of homosexuals, but a major impulse came from Senator Joseph McCarthy. Congress pressured the chief executive to strengthen federal personnel security. Truman created a new Loyalty Program to "root out" political subversives and those deemed disloyal or potentially disloyal.[127]

According to Truman, "maximum protection must be afforded the United States against infiltration of disloyal persons into the ranks of its employees, and equal protection from unfounded accusations of disloyalty must be afforded the loyal employees of the Government."[128] Although Truman did not make explicit reference to sexual orientation in his executive order, the term "disloyalty" implied homosexuals.[129] From 1947 to 1950, 1,000 employees were fired every month under this program.[130] In a majority of these cases, the reason for termination was sexual orientation.

Under Truman's Loyalty Program the CSC was directed to ask applicants whether they had "homosexual tendencies."[131] It also led the FBI to run background checks on more than 2 million federal employees. As a result of those checks, the FBI launched investigations into the personal lives and political beliefs of more than 14,000 employees.[132] Truman issued additional executive orders that promoted discrimination against homosexuals in the federal government.[133] In a sign of the complex nature of history, even as he boldly desegregated the military, Truman listed sexual perversion as a disqualifying condition for the armed forces.[134] Truman also made it easier to question civil servants' loyalty and to remove them from their positions.[135] Under Truman's executive order, there only had to be a "reasonable doubt" of loyalty for termination to take place.

The 1952 election highlighted concerns about the sexual orientation of employees within the federal government. Republicans ran a "Let's Clean House" campaign designed to suggest that the federal government under Truman was "rife with homosexuals and communists."[136] Eisenhower replaced Truman's Loyalty Program with an even stricter one.[137] Eisenhower demanded that all federal employees exhibit loyalty and that any employee who is "disloyal" or "untrustworthy" would be dismissed. Disqualifying behaviors were listed, and for the first time, "sexual perversion" was included.[138] Before each appointment, Eisenhower required an investigation to gather information as to whether employment of a given individual in the federal service was clearly consistent with the interests of the national security.[139] Prohibited practices included "any criminal, infamous, dishonest, immoral, or notoriously disgraceful conduct, habitual use of intoxicants to excess, drug addiction, or sexual perversion."[140]

During the 1950s, federal courts followed the doctrine that "since federal employment was not a right, the federal government as an employer could impose essentially any conditions it chose on that employment."[141] Throughout the 1960s, the application for federal civil service employment contained the question for all applicants: "Have you ever had, or have you now, homosexual tendencies?"[142] As the various liberation movements for blacks, women, gays, and other marginalized groups flowered, however, the CSC announced a new approach for determining the suitability of homosexual applicants for federal employment.[143] In 1975 the CSC issued a new rule stating that employees could not be dismissed based on "conduct that does not adversely affect their job." This rule was eventually listed as one of thirteen "Prohibited Personnel Practices," or PPPs, and was commonly interpreted as covering employees' sexual orientations—that is, homosexuality would not be a reason for termination if it did not adversely affect the person's ability to do their job. Carter affirmed this rule.[144] Carter also stated that federal employees or applicants for employment were protected from actions based on or inquiries into matters such as religious, community, or social affiliations or sexual orientation.[145]

Despite this slight softening of the barriers to homosexuals, by the 1990s the federal government still did not have an explicit nondiscrimination policy regarding sexual orientation. Clinton used executive orders to address that. He reaffirmed the existing agency interpretation: "OPM has long taken the position that [the tenth PPP] applies directly to discrimination on the basis of sexual orientation."[146] Clinton also advised federal agencies that federal employees were protected against actions taken in response to non-job-related conduct, including sexual activities.[147]

A major issue for gay rights groups at the time was the federal government's policy, dating to Truman's loyalty oath, of using sexual orientation as a reason to deny security clearance to federal employees. Clinton, in response to key organized groups, issued new guidelines for determining employees' suitability for security clearance, stating that "the United States Government does not discriminate on the basis of race, color, religion, sex, national origin, disability, or sexual orientation in granting access to classified information."[148]

Using executive authority to lead the nation in a new direction, Clinton worked to prohibit discrimination against gays and lesbians at a time when Congress and much of the public resisted legislation prohibiting discrimination based on sexual orientation. Actions Clinton took included support for a proposed Employment Non-Discrimination Act, which would have extended antidiscrimination protections to gays and lesbians.[149] More broadly, Clinton added "sexual orientation" to the federal government's equal opportunity statement.[150]

Linking his actions with earlier efforts of presidents to advance civil rights, Clinton hoped the new rules might pressure Congress to pass the Employment Non-Discrimination Act.[151] Clinton's EO on equal opportunity did not contain any enforcement muscle because "those rights (of enforcement) can be granted only by legislation passed by the Congress, with the Employment Non-Discrimination Act."[152]

PROHIBITING DISCRIMINATION BASED ON AGE, STATUS AS PARENT, OR GENETIC INFORMATION

As American politics and demography continued to change during the mid- and late twentieth century, presidents applied their long-established authority to new areas. Dramatic increases in life expectancy made age discrimination in employment a new and important issue. Federal employees did not enjoy any protection from age discrimination until 1956, when the CSC banned age limits on entry into federal employment.[153] It took seven more years before Kennedy became the first chief executive to prohibit discrimination based on age in federal employment. Kennedy issued a memorandum which declared that the "policy of the federal government as an employer is to evaluate each job applicant on the basis of ability, not age."[154]

Johnson also declared a policy against discrimination on the basis of age and prohibited age-based discrimination in federal employment.[155] Nixon issued a memorandum stating, "As the largest employer in the nation, the [federal] government has a special responsibility to [take] the lead in eradicating age discrimination in the world of employment." For Nixon, the time had come for the federal government to recommit to its long-held position "that age, by itself, shall be no bar to a Federal job which an individual is otherwise qualified to perform." Nixon directed all agencies to take immediate steps to cease any "practice that denies older citizens fair and full consideration for employment and advancement" in the federal workforce.[156]

Facing a changing landscape, Clinton was the first president to use executive authority to protect parents from discrimination. As part of his working families agenda—including the flextime reforms described in the previous chapter—Clinton aimed to prohibit discrimination against parents "striving to meet their responsibilities both at home and at the office," by supporting the Ending Discrimination against Parents Act. That reform prohibited "employment discrimination against private sector and public employees because they are parents." Clinton added "status as a parent" as a protected class under the federal government's equal opportunity policy.[157]

Clinton faced another new challenge as advancements in genetic testing raised concerns that this private medical information might be accessed and exploited by health insurance companies and employers for discriminatory purposes.[158] In response to demands by key advocacy groups, Clinton banned all federal agencies from requiring employees to submit a genetic test, and if an employee did take such a test, the information must be kept confidential. Clinton identified two familiar goals with his pioneering action: to set an example for every employer in America and to provoke congressional action.[159] In sum, Clinton updated Nixon's order to protect employees from discrimination on the bases of sexual orientation, status as a parent, and genetic information.[160]

CONCLUSION

As the number of federal employees has grown and groups that demand nondiscrimination and even preferential treatment in hiring have proliferated, preferences have evolved, and presidents have used the power of employer-in-chief to eliminate discrimination and expand equal employment opportunities for new political groups and interests. Executive power truly served as a model, allowing government the flexibility to test out new policies that the nation—or parts of it—resisted or hadn't fully considered. Presidents have taken the initiative, using their executive power to issue executive orders and memos to expand equal opportunity and limit discrimination in federal employment. Many of these orders were later affirmed by Congress. Of course, not every president was a champion of civil rights, or thought government decrees were the best way to achieve equality and opportunity. And, especially during the darkest days of the Cold War and the McCarthy era, some presidents acted to exclude particular groups from federal employment, including homosexuals. But, in the sweep of American political history, presidents have more often used the power of the employer-in-chief to advance more inclusive views that eventually gained wider support. This sensitivity may be due in part to the fact that the president is the only official chosen in a national election and must appeal to broad political constituencies.

It is useful to highlight a few examples that demonstrate how executive orders have inspired important congressional action regarding equal employment policies for racial minorities and other protected classes. Congress, under the 1964 Civil Rights Act, both affirmed and expanded upon earlier presidential orders that promoted the recruiting and hiring of minorities in the federal workforce. Indeed, it is hard to imagine the language and intent of that landmark bill without acknowledging the legacy of those efforts (even though soaring language was often paired with weak enforcement mechanisms). Efforts to battle age discrimination powerfully illustrate how presidents can influence Congress. Kennedy was the first chief executive to address this issue; Johnson continued this work. When Congress first took action, it affirmed Johnson's EO 11141 when it passed the 1967 Age Discrimination in Employment Act, which prohibited age discrimination in employment against individuals over forty years of age.[161] In 1972, Nixon issued a memorandum that extended those protections, which Congress affirmed in 1974 when it amended the Age Discrimination in Employment Act to include employees of state and local governments.[162] In the years that followed, Congress extended age discrimination protections to cover public and private workers. In amendments to the Age Discrimination in Employment Act passed in 1986, Congress ended mandatory retirement solely on the basis of age for most American workers and eliminated the upper age limit of seventy on all other protections of the act.[163]

Presidents also led the way in expanding rights to other marginalized groups. Kennedy's EO 10980, concerning discrimination of women in federal employment, set the precedent for the sweeping 1963 Equal Pay Act, which extended equal opportunity for women beyond federal employment, when Congress required that men and women be given equal pay for equal work in the same establishment.[164]

In 1944 Congress passed the Veterans' Preference Act, which required the federal government to favor returning war veterans when hiring new employees. This far-reaching law consolidated and affirmed veteran preference provisions already in effect as a result of executive orders and civil service rules. As the historical pattern unfolded again, Congress reaffirmed the executive orders of another wartime president, George H. W. Bush, when it passed the Uniformed Services Employment and Reemployment Rights Act of 1994, building on Bush's order that military reservists, including Coast Guard and National Guard Reserve, had the right to return to the civilian jobs they had held prior to leaving for active duty.

Another landmark example was Congress's affirmation of Nixon's EO 11478 when it passed the 1972 Equal Employment Opportunity Act, which provided equal opportunity in federal employment on the basis of merit and fitness and prohibited discrimination on the basis of race, color, religion, sex, or national origin.[165] It also affirmed prior executive orders by adopting the 1973 Vocation Rehabilitation Act, which prohibited discrimination based on disability in federal employment as well as contracts and programs receiving federal funds. The Vocation Rehabilitation Act remained the only reform regulating the rights of employees with disabilities until Congress passed the Americans with Disabilities Act in 1991, which prohibited discrimination against individuals with disabilities and mandated "reasonable accommodation" for employees. Finally, Clinton's EO 13145 set a precedent for the more expansive definition included by Congress in the Genetic Information Nondiscrimination Act of 2008.[166]

Carter was the first chief executive to require that federal employees or applicants for employment be protected from actions based on or inquiries into matters such as religious, community, or social affiliations or sexual orientation.[167] Congress codified the OPM's tenth "Prohibited Personnel

Practice" as part of the Civil Service Reform Act. Over the years, the OPM interpreted the PPP as prohibiting discrimination based on sexual orientation.[168] Presidents embraced this guideline, as it spared them from having to take a more political risky position.

Presidents, with preferences evolving over time, have successfully used the power of the employer-in-chief to address equal opportunity in federal employment and, through this behavior of the federal government as the model employer, also to influence Congress and the private sector. Obama built on this legacy, using the power of the employer-in-chief to dictate the terms and conditions of the employment relationship between the federal government and its employees, to expand protections to emerging groups, and to hold up the federal government as a model for the private sector.

SIX

Barack Obama and the Power of the Employer-in-Chief

Barack Obama was remarkably consistent in the political and policy goals he pursued throughout his presidency. Indeed, during his final year and months in office he was working to fulfill campaign promises he had made as a candidate in 2008. But Obama addressed his agenda in two very different environments. During his first two years in office he focused on passing legislation with a Democrat-controlled Congress. After Republicans took political control of the House in 2011 and the Senate in 2015, Obama asserted the power of the employer to achieve political and policy priorities actively opposed by Congress. Republicans complained often and bitterly about these efforts. Obama tried to defuse their charge in 2014 when he noted, correctly, that he had issued the fewest number of executive orders of any president since Grover Cleveland. What he did not say was that he had issued more presidential memoranda than any chief executive before him. Indeed, many of Obama's memos accomplished the same things prior presidents had by executive order.[1] In the era of immensely complicated and often divided government, presidents increasingly believe they must call the shots via executive orders and memoranda.

Obama, like his predecessors, used the power of the employer-in-chief to dictate the terms and conditions of the employment relationship between the federal government and its employees. More specifically, Obama issued orders and memos to expand the reach of the federal government as a "diverse and inclusive" employer (see chapter 5) and to deliver political benefits to federal employees (see chapter 4). As employer-in-chief, he acted in a range of existing and new areas: labor-management cooperation, employee pay, worker health and safety, domestic violence prevention in the workplace, and efforts to encourage a flexible, family-friendly workplace. Obama gave special attention to promoting equal opportunity by addressing diversity and inclusion in the federal workforce, reemployment of veterans, reemployment of the long-term unemployed, employment of individuals with disabilities, employment of younger workers, federal employee benefits for same-sex couples, and prohibiting discrimination based on sexual orientation and gender identity.

LABOR-MANAGEMENT PARTNERSHIPS, PAY FREEZES, AND EMPLOYING THE LONG-TERM UNEMPLOYED

Obama received significant political support from organized labor during the 2008 and 2012 elections, and he subsequently resolved to "do everything we can do to strengthen unions in this country."[2] His predecessor, George W. Bush, had revoked Bill Clinton's order requiring federal agencies to form labor-management partnerships.[3] Obama reversed this reversal, strengthening collective bargaining in the federal workplace by "establishing a cooperative form of labor-management relations throughout the executive branch."[4] Expanding upon Clinton's order, Obama created the National Council on Federal Labor-Management Relations to "support the creation of department- or agency-level labor-management forums." Obama requested that forum members collaborate on solving federal workplace issues within their organizations to improve federal government services. Obama's order aimed to support creation of labor-management forums, promote partnership efforts between labor and management, develop metrics to evaluate its effectiveness, provide guidance on labor-management relations improvement efforts, use training methods to further dispute resolution and cooperation, and "develop recommendations for innovative ways to improve delivery of services and products to the public while cutting costs and advancing employee interests."[5] Each federal agency responded with an implementation plan.[6]

With the national economy facing what turned out to be the Great Recession, Obama sent a political message that he understood the challenges ordinary Americans were facing by issuing a pay freeze for White House officials on his first day in the White House in 2009.[7] Obama wrote a memorandum in which he directed his chief of staff and heads of all federal agencies "to suspend cash awards, quality step increases, bonuses, and similar discretionary payments or salary adjustments to any politically appointed federal employee."[8] Republicans in Congress went a step further, pushing Obama to freeze federal pay for all federal employees. In response, he mandated a two-year freeze in the pay of all civilian employees of the federal government.[9] However, as the economic recovery began, Obama ordered a 1 percent pay raise for federal employees in 2014 and again in 2015, giving them only their second wage increase in five years after what turned out to be a three-year pay freeze.[10] Obama issued an additional executive order to strengthen the Senior Executive Service (SES) in an effort to streamline recruiting and hiring.[11] Members of the SES serve in the key positions just below the top presidential appointees, linking political appointees with the rest of the civilian federal workforce.[12] Obama raised the aggregate spending cap on executive performance awards from 4.8 to 7.5 percent.[13] His motivation for the increase was to "retain and reward more top performers" among SES and senior-level scientific or professional employees.[14]

FEDERAL EMPLOYEE HEALTH AND SAFETY

Obama, like some of his predecessors, issued a memo to protect the health and safety of federal employees. Under his Protecting Our Workers and Ensuring Reemployment initiative, Obama directed federal agencies to prioritize the implementation of health and safety management programs that had proved effective in the past.[15] Federal agencies were required to improve performance in seven areas of workplace health and safety, including the reduction of total injuries and illnesses, the timeliness of workers' compensation claims, and the reduction of lost time injury case rates. Federal agencies except the U.S. Postal Service were to coordinate with the DOL's Occupational Safety and Health Administration and Office of Workers' Compensation Programs to establish performance targets in each category. In addition, Obama issued an executive order focused on the reemployment of federal employees who had sustained work-related injuries and illnesses as defined under the Federal Employees' Compensation Act (FECA).[16] Obama's purpose was to increase the availability of job accommodations and light- or limited-duty jobs and remove disincentives for FECA claimants to return to work.[17]

The rise of cellular phone technology created a new workplace health and safety issue: distracted driving. While Congress began to consider this problem, Obama convened the Distracted Drivers Summit in 2009.[18]

Obama, acting as employer-in-chief, directed the nearly 4 million federal employees to refrain from texting or using government-issued electronic devices while driving for work.[19] Obama claimed that "a Federal Government-wide prohibition on the use of text messaging while driving will help save lives, reduce injuries, and set an example for state and local governments, private sector employers, and individual drivers."[20] Again, the president hoped Congress and the private sector would follow his lead with legislation.

After the 1994 Violence Against Women Act expired in 2011, Obama affirmed his support of the role of the federal government as a model employer in supporting employees facing domestic violence.[21] Under the banner of health and safety, Obama proclaimed that it is the policy of the federal government to promote the health and safety of its employees by responding to the effects of domestic violence, sexual assault, and stalking in the workplace and by providing support and assistance to federal employees whose working lives are affected by violence.[22] Obama, as first mover, hoped these policies within the federal workforce would serve as a model for private sector employers.

EQUAL PAY FOR EQUAL WORK AND A FLEXIBLE, FAMILY-FRIENDLY WORKPLACE

Women were a key part of Obama's electoral coalition. He won the presidential vote among female voters in the 2008 election by fourteen points and by twelve points in 2012.[23] To maintain political advantage, Obama and Democrats in Congress took of series of actions to counter what they described as a "Republican war on women." After Congress passed the 2009 Lilly Ledbetter Fair Pay Act, which prohibits sex-based wage discrimination between men and women in the same firm who perform jobs that require substantially equal skill, effort, and responsibility under similar working conditions, Obama issued a memo to address the wage gap between men and women working for the federal government.[24] While acknowledging his limited capacity to influence the wage gap—Congress sets federal employee pay levels—Obama asserted the power of the employer by noting that "the fixing of individual salaries and other types of compensation can be affected by the exercise of administrative discretion." Obama directed federal agencies to provide very specific data to the OPM, including agency-specific policies for setting starting salaries for new employees;

agency-specific policies that may affect the salaries of individuals who are returning to the workplace after having taken extended time off from their careers; agency-specific policies for evaluating individuals regarding promotions, particularly individuals who work part-time schedules; additional agency-specific policies that may be affecting gender pay equality; and any best practices the agency has employed to improve gender pay equality.[25]

During the 2008 campaign, Obama supported reforms to assist Americans in meeting work and family responsibilities. Obama saw economic stability for American families as depending on policies that help them balance work and caregiving obligations.[26] Throughout his presidency, Obama took unilateral action to advance flexible, family-friendly workplace reforms, including paid and unpaid family and medical leave and flexible work schedules. At a White House Workforce Flexibility Forum, Obama noted: "Workplace flexibility isn't just a women's issue. It's an issue that affects the well-being of our families and the success of our businesses. It affects the strength of our economy, whether we'll create the workplaces and jobs of the future we need to compete in today's global economy."[27] Obama issued several memoranda aimed at modernizing the federal government's workplace flexibility policies, including flexible work schedules, family medical leave, and sick leave. He established a pilot program on workplace flexibility.[28] Obama, as employer-in-chief, directed all federal agencies to keep their employees well informed about their rights to request work schedule flexibility under current federal law. Federal agencies were required to provide employees with the ability to request work schedule flexibilities, including telework, part-time employment, or job sharing. Obama also directed the OPM to initiate emergency leave transfer programs for federal employees impacted by natural disasters.[29]

Obama's family-friendly goals included paid sick leave and vacation time for federal employees.[30] Congress did not act in 2015 on either the Health Families Act, which would have allowed private sector employees to earn up to seven days of paid leave to take care of children or other sick family members, and the Federal Employee Paid Parental Leave Act, which would have allowed federal workers to accrue up to six weeks of paid sick leave annually.[31] Undeterred, Obama directed all federal agencies to offer up to six weeks of paid sick leave for parents with a new child, employees caring for ill family members, and other sick-leave-eligible uses.[32] Obama also mandated, in a memo in January 2015, that annual leave be made available to employees for placement of a foster child in their home.[33] Absent support from Congress for these initiatives, Obama took executive action as employer-in-chief.

EQUAL EMPLOYMENT OPPORTUNITY AND A DIVERSE
AND INCLUSIVE FEDERAL WORKFORCE

When Obama was elected the forty-fourth president of the United States in 2008, he swept away "the last racial barrier in American politics with ease as the country chose him as its first black chief executive."[34] Prior to Obama's historic election, the power of the (equal opportunity) employer evolved through decades of prior executive orders and/or congressional statutory affirmation. Affirming these efforts, Obama issued an executive order to promote diversity and inclusion in the federal workforce. Obama instructed federal agencies to "draw upon talents found in all parts of society and to tap diverse perspectives to overcome the nation's greatest challenges."[35] Obama ordered each federal agency to issue its own agency-specific Diversity and Inclusion Strategic Plan.[36]

If there is one thing just about every president has supported—besides, of course, the expansion of his own authority—it is preferences for veterans in federal employment. Obama was no different.[37] This was an especially important issue for Obama for at least two reasons: because he inherited wars in Iraq and Afghanistan and because of the effects of the long tradition of hiring preference maintained by both Congress and presidents. In 2012 the federal government was the nation's largest employer of "citizen-soldiers": about 123,000—or about 14 percent—of the 855,000 men and women serving as active duty or reservists in the National Guard had civilian jobs with the federal government. Over a fourth of federal employees were veterans.[38]

Obama had pledged to end those two wars in the Middle East, and he also wanted to assure returning veterans that he would support them. Congress, with the 1994 Uniformed Services Employment and Reemployment Rights Act (USERRA), had already ensured that service members would not experience disadvantages in their civilian careers due to their service. Just before his first Veterans Day as president, Obama, with clear political motivations, created the Council on Veterans Employment as part of an "effort to increase the number of veterans employed by the federal government by enhancing recruitment and training."[39] Affirming the power of the employer-in-chef, Obama noted: "The Federal Government, as our Nation's largest employer, has a responsibility to adopt best practices with respect to employing returning service members." Veterans already enjoyed preferences in federal hiring, but Obama went a step further, mandating in an EO that the progress be tracked and reported to the president.[40] Obama directed federal agencies to ensure compliance with USERRA's employment and reemployment protections across the federal government through outreach, education, and oversight. Organized veterans groups welcomed the action, which came just days after Obama signed a defense authorization bill that included new programs designed to assist service members and recent veterans.[41]

Despite prior executive orders and congressional support to promote the employment of individuals with disabilities, the number of these employees in the federal government remained largely unchanged even after passage of the Americans with Disabilities Act in 1990. Although an executive order of Bill Clinton's in 2000 called for an additional 100,000 individuals with disabilities to be employed by the federal government between 2000 and 2005, Bush took few steps to achieve this goal.[42] This revealed once again that issuing an order is one thing—implementing it successfully and effectively, another. Marking the twentieth anniversary of the Americans with Disabilities Act in 2010, Obama directed federal agencies to "improve their efforts to employ workers with disabilities and targeted disabilities through increased recruitment, hiring, and retention of these individuals."[43] Echoing Clinton, Obama restated the goal of hiring 100,000 individuals with disabilities in the federal workforce by 2015.[44]

Despite a recovering economy, job growth and labor participation rates remained low throughout Obama's presidency. In response, Obama extended protections to a new group: the unemployed. Obama issued a three-part call to action—by employers, by communities, and by federal agencies—to help Americans find jobs. In asking the private sector to not discriminate against the unemployed—especially the "long-term unemployed," defined as those who had been out of work for twenty-seven weeks or more—Obama as employer-in-chief acknowledged that the federal government must be a model employer.[45] Although federal agencies generally can, and do, take applicants' employment history and other factors into account when making hiring decisions, Obama reiterated that applicants "should not face undue obstacles to federal employment because they are unemployed or face financial difficulties."

Seeking to make the government workforce more diverse and inclusive, and to recognize his strong support from young voters, Obama claimed that the federal government was at a competitive disadvantage in trying to hire new talent—students and recent graduates; these applicants were often excluded from hiring because most positions with the federal government required prior work experience. In order "to compete effectively for students and recent graduates," Obama consolidated several initiatives into a Pathways Program, which offered a clear path for college graduates to federal internships and careers.[46] Obama's order represented a major personnel policy change by allowing recent graduates to receive "noncompetitive eligibility" once they completed the Pathways Program, which made it easier for them to land a job with the federal government.[47]

FEDERAL EMPLOYEES AND BENEFITS FOR SAME-SEX SPOUSES

Few aspects of American politics and policy have changed more profoundly during the last decade than views on same-sex marriage. Once again, executive power has been instrumental in this process. In 1996, under the Democratic president Bill Clinton, a Republican-majority Congress passed the 1996 Defense of Marriage Act (DOMA), whose purpose was "to define and protect the institution of marriage." DOMA defined marriage as the union of one man and one woman and prohibited the extension of any spousal benefits to the same-sex partners of federal employees.[48]

The federal government provides a variety of benefits to 4.4 million civilian and military employees and 4.7 million civilian and military retirees, including health insurance, dental and vision benefits, survivor benefits, retirement and disability benefits, reimbursement of relocation costs, and family, medical, and emergency leave. Federal employees may extend these benefits to eligible spouses and children. As of 2013, among these were an estimated 34,000 federal employees in same-sex relationships, including state-recognized marriages, civil unions, or domestic partnerships.

Both Barack Obama and Hillary Clinton as candidates for the Democratic nomination in 2008 explicitly declared their opposition to same-sex marriage, although they supported "civil unions." A civil union was a legal relationship between two people that provides legal protections to the couple only at the state level. A civil union is not a marriage: they do not provide federal protections, benefits, or responsibilities to couples, and a civil union may not be recognized by all states. Civil unions were established primarily as an alternative for same-sex couples in states where marriage was unavailable.

Three years later, as he was preparing to seek reelection in a very different political environment, Obama proclaimed his support for same-sex marriage, leading *Newsweek* magazine to portray him on its cover with a rainbow halo and a headline dubbing him the "first gay president."[49] Obama, responding to demands from his political base, took bold action. Obama hoped Congress would extend benefits to the same-sex partners of federal employees under the proposed Domestic Partnership Benefits and Obligations Act.[50]

With Congress unlikely to act, Obama issued two memoranda to expand benefits for same-sex couples in the federal workplace. First, Obama identified the existence of delegated, narrow, statutory authority to extend the benefits to same-sex domestic partners of federal employees that were available to heterosexual spouses. Obama directed the secretary of state and the Office of Personnel Management (OPM) to grant benefits to the same-sex partners of federal employees "where doing so can be achieved consistent with Federal law."[51] The OPM and the Department of Justice recommended a few specific federal benefits that could be legally extended to the partners of federal employees in same-sex relationships. Obama requested federal agencies to review the benefits offered by the agency, including workplace flexibilities and policies, and determine whether they already are available to—or could be extended to—the same-sex domestic partners of employees.[52] Obama also detailed which benefits OPM and the Department of Justice had recommended for extension to same-sex partners, but could only extend benefits to federal agencies whose authorizing statutes do not use the term "spouse" to define or limit potential recipients of the benefit.[53] The legal necessity of this constraint became clear when Secretary of Defense Leon Panetta, in a memorandum to the secretaries of all military departments in February 2013, extended many benefits to same-sex partners of military members.[54] But Panetta could not offer benefits that were available only to spouses, because the DOMA had defined "spouse" as a person of the opposite sex who was a husband or a wife.[55]

The U.S. Supreme Court removed this constraint in 2013 when it ruled that the federal government must treat all married couples equally and the DOMA discriminates against same-sex couples.[56] Obama immediately directed the attorney general "to review all relevant federal statutes to ensure the Court's decision, including its implications for federal benefits and obligations, is implemented swiftly and smoothly."[57] Obama then directed the OPM to extend health insurance, life insurance, dental and vision insurance, long-term care insurance, and flexible spending accounts to all same-sex spouses and annuitants of federal employees. After gay married couples were blocked from receiving the same benefits as their heterosexual counterparts, Obama as employer-in-chief, treated all married couples alike.[58]

PROHIBITING DISCRIMINATION BASED ON SEXUAL ORIENTATION AND GENDER IDENTITY

During the 2008 presidential campaign, Obama expressed his political support for legislation protecting all employees regardless of sexual orientation or gender identity.[59] While campaigning for the presidency in 2008, he promised to write an executive order banning workplace discrimination on the basis of sexual orientation. Once in office, Obama urged Congress to pass the Employment Non-Discrimination Act (ENDA). This reform would provide strong federal protections against discrimination, making it explicitly illegal to fire lesbian, gay, bisexual, transgender, or queer (LGBTQ) employees.[60]

The Obama administration adopted an equal employment opportunity policy that included both sexual orientation and gender identity from the outset, stating on its website in January 2009, regarding presidential appointments: "The Obama-Biden Administration does not discriminate on the basis of race, color, religion, sex, age, national origin, veteran status, sexual orientation, gender identity, disability, or any other basis of discrimination prohibited by law."[61]

With the House failing to act on ENDA in 2013 and 2014, Obama—building on Bill Clinton's EO barring discrimination on the basis of sexual orientation with his EO 13087 in 1998—issued an order to prohibit discrimination in the federal government based on gender identity.[62] Obama, claiming the federal government as an equal opportunity employer, stated: "This executive order is part of a long, bipartisan tradition. Roosevelt signed an order prohibiting racial discrimination in the national defense industry. Eisenhower strengthened it. Johnson expanded it. Today I'm going to expand it again. . . . I'm going to do what I can, with the authority I have, to act."[63]

Obama also required all agencies to review their antidiscrimination policies to ensure that they offered a nondiscriminatory work environment to employees, irrespective of their gender identity or perceived gender nonconformity. Obama's OMP stated: "The federal government does not and will not condone workplace discrimination against lesbian, gay, bisexual, and transgender Federal employees." Several federal agencies—OPM, the Equal Employment Opportunity Commission, the Office of Special Counsel, and the Merit Systems Protection Board—released a guide on the rights and processes available to applicants and employees who alleged that they had been discriminated against on the basis of sexual orientation or gender identity.[64] All federal employees—including LGBT individuals—would be able to perform their federal jobs free from unlawful discrimination. As of 2011, the federal government's equal employment opportunity policy read: "The United States Government does not discriminate in employment on the basis of race, color, religion, sex, national origin, political affiliation, sexual orientation, gender identity, marital status, disability and genetic information, age, membership in an employee organization, or other non-merit factor."[65]

Obama's decision to act unilaterally has been described as a matter of personal values as well as political considerations—namely, the need to mobilize young voters and solidify his liberal base. It wasn't until 2012 that Obama publicly voiced his support for same-sex marriage, concluding that civil unions were not a sufficient substitute for marriage. However, as Andrew Sullivan, a prominent gay journalist, concluded, "There was, of course, cold politics behind it. One in six of Obama's fundraising bundlers is gay, and he needs their money."[66] Bundlers organize and collect campaign contributions from other donors. This distinguishes them from writers of checks.[67] Another commentator noted, "Additionally, supporting equality is a smart, rationale strategy for him in terms of holding on to his base, of making sure that a large part of his base that is very invested in domestic policy remembers this enormous commitment he's made and the actions he's taken."[68]

CONCLUSION

Executive orders and memos are a paradox. In one regard they are timeless tools of continuity. Since the early days of the republic, presidents of all parties and persuasions have used them to expand the power of their office. An unintended consequence, of course, is that they have empowered successors who might have very different priorities and beliefs. In addition, presidents have used these tools to pursue their agendas, with or without the consent of Congress. This suggests a further paradox: presidents, who are the only officials who face a national electorate, often take these unilateral actions to overcome the resistance of other, democratically elected officials. Despite the timeless quality of *how* presidents act, *what* they choose to act on is deeply reflective of the specific time in which they serve.

Thus, presidential orders and memos often reflect the political and electoral concerns of their times. This was certainly true of Barack Obama. Indeed, his historic use of orders and memos indicated the growing political divide, as he sought to assert his agenda over the resistance of a hostile Congress. Like his predecessors, Obama took unilateral action to respond to the needs of his political supporters, delivering political benefits to key allies, including unions. Reversing the actions of George W. Bush, Obama supported labor-management cooperation as well as new efforts to support worker health and safety, including efforts to prevent domestic violence, sexual assault, and stalking in the federal workplace. As the leader of a country mired in a recession, Obama initially issued orders and memoranda on federal employee compensation, including a recession-based pay freeze for political appointees. When the economy improved, he authorized a post-recession pay increase for federal employees and the SES and ensured the re-employment of the long-term unemployed.[69] Obama also paid attention to issues affecting women and working families: he issued directives concerning equal pay and made the federal workplace more flexible and family-friendly.[70]

As the employer-in-chief, Obama initiated new efforts to improve diversity and inclusion in the federal workforce; to bring recent college graduates and young, less-experienced employees into the federal workforce, and to support employment of individuals with disabilities. As a wartime leader, Obama used his authority as employer-in-chief to affirm prior chief executives' efforts to extend preferences to veterans and facilitate their reentry into federal employment as well as to ensure that the federal workforce was diverse and inclusive.

Obama's most groundbreaking efforts revolved around the social and legal support for LGBT constituencies, which expanded with remarkable speed during his presidency. For the first time ever, a president used the power of the employer to extend benefits to same-sex partners of federal employees and used the power of the employer to extend protections to federal employees, regardless of sexual orientation and gender identity. After Republicans in Congress were unwilling to move on any of Obama's proposed reforms after the 2014 midterm election, the president relied on the power of the employer to achieve his political and policy goals.

SEVEN

The President and the Power
of the Ethical Employer

Few issues illuminate the political dimensions and tensions of the modern presidency more clearly than ethics. As the CEO of the federal bureaucracy and as its employer-in-chief, the president can define principles of ethical conduct for political appointees and federal civil service employees. The U.S. Office of Government Ethics defines a political appointee as "any employee who is appointed by the President, the Vice President, or agency head."[1] Federal civil service employees work under one of the independent agencies or one of the fifteen executive departments.

Throughout much of American political history, however, presidents have been hesitant to issue high-minded rules that might hamstring their political appointees. The executive orders they have issued have usually been in response to highly visible ethical scandals that occurred during the previous administration and generated public calls for reform.[2] These orders have allowed presidents to signal their ethical compass and their resolve to restore integrity within the federal government. Several factors—including the Watergate scandal, the growth of the federal government (which has increased the role and influence of lobbyists), and the development of far more scrutiny of public trust issues—have made establishing ethics standards a central feature of the modern presidency. At least since Gerald Ford, every president has made ethics and transparency features of his campaign and a stated value of his administration. But even as they have imposed new ethics rules, presidents have also carved out exemptions and waivers from their own standards. Presidents have also sought to control this potentially explosive issue by investing the Office of White House Counsel with greater influence over federal ethics policy.[3]

FEDERAL ETHICS RULES FROM PARTY PATRONAGE TO PRE-WATERGATE

Historically, Congress was often the first mover in dealing with corruption in the federal bureaucracy and initiating federal ethics reforms. Late nineteenth-century congressional ethics actions prohibited federal employees from receiving payment or anything else of value in exchange for offering to help private parties prosecute claims against the federal government. Congress also passed legislation containing prohibitions to reassure the public that federal employees and political appointees were not using their privileged access to government information to gain windfall profits or enrich themselves.[4] The 1872 Civil Post-Employment Act was the first time Congress paid attention to the issue of the revolving door and articulated a policy regarding conflicts-of-interest and outside compensation and mandated the reporting of financial interests for individuals who had left government service.[5] Under the 1883 Pendleton Act, Congress enshrined in law rules concerning unethical activity within the federal government. Congress extended the revolving door policy to all federal agencies and added a criminal penalty for any violations. The new federal merit system prohibited the practice of requiring federal employees to contribute part of their salaries to political candidates and parties. Under the 1916 Federal Employees' Compensation Act, Congress prohibited any outside supplementary contributions to a federal employee's salary for services performed by the federal government. In 1917 Congress also prohibited any supplementation for salaries of federal employees.[6]

World War I and the growing size of the federal government led Congress to impose new restrictions on the ability of former War Department employees to do business with the federal government and, perhaps, profit from their access to secret national security information. In 1919 Congress banned War Department officials from engaging in any private business dealings with the federal government for two years after leaving federal service.[7] In 1957–58, Congress adopted the general Code of Ethics for Government Service, which required all federal employees to avoid conduct that raised questions about their objectivity or impartiality, but the code didn't include any penalties for violations. The code, for example, stated that federal employees should never dispense special favors or privileges, and never accept favors. These provisions were not legally binding because the code was adopted by congressional resolution rather than by public law. Nonetheless, the standards in the ten-point code are considered ethical guidance in the House and Senate.[8]

THE PRESIDENT AS CEO AND ETHICAL EMPLOYER-IN-CHIEF

Although ethics were not a central concern for presidents until after World War II, before then, as now, their executive orders on ethics were driven largely by the political motivation to persuade the public of their commitment to high ethical standards. Nearly without exception, ethics scandals associated with the executive branch have involved money—that is, political appointees or federal employees have been accused of betraying the public trust for private gain.[9] A post office scandal during Andrew Jackson's term—Jackson was known for maneuvering his political standing in order to garner favors—led the postmaster general to issue the first rules of ethical conduct for federal employees (1829).[10] Formal ethical rules within the federal government continued to evolve in the post-Jacksonian era.

Ethical conduct challenges during the 1930s and 1940s centered on World War II procurement issues.[11] Harry S. Truman, especially in his second term, faced scandals involving both political appointees and federal civil service employees.[12] As a direct result, Congress placed political pressure on Truman to take action, recommending an ethics code for federal employees and calling for the president's support of "the ten golden rules of ethics." Truman did not respond to Congress's initial demands, contending that ethics "has to be in a man's heart to start with."[13] Eventually, he agreed to support public disclosure of personal finances by senior members of all three branches of federal government. But Republicans in Congress blocked action to prevent Truman from being able to score political points for addressing ethics issues.

In response to Cold War pressures, Dwight D. Eisenhower became the first chief executive to act on an ethics-related challenge by requiring security checks—full-field investigations by the FBI—on all senior political appointees.[14] The full-field background investigation (FFI) is required for all employees assigned to high-risk positions. Focused on national security clearance, Eisenhower addressed the suitability for federal employment or service based on "any behavior, activities, or associations which tend to show that the individual is not reliable or trustworthy" or "any deliberate misrepresentations, falsifications, or omissions of material facts."[15] Eisenhower established the FBI's National Name Check Program to examine personnel security issues and mandated National Agency Checks as part of the pre-employment vetting and background investigation process.[16]

John F. Kennedy did not confront any particular ethical scandal, but felt the need for reform, noting in April 1961 that "in the past two decades, incidents have occurred to remind us that the laws governing ethics in government are not adequate to the changed role of the federal government, or to the changing conditions of our society." Kennedy asserted that "high level officials owe a special responsibility to the government and to their employees to set a high standard of ethical and moral behavior." Kennedy took the lead by appointing the Advisory Panel on Ethics and Conflict of Interest in Government. Reflecting his aggressive vision for executive action, Kennedy affirmed that the problems of ethics in the federal government could be addressed without the participation of Congress—by "presidential order, memoranda or other form of action." Kennedy issued a special message to Congress on conflicts of interest and other ethical issues among federal government employees, recommending comprehensive reform of existing conflict of interest statutes—the Executive Employees' Standards Act.[17]

Acting unilaterally, Kennedy prohibited unethical behavior including outside employment or activity incompatible with the proper discharge of official responsibility, outside compensation for any activity within the scope of official duty, and receipt of compensation for any lecture, article, public appearance, and so forth, devoted to the work of the department or based on official information not yet a matter of general knowledge.[18] He also attempted to prohibit conflicts of interest on the part of advisers or consultants to the federal government.[19] Congress followed his lead, passing the 1962 Ethics in Government Act, a comprehensive reform of the conflict-of-interest laws covering federal employees. Congress set forth conflict-of-interest regulations for part-time employees, tightened and closed loopholes in conflict-of-interest rules affecting full-time workers, and relaxed restrictions affecting part-time employees in an effort to draw more part-time or consultative talent into federal service. The law prohibited members of Congress and federal employees from receiving compensation for services pertaining to federal service (prohibiting the payment as well as receipt of such compensation); prohibited nepotism; clarified existing law, which prohibited the payment and receipt of salary from private sources as compensation for services as an employee of the executive branch; and continued existing law prohibiting a federal officer of employee from acting as an agent or attorney in the prosecution of claims against the federal government. Congress emphasized and strengthened the revolving-door policy. Federal employees were prohibited, for a period of two years after leaving the federal service, from representing anyone before a court or federal agency in any matter in which the United States had an interest that had been under the former employee's official responsibility.

In addition, some ethics provisions that applied to federal executive branch employees applied differently to an employee who qualified as a "special Government employee" (SGE), or did not apply at all. Congress created the SGE category in 1962, recognizing the need to apply appropriate conflict-of-interest restrictions to experts, consultants, and other advisers who serve the federal government on a temporary basis. On the other hand, Congress determined that the federal government cannot obtain the expertise it needs if it requires experts to forego their private professional lives as a condition of temporary service. Since 1962, the SGE category has been used in a number of statutes and regulations as a means of tailoring the applicability of some restrictions.[20]

Lyndon B. Johnson not only affirmed Kennedy's action but also moved beyond anything attempted by prior chief executives. Johnson's goal was for federal employees to avoid any action—whether or not specifically prohibited—that might result in or create the appearance of public offices being used for private gain. This included preferential treatment being given to any organization or person; impediments to government efficiency or economy; the loss of complete independence or impartiality of action; government decisions being made outside of official channels; or other adverse effects on the public's confidence in the integrity of their government. In pursuit of these goals, Johnson required federal employees to report the details of their *personal* finances. The order not only expanded the ethics management activities of the Civil Service Commission, but also prohibited federal government officials from holding financial interests, direct or indirect, that conflicted with their responsibilities as civil servants.[21] Richard Nixon expanded Johnson's order to include all federal employees at the U.S. Postal Rate Commission and the U.S. Postal Service.[22]

POST-WATERGATE POLITICIZATION AND
CENTRALIZATION OF FEDERAL ETHICS POLICY

The Watergate scandal and Nixon's resignation radically altered the political landscape, helping transform ethics into a central issue for all future chief executives. His successors faced two fundamental, intertwined challenges: issuing executive orders that signaled their political commitment to ethics to an increasingly mistrustful public, and using the Office of White House Counsel—a team of high-powered lawyers, who are often selected for their loyalty to the president—to exert political control over the entity charged with overseeing ethics rules within the federal bureaucracy since the late 1970s, the Office of Government Ethics.[23] Nixon's immediate successor, Gerald Ford, who took over after Nixon resigned, faced the difficult political task of beginning to restore public trust in the federal government.[24] This was especially challenging as federal government reports exploring corruption indicated that violations of the conflict-of-interest laws and rules had not resulted in any punishment.[25]

As the first chief executive elected after Watergate, Jimmy Carter ordered strict conflict-of-interest guidelines for his political appointees,[26] having concluded that "under the existing [Johnson] executive order, guidelines have often been unclear, and enforcement has been ineffective in some agencies."[27] Carter required all presidential appointees to disclose their business and financial interests and to remove any possibility of hidden conflicts of interest.[28] Carter demanded a commitment from these officials to adhere to tighter restrictions after leaving the federal government in "order to curb the revolving door practice that has too often permitted former officials to exploit their government."[29]

Carter proposed an Ethics in Government Act to "establish far-reaching safeguards against conflicts of interest and abuse of the public trust by [federal] government officials."[30] Democrats in Congress, seeking to restore public confidence and score political points, passed that reform in 1978. Congress established the Office of Government Ethics (OGE) to oversee the introduction of new ethics programs designed to prevent and resolve conflicts of interest in the executive branch. The Office of Government Ethics was to take charge of an expanded financial disclosure system, ensure education of executive branch employees, and review agency programs to guarantee compliance with ethics laws. It was charged with coordinating policy through designated federal agency ethics officials, who would be appointed within each agency in the federal government.[31] For the first time in American political history, the entire executive branch had one oversight system and a single set of standards for ethical conduct.[32] Congress initially recognized the chief executive's authority, making the OGE part of the Office of Personnel Management. The OGE is headed by a director who is appointed to a five-year term by the president, following confirmation by the U.S. Senate. The rest of the OGE employees are federal civil service employees. The director was charged with providing direction on executive branch policies of disclosure and collaborating with the U.S. attorney general in investigations of ethics violations.[33] Carter continued the pattern of securing political control and influence, saying, "The ultimate authority for—or responsibility for—endorsing and interpreting the provisions of the act lies in the executive branch of government."[34]

Ronald Reagan established a confidential financial reporting system for officials and employees of the executive branch.[35] Nevertheless, Reagan's term was plagued by ethics scandals, many involving grant rigging and influence peddling. Between 1981 and 1989 more than one hundred Reagan officials or former Reagan officials found themselves subject to allegations or improper or illegal conduct.[36] Democrats in political control of Congress became so concerned about Reagan's political control and influence over the OGE and the lax enforcement of federal ethics rules that in 1988 it made the OGE an independent agency when it passed the Office of Government Ethics Reauthorization Act.[37]

George H. W. Bush was determined to tackle early "an issue that became a millstone" for the man he had served as vice president—the conflict-of-interest questions about several of Reagan's closest advisers.[38] To distance himself from those ethical issues, in 1989 Bush created the Commission on Federal Ethics Law Reform, which recommended that individual federal agency standards of ethical conduct be replaced with a single regulation applicable to all executive branch employees.[39] Bush issued an executive order in which he declared fourteen basic principles of ethical conduct for executive branch employees. In consultation with the attorney general and the director of the OPM, Bush also directed the OGE to establish "a single, comprehensive, and clear set of executive branch standards of conduct that shall be objective, reasonable, and enforceable."[40] With this action Bush replaced hundreds of conflicting ethics rules across federal agencies with a uniform code that applied to all federal executive branch employees.[41]

With passage of the Ethics Reform Act of 1989, Congress affirmed the OGE as the supervising ethics office for the executive branch, granting it oversight of public and confidential financial disclosure reporting by federal agency employees. Congress expanded the restrictions on employment established by the 1978 reform beyond federal employees to include members of Congress and staff in the executive branch: these people, too, faced a year of non-employment in positions in private companies that used their former service in government to lobby on behalf of special interests. Employees were to disclose waste, fraud, abuse, and corruption to appropriate authorities.[42] Over time the OGE has evolved with a level of professionalism and political independence, working as a partner with all other executive branch agencies in developing, interpreting, and enforcing ethics laws and regulations. However, its authority has limits, for George H. W. Bush reasserted presidential authority by empowering the Office of White House Counsel to grant exemptions or approvals for presidential appointees to committees, commissions, boards, or other groups established by the president.

As a candidate in 1992, Bill Clinton assailed the Bush administration's standards of behavior in office, promising that he would lead "the most ethical administration in the history of the Republic."[43] During the presidential transition, Clinton issued ethical guidelines intended to close the revolving door between federal government service and private lobbying activities. Clinton's transition director, Warren Christopher, characterized these restrictions as a "dramatic step" that offered a forceful response to Americans who wanted to "take their government back."[44]

After assuming the presidency, Clinton applied the ethics standards to all top officials.[45] The most significant change was extending from one to five years the lobbying ban; officials could not lobby any officer or employee involved in a matter in which the former official had held significant responsibility. Clinton placed similar prohibitions on senior White House officials. The Clinton ethics standards applied to 1,100 of the president-elect's 3,500 political appointees. The new regulations, far tougher than those imposed by any previous administration, required Clinton's top appointees to sign pledges agreeing to refrain from lobbying their agencies for five years after leaving office.

Under the Clinton order, the president could grant a waiver of any of these restrictions. A request for a waiver had to be submitted to the head of the affected agency in order to be referred to the president through the Counsel to the President. A waiver required the president's written certification and publication in the *Federal Register* if a statement that the waiver would be in the public's best interest for the waiver to be granted.[46]

As one of his first official executive actions, George W. Bush issued a presidential memorandum directing all federal employees to become familiar with "and faithfully observe" existing ethics laws and rules.[47] Bush formally reaffirmed George H. W. Bush's Standards of Ethical Conduct for Employees of the Executive Branch.[48]

Continuing a predictable post-Watergate action, Barack Obama, during the 2008 presidential campaign, promised to have the most ethical presidency in American political history.[49] As a candidate Obama decided not to take campaign contributions from lobbyists registered under the 1995 Lobbying Disclosure Act.[50]

Obama acted to put his stamp on federal ethics rules in his second day in office with EO 13490, which affirmed Clinton's ethics order, but with some changes—most (but not all) in the direction of stricter federal ethics rules. The centerpiece of Obama's order was the Ethics Pledge, a seven-point commitment required of all executive appointees. Obama's order, which applied to "every appointee in every executive agency," barred them from leaving and then lobbying any other executive branch official or senior appointee for the remainder of his administration. Obama barred new officials from making policy on any matter involving their former employer or clients for a period of two years, or from working at an agency they lobbied within those two years. The definition of "appointee" included all full-time, political appointees regardless of whether they are appointed by the president, the vice president, or an agency head. Obama demanded signed pledges, and political appointees were required to write personalized letters promising to live up to these standards.[51]

Through this executive order, Obama prohibited federal executive branch employees from accepting gifts from lobbyists, closed the revolving door that allowed federal government officials to move to and from private sector jobs in a manner that gave those sectors undue influence over the federal government, and required that federal government hiring be based upon qualifications, competence, and experience rather than political connections.[52] Obama directed the OGE to issue a memo on the new rules he had imposed on executive branch officials.[53]

Obama informed federal agencies that it was his administration's aspiration "that federally-registered lobbyists not be appointed to agency advisory boards and commissions." Although Obama's order did not apply to federally registered lobbyists appointed by agency or department heads, its spirit and Obama's word conveyed that political message. In June 2010 Obama issued a memo formally directing agencies not to appoint or reappoint federally registered lobbyists to advisory committees and other boards and commissions.[54]

THE POLITICIZED PRESIDENCY AND
THE NOT-SO-ETHICAL CEO

Since Watergate, presidents have exerted political control and influence over executive branch ethics in two chief ways: via appointment of the head of the OGE (although it is technically independent) and by placing the Office of White House Counsel at the center of presidential political control and influence over federal ethics rules. The White House Counsel, a presidential appointee, has no statutory duties, and no statute even acknowledges the existence of the office. Nevertheless, the White House Counsel carries out many tasks, such as vetting all presidential appointments and advising on the application of ethics regulations to White House staff and executive branch officials. It also operates as a command center when political crises or ethical scandals erupt.[55] The political challenges of dealing with ethics have been central to the expansion of the Office of White House Counsel.[56] During any modern presidential transition, the White House Counsel seeks to ensure that all White House staffers and political appointees are informed of the ethics statutes, executive orders, and other administration rules under which they must work.[57] The president's counsel is attentive to legal issues that may arise within both the political and policy contexts in which the president plays a role.

Orders and commitments on ethics receive considerable attention in the chief executive's first months in office, but with time, public interest can wane. A White House ethics lawyer, Richard Painter, under President George W. Bush, explained the political challenge of ethics rules at the end of a term: "It's a big problem because people want to sort of cash in towards the end of the president's term. Things get sort of loosey-goosey the last two years. . . . Everybody's looking for lucrative opportunities in the private sector." In other words, presidents who participate in the construction of ethics orders do so "with an eye on their public appearance, often more than on their practical impacts."[58] Thus, presidents have moved unilaterally to skirt the standards they themselves had just trumpeted.

George H. W. Bush delegated authority to the heads of federal agencies, committees, and commission boards to issue exemptions and waivers of his ethics rules and also empowered the Office of White House Counsel to grant exemptions.[59] The key point is that the president's counsel has direct political influence to apply ethics rules to political appointees.[60] The OGE developed guidelines for granting waivers for political appointees and federal employees from the conflict-of-interest laws governing future employment, but they were just that: only guidelines. Each federal agency promulgated its own waiver procedures, which were interpreted and enforced by the specific ethics officer appointed within the agency. As a result, there was no single set of procedures for seeking and receiving waivers from conflict-of-interest laws, and different federal agencies interpreted each set of waiver rules differently.[61]

Clinton, as he was preparing to leave the presidency, revoked his own ethics order, which had barred senior officials of the White House and other agencies from lobbying former colleagues for five years.[62] Clinton's order became effective just as George W. Bush took political control of the federal bureaucracy. Clinton claimed the five-year ban would have remained in place if Vice President Al Gore had won the election—Clinton changed it because former Clinton appointees would "face a tough labor market as Republicans had taken control of both the White House and Congress."[63] During the chief executive's exit, the political calculation had changed.

Due to the lack of clarity surrounding federal ethics rules, George W. Bush required that all waivers be reviewed by the Office of White House Counsel. Exerting more direct political control and influence over waivers, Bush prohibited federal agencies from granting waivers to presidential appointees for the purpose of negotiating for outside employment unless the federal agency consulted with the Office of White House Counsel.[64]

Obama in his turn also issued an executive order that allowed any current or former political appointee to receive a written waiver of any restrictions contained in the ethics pledge if "the literal application of the restriction is inconsistent with the purposes of the restriction or [if] it is in the public interest to grant the waiver." According to Obama, "The public interest shall include, but not be limited to, exigent circumstances relating to national security or to the economy."[65]

Generally speaking, Obama allowed waivers when the "literal application of the pledge did not make sense or was not in the public interest."[66] Or, more to the point, when it was not in the president's interest. In sum, Obama created flexibility and discretion for the CEO of the federal bureaucracy.[67]

In fact, the first waiver was granted the day after Obama issued his order on ethics, with the nomination of William Lynn as deputy secretary of defense.[68] William Lynn's former position as a lobbyist violated the ethics pledge. Due to public interest and "the current national security situation," the White House deemed Lynn's years as a security lobbyist necessary to the administration. Obama also granted a waiver for selection of his White

House Counsel.[69] At several other points during his presidency, Obama waived his own ethics rules to appoint certain new officials to positions in the executive branch.[70] In the end, Obama appointed several lobbyists.[71] In 2014 Obama also reversed key parts of his 2010 memo banning lobbyists from serving on boards and commissions.[72] He also issued revised guidance regarding the prohibition on appointing or reappointing federally registered lobbyists.[73] The Center for Responsive Politics reported that hundreds of Obama appointees entered government service through the revolving door; many others left the Obama executive branch to move into private sector jobs.[74] Thus, their very own ethics rules are no obstacle to presidents' meeting their political objectives.

CONCLUSION

When it comes to ethics, modern presidents are often beset by their own conflict of interest. On the one hand they want to assure federal employees are only serving the public interest. On the other hand, presidents must display loyalty to their political appointees. This has become an especially fraught issue since Watergate, as public demands for integrity have become loud at the same time as the scope and complexity of federal government has made experts with private sector experience more attractive to government— and conversely, high-wage private sector jobs have become more attractive to political appointees leaving government service.

This tension is resolved somewhat by the fact that the ethical conduct of executive branch employees is governed first and foremost by criminal and civil statutes as well as an administrative code of conduct and certain other legal authorities. Currently, political appointees are subject to more significant ethics restrictions than federal civil service employees. However, the president as employer-in-chief has the power to delimit principles of ethical conduct for political appointees and federal employees.

Public concerns about ethics have led presidents to exercise this authority in ways that provide confidence to voters while providing some protection to their appointees.[75] As the size of the federal bureaucracy expanded, every modern president has found his administration disrupted by major episodes of ethical conduct breaches. Successors often act to portray themselves as restorers of the public trust—the new "ethical" chief executive. New ethics restrictions typically stay in effect unless or until they are lifted by the current president or modified by a future president.

Ethics, which generally involves rules and constraints, can seem to involve the surrender of power. Presidents, however, have sought to command the process through influencing the OGE and giving more control over ethics to the Office of White House Counsel. This has allowed presidents to offer waivers and exemptions to their own rules.

Obama offered a tougher approach not only to the usual problems, such as conflict of interest and the revolving door, but also to broader challenges such as political influence exerted on career federal civil service employees and the lack of transparency in the federal government.[76] Unknown is whether his successor will adopt a similar ethics order, since it will expire once Obama leaves office. The nonprofit organization Public Citizen has stated: "We would love to see the [Obama] ethics order put into statute, because if we don't, whoever is going to be elected next is immediately going to throw this ethics order out the window."[77]

All presidents back away from some of their most dramatic campaign promises and initial executive orders. However, it can be politically difficult and risky for a president to repeal the ethics order of his or her predecessor.[78] At times the president is motivated to change the ethics rules or just to do and say the right thing before and right after an election. But, the political scientist Bruce Cain warns, "The problem that you have is that the political actors strategically adapt to the [ethics] rules that you have. You have to realize you're never going to completely close that influence gap."[79] Presidents, the "ethical" CEOs of the federal bureaucracy, write and rewrite the ethics rules for their own political and instrumental advantage.

EIGHT

The President and the Power of the Payer

Since Franklin D. Roosevelt, several U.S. presidents have struggled to enact health-care reform; most failed.[1] Barack Obama made health-care reform one of his first priorities: he succeeded on his campaign promise to make coverage available to more Americans.[2] Between the presidencies of FDR and Obama, health care emerged as a central issue of American politics and policy. Presidents responded as they have in so many areas, viewing this new challenge as an opportunity to serve the public, expand their authority, and score political points.

Although this chapter will focus specifically on health care, it is important to note that it was one of a number of complex policy issues that strained existing governance structures during the second half of the twentieth century. This led presidents to seek more political control and influence over the domestic policymaking process by centralizing it in the White House, ensuring that programs were consistent with the president's goals. Health care was no exception.

Presidents since Lyndon B. Johnson have had staff in the White House devoted to developing domestic policy.[3] Richard Nixon was the first chief executive to develop a formal structure for coordinating domestic policy, establishing the Office of Policy Development in 1970. Jimmy Carter referred to his domestic policy staff as the Domestic Policy Group; Ronald Reagan established a Domestic Policy Council in 1985; and George H. W. Bush continued the council in 1989. Bill Clinton formally created the Domestic Policy Council, and George W. Bush maintained it.[4] Obama established the White House Office of Health Reform. After Congress approved the 2010 Patient Protection and Affordable Care Act, Obama abolished the Office and transferred its work to the Domestic Policy Council.[5]

A primary focus of the Domestic Policy Council has been the federal government's role in health care. As federal agencies shaped more and more health policy decisions outside direct presidential control, presidents responded predictably—by seeking to politicize and centralize health-care policy within the executive branch of the government.[6]

THE EMERGING POWER OF THE PAYER-IN-CHIEF

Health care was not a major issue on the president's agenda in the early twentieth century. Private health insurance emerged prior to World War I, and the first large medical insurance company, Blue Cross, was established in 1929. Two world wars and the creation of Military and Veterans Health Systems, the Federal Employees Health Benefits Program (FEHBP), and Medicare and Medicaid made the federal government the largest payer of health care in the United States, accounting for more than a quarter of all U.S. spending on health care. As a single entity that provides so much revenue for the health industry, the federal government has outsized influence on the industry. Consequently, as the nation's largest payer, the federal government is able to significantly shape and move the health-care market.[7] In addition to all of his other duties as CEO of the federal government, the president now sits atop a large health-care bureaucracy.[8]

As payer-in-chief, the president oversaw federal health spending of $1.13 billion in FY 2015, accounting for 30 percent of all federal budget outlays and 6.3 percent of GDP.[9] These outlays included $620 billion on Medicare, $333 billion on Medicaid, $48 billion on the Defense Health Program, $61 billion on the Veterans Health Administration, $48 billion in spending on the Federal Employees Health Benefits Program, and $29 billion on health insurance assistance.[10] Currently, the federal government subsidizes health insurance for most Americans through a variety of federal programs and tax preferences.[11] Federal payments for health-care services will almost certainly be pushed up in the future by a sharp increase in the number of people receiving benefits from federal government health programs. That increase can be attributed to two main factors. The first is the aging of the population—in particular, the aging of the baby boom generation, people born between 1946 and 1964—which will increase the number of people receiving benefits from Medicare by more than one-third over the next decade. The second is the expansion of federal support for health insurance under the Affordable Care Act, which will significantly increase the number of people receiving benefits from the federal government.[12]

Managing the federal health bureaucracy involves a series of connected yet different responsibilities. The president and his political appointees oversee several federal agencies that pay for health care: the Department of Veterans Affairs funds veterans' health care, and the Department of Defense pays for health benefits through TRICARE, which is the health-care program for uniformed service members.[13] The president is also the largest payer of employer-sponsored group health insurance in the United States, the FEHBP. Currently, the Office of Personnel Management pays for health benefits for federal government employees and retirees. Federal retirees and surviving spouses retain their eligibility for FEHBP at the same cost as current employees.[14] Presidents use the power of the payer to dictate the terms and conditions of private health plans available to federal employees in the FEHBP.[15] As the largest employer-sponsored health plan in the nation, the FEHBP often serves as a standard for private employers shaping their employee health plans.[16]

Perhaps most important, the president exercises control over the Centers for Medicare and Medicaid Services, the largest single payer of health-care costs in the United States, comprising Medicare, Medicaid, and the Children's Health Insurance Program (CHIP), which pay almost one-third of all the nation's health expenditures.[17] At first, the Social Security Administration managed Medicare, and the Social and Rehabilitation Service managed Medicaid. The bare-bones staffing of the original federal agency that oversaw Medicare—which was housed in the Social Security Administration until the creation of the Health Care Financing Administration within the Department of Health and Human Services (HHS)—was possible because federal agencies were not directly responsible for paying claims. The managerial and oversight role was to manage relationships with those outside stakeholders that actually processed Medicare claims.

Over time, Congress delegated managerial authority over these federal health programs to the executive branch. In recent decades, through delegated authority, executive orders, or memoranda, presidents have exercised more and more political control over these federal health programs and political influence on the private sector health-care industry.

THE PRESIDENT AS PAYER-IN-CHIEF OF VETERANS AND MILITARY HEALTH

As in so many other areas, the federal government's involvement in health care began with veterans and active-duty military. As the country entered World War I, Congress approved a system of veterans' benefits that included programs for disability compensation and insurance for military service personnel and veterans. At first, in 1919, Congress charged the executive branch—the Bureau of War Risk Insurance and Public Health Service, within the U.S. Treasury Department—with operating hospitals for returning World War I veterans. Congress centralized programs for World War I veterans by creating the Veterans Bureau in 1921.[18] Congress also specifically authorized the president "to consolidate and coordinate any hospitals and executive and administrative bureaus, agencies, or offices, created for or concerned in the administration of benefits provided to former members of the U.S. military and naval establishments."[19] Herbert Hoover elevated the Veterans Bureau to a federal agency, creating the Veterans Administration to "consolidate and coordinate federal government activities affecting war veterans."[20] The Veterans Administration would provide benefits and medical care to honorably discharged persons. Congress later elevated the Veterans Administration to be known as the Department of Veterans Affairs (VA).[21] The president and his appointees now manage the largest integrated health-care system in the United States, the Veterans Health Administration (VHA).[22]

Following World War II and the Korean War, Congress authorized medical care for dependents of military personnel as an incentive to help retain soldiers and doctors. Via the 1956 Dependents' Medical Care Act, Congress delegated authority to the Department of Defense to contract with civilian health-care providers.[23] Before 1956, active-duty members received first priority for health care at the military's medical treatment facilities; their dependents were eligible for health-care services on a space-available basis. Congress broadened the DOD's authority to contract with civilian providers by creating the 1966 Civilian Health and Medical Program of the Uniformed Services. This program is now known as TRICARE, an effort of the DOD, beginning in 1995, to coordinate all medical care efforts and to institute managed care in one program.[24] At first, an entity called TRICARE Management Activity (TMA) managed the TRICARE health-care program for active-duty members and their families as well as others entitled to receive medical care through the DOD. The Defense Health Agency, an agency of the DOD, replaced the TMA as the U.S. military entity responsible for providing TRICARE (2013).[25] The president and his appointees manage the Military Health Services System, which is the enterprise within the U.S. Department of Defense that provides health care to active duty and retired U.S. military personnel and their dependents. The increasing importance of health care has provided presidents with a powerful political tool for responding to the needs of various groups. Veterans have, of course, been particularly important.[26] Exercising the authority to declare a national emergency during a period of armed conflict, George H. W. Bush directed the Department of Veterans Affairs to expand its health-care services by providing care to members of the military on active duty in Operation Desert Storm.[27] Bush also required the VA to establish additional contracts with private sector providers for hospital care and other medical services.[28]

Clinton worked to repair his strained relations with veterans groups by ordering the VA to expand its health coverage to those who had served in Vietnam and suffered from prostate cancer or a nerve disease that might be associated with the defoliant Agent Orange, resulting in expanded coverage to 2.6 million veterans.[29] Further embracing veterans' causes, Clinton promised to propose legislation to Congress to provide new health benefits for children of Vietnam veterans who suffered from spinal bifida, a congenital birth defect. This would be the first time health coverage would be extended to offspring of veterans who may have been exposed to Agent Orange where this could have resulted in a birth defect in their children.

George W. Bush also sought to improve relations with veterans by addressing health care.[30] Bush had been accused by veterans groups of seeking inadequate funds for health care.[31] In response, Bush established the President's Task Force to Improve Health Care Delivery for Our Nation's Veterans.[32] Bush's commission concluded that "the system was insufficient for the demands of two modern wars [in Afghanistan and Iraq] and called for improvements, including far-reaching changes in the way the government determines the disability status and benefits of injured soldiers and veterans." However, the commission co-chairs expressed concern about Bush's actual implementation of their recommendations. As two *New York Times* journalists concluded, "Bush spent his presidency pledging support for the troops, and reports of problems in their care had exposed political and policy vulnerabilities that the Democrats seized upon."[33]

Obama, reaching out to a growing political constituency of veterans and military families amid rising concerns about Post Traumatic Stress Disorder (PTSD), issued an executive order to improve access to mental health services for veterans, service members, and military families. Obama directed the DOD, the VA, and the Department of Health and Human Services to strengthen suicide prevention efforts across the military services and in the veteran community.[34]

Presidents have used their executive authority to dictate additional terms and conditions of coverage within and eligibility for health plan choices available to federal employees under the FEHBP.[35] The concept of the federal government as an employer that pays for health insurance gained traction when Truman formed the Commission on the Health Needs of the Nation in 1951, which recommended that the federal government offer health insurance to its employees.[36] Eisenhower also called for better benefits for federal employees, stating, "I have been long convinced that a program combining the best practices of progressive private employers with the special demands of public service would greatly benefit our Federal career system and its employees."[37] Specifically, he proposed a Medical Care and Hospitalization Insurance program open to all federal employees on a voluntary contributory basis.[38]

Congress subsequently passed the Federal Employees Health Benefits Act (1959), establishing a prepaid, voluntary health insurance plan for 2 million federal employees and their families, with costs shared equally by the federal government and employees.[39] Congress established basic rules for FEHBP benefits, enrollment, and participation, and other general requirements.[40]

Congress delegated authority to the Civil Service Commission—subsequently renamed the Office of Personnel Management—"to contract for the best possible program" and to prescribe rules to manage the FEHBP.[41] Currently, the OPM, which is under the president's direction, is authorized to contract on behalf of the federal government with health insurance carriers.[42]

Presidents have used this authority to expand the range of coverage offered federal employees regarding mental health. Kennedy, in response to employee groups, was the first chief executive to expand federal employee health coverage to include mental health. He directed the Department of

Health, Education, and Welfare (since renamed the Department of Health and Human Services) to explore steps for "encouraging and stimulating the expansion of private voluntary health insurance to include mental health care."[43] Kennedy initiated a review of all federal programs, including the FEHBP, to determine whether "further efforts were needed to increase the provision for mental health care."[44] Kennedy also directed the Civil Service Commission to modify the FEHBP and handle mental illnesses the same as physical illnesses.[45] In response to Kennedy's order, the FEHBP's two nationwide health insurance plans offered parity in mental health benefits between 1967 and 1975.[46] The term "parity" means that specified mental health and substance abuse (MH/SA) insurance benefits are equal to the benefits for general medical services. However, beginning in 1975, when more flexibility in benefit design was permitted, MH/SA coverage began to erode. The diminution of benefits continued into the early 1980s. After 1982, the OPM allowed plans to vary levels of mental health benefits offered. In the mid- to late 1990s, the OPM began to take steps to move federal employee mental health and substance abuse benefits nearer to parity.

Decades later, Reagan made it a condition of employment for all federal employees to refrain from using illegal drugs on or off duty.[47] As part of this effort, Reagan directed the OPM to ensure that appropriate coverage for drug abuse was offered for employees and their families under the FEHBP. Reagan directed the OPM to provide information about the effects of drug abuse, guidelines for drug testing and treatment, training of supervisory personnel, and technical assistance in support of Employee Assistance Programs.[48] Since 1986 the federal government has mandated a comprehensive drug-free workplace program to address illicit drug use by federal employees.[49]

After the passage of the 1996 Mental Health Parity Act, Bill Clinton required that the "nation's largest private insurer, the FEHBP, provide full parity for mental health."[50] Clinton directed the OPM to implement "full" mental health parity for mental health and substance abuse benefits. As implemented by the OPM, "full" mental health parity meant that in-network benefits coverage for mental health, substance abuse, medical, surgical, and hospital services would have the same limitations and cost-sharing requirements (such as deductibles, co-insurance, and co-payments).[51] George W. Bush declared support for people with mental and physical disabilities, pledging to "tear down barriers to equality that existed for many of the 54 million Americans with disabilities."[52] While a recommendation in support of mental health parity appeared in the President's New Freedom Commission on Mental Health final report (2003), Bush did not expand mental health parity for federal employees.[53] Obama's OPM, with a formal memo, encouraged FEHBP plans to offer Applied Behavior Analysis benefits for children with autism spectrum disorders.

Along with mental health, presidents have acted to expand federal employee coverage in new areas, including women's and children's health. Clinton directed the OPM to require all federal health benefit plans to comply with the National Cancer Institute Advisory Board's recommendations on mammogram screenings. Clinton, aiming to influence private health plans, concluded, "The federal government is doing its part to make sure women have both coverage and access to this potentially lifesaving test. I want to challenge private health insurance plans to do the same."[54]

Clinton expanded access to preventive health services for federal employees, including screening for prostate, cervical, colorectal, and breast cancer; screening for sickle cell anemia, blood lead level, and blood cholesterol level; all recommended childhood immunizations; well childcare; and adult preventive care visits. In addition, Clinton called on the federal government to provide employees with "considerable flexibility in scheduling their hours of work and taking time off for medical needs, including routine examinations and preventive screenings." Clinton directed federal agencies to "expand worksite programs to help employees understand their risks for disease, obtain preventive health services, and make healthy lifestyle choices."[55] Clinton also directed FEHBP plans to offer full coverage, with no cost sharing for enrollees, of a number of preventive health services, including childhood immunizations, tobacco cessation services and medications, and screenings for cancer, diabetes, and high blood pressure.[56]

Although it covered many prescription drugs and devices, the FEHBP did not initially include contraception.[57] Clinton's OPM changed that, requiring all FEHPB plans to cover the full range of contraceptive drugs and devices approved by the Food and Drug Administration.[58] The FEHBP has offered this coverage every year since 1999. However, in 1998 Congress did allow an exception for a few specified health insurance coverage plans and any other existing or future plan that objected to offering such coverage on religious grounds.[59] FEHBP coverage of abortion services also has been highly politicized. Since Congress can place conditions on the use of federal funds, it can impose conditions on health insurance coverage for political reasons. In 1997, Congress prohibited the OPM from contracting with health plans that included any abortion-related benefits and services.[60]

Obama expanded new protections to federal employees regardless of sexual orientation. Obama's OPM required FEHBP health plans to allow individuals who identified as transgender to select their preferred gender designation for health records (although no formal memo was issued).[61] In 2014, OPM removed the requirement that FEHBP exclude "services, drugs, or supplies related to sex transformations." In the past, FEHBP plans had generally excluded services "related to sex reassignment." Obama's State Department—which offered about twelve health plans—also asked each of its plans to lift the transgender exclusion.[62]

Obama also broke new ground, and extended presidential authority, by expanding FEHBP eligibility. Since 1959, only Congress has extended eligibility to new categories of federal employees, annuitants, and their family and ex-family members.[63] However, Congress delegated authority to the OPM to prescribe the conditions under which federal employees are eligible to enroll in the FEHBP. The OPM reserves the right to include or exclude employees on the basis of the nature and type of their employment or conditions pertaining to their appointments, including the duration of the appointment.

Under existing OPM rules, individuals serving under temporary appointments have been excluded from the FEHBP, with limited exceptions.[64] Obama became the first chief executive to expand eligibility when he directed OPM to extend coverage to temporary firefighters and fire protection personnel working on wildland fires across the country.[65] Obama's OPM also recognized that there might be other groups of federal employees who were not currently covered by the FEHBP due to the temporary nature of their appointments, but who also performed emergency response services.[66] As a result, Obama's OPM amended enrollment rules to permit federal agencies to request that OPM extend coverage to additional federal employees.[67]

Obama's OPM, responding to two Supreme Court rulings bolstering gay marriage in 2013, affirmed that legally married same-sex spouses were eligible for all federal government benefits available to family members, regardless of their state of residency.[68] Obama's OPM also directed in 2013 that the children and also stepchildren of same-sex married couples should be treated the same as the children of opposite-sex marriages. This is a most recent example of Obama's efforts to extend civil rights protections to gay and lesbian families.[69]

THE POWER OF A POLITICALLY RESPONSIVE PAYER:
SENIORS, THE POOR, AND THE WORKING POOR

The idea that health care is a basic and necessary service that the government should provide, especially to seniors and the poor, sparked lasting reforms during the 1960s. President Johnson's Great Society programs passed by Congress authorized the Medicare and Medicaid programs as Title XVIII and Title XIX of the 1965 Social Security Act.[70] Medicare meets the medical care needs of the elderly, and Medicaid does the same for the poor. Medicaid is a cooperative program between each state and the federal government, and is financed by both federal and state funds.[71]

The Medicare statute contains an express delegation of authority to the Department of Health and Human Services, and to the Centers for Medicare and Medicaid Services (CMS) to make and publish rules necessary to the efficient administration of the Medicare program. Medicare establishes and updates its rules governing the systems that it uses to pay providers and suppliers of Medicare-covered items and services, including hospitals, doctors, durable medical equipment suppliers, and others.[72] The CMS and its politically appointed administrator exercise influence over the private sector health-care industry through the certification, coverage, and payment rules it enforces in administering hundreds of billions of dollars paid for health-care services provided to professionals, suppliers, and providers.[73]

Congress in 1997 established the Children's Health Insurance Program (CHIP) to cover the health-care needs of uninsured children. CHIP is a means-tested program that provides health coverage to targeted low-income children and pregnant women in families that have annual income above Medicaid eligibility levels but do not have health insurance. The program is jointly financed by the federal government and states, and the CMS administers the CHIP program.[74]

Congress expanded CMS's responsibilities under the 2010 Affordable Care Act, which contains numerous provisions that influence CMS's traditional role as the overseer of federal health programs.[75] Under the ACA, Congress delegated authority to the CMS to prohibit health-care consumers from being denied health services or health coverage or discriminated against in other ways in health services or coverage because of race, color, national origin, sex, age, or disability.[76]

Johnson, as the CEO of the new Medicare program, was the first chief executive to deal with a potential shortage of health-care professionals. With more than 19 million new seniors eligible for health coverage under Medicare, he established the President's Committee on Health Manpower to address the looming health manpower shortage.[77] Prior to Congress adopting a 1968 Health Manpower Act, Johnson directed all federal agencies to "intensify their efforts to relieve health manpower shortages through federal programs."[78]

The creation of the Medicare and Medicaid programs gave the federal government a major role in paying for health care in the United States.[79] Over time, seniors emerged as a politically important constituency for presidents, not only because they vote more reliably than other voters, but also because they are a key voting bloc in swing states.[80] Clinton, addressing this powerful bloc of voters, was the first chief executive to revise Medicare payment policy to cover most of the costs related to clinical trials testing new drugs and medical treatments. Medicare rules had been widely interpreted as barring payment for the routine medical care that beneficiaries needed when they participated in clinical trials. Many private health insurers had also denied coverage, saying the treatments were experimental or investigational. Clinton, in the middle of Vice President Al Gore's 2000 presidential campaign, issued and executive order whose aim was to increase the number of elderly people who participate in studies investigating ways to prevent, detect, and treat ailments, including cancer, heart disease, stroke, Alzheimer's disease, arthritis, diabetes, and eye disorders.[81] Clinton's EO, after years of debate and failed legislation, was significant not only because Medicare covered 39 million Americans in 2000 but also because many private health insurers follow the federal government in deciding what to include in their health coverage.[82]

Under the 1997 Children's Health Insurance Program, Congress encouraged states to provide health coverage for uninsured children in families whose incomes were too high to qualify for Medicaid but too low to afford private health insurance. Congress also gave states the authority to set their CHIP income eligibility levels, subject to available funding. Clinton, to promote his working families agenda, issued a memo to promote children's health insurance enrollment and outreach, and also took further executive actions to target and enroll millions of uninsured children who might not know they were eligible for Medicaid and CHIP.[83] However, George W. Bush, with different preferences, limited the flexibility of states to set income eligibility standards for their CHIP, formerly the State Children's Health Insurance Program (SCHIP).[84] Bush eliminated CHIP for children in households earning more than 250 percent of the federal poverty level—$42,925

for a family of three in 2007. Bush described the directive as a "clarifica-
tion," but in fact it was a change of long-standing CHIP policy that had
allowed states to determine the income eligibility level for their SCHIP programs.[85] Obama, motivated by a political goal to expand health coverage to
working families, issued a memo to withdraw the Bush directive and to
implement CHIP without additional requirements.[86]

THE POWER OF THE ALL-PAYER-IN-CHIEF
AND HEALTH-CARE REFORM

Clinton, after losing battles with Congress over health-care reform and the
regulation of managed care in 1993–94, pursued change through unilateral
action.[87] During the 1996 campaign, he promised to examine how consumers could be protected in a health-care market that many saw as offering
higher costs and fewer options. Clinton established the President's Advisory
Commission on Consumer Protection and Quality in the Health Care Industry and charged the commission to draft a "consumer bill of rights."
The rules were a list of universal non-waivable contract provisions that
managed-care organizations would be required to include in their arrangements with subscribers and providers.[88]

Clinton directed all federal payer agencies—the Departments of Health
and Human Services, Defense, Veterans Affairs, and the OPM—to bring
their federal health programs in compliance with the Consumer Bill of Rights
and Responsibilities, meaning that unilaterally extended consumer rights and
protections to an estimated 75 million enrollees (Medicare, Medicaid, CHIP,
military, veterans, other federal health-care programs) and 9 million federal
employees (FEHBP).[89] Clinton concluded that federal agencies "will serve
as strong models for health plans in the private sector." He was correct, as
many large public and private group payers as well as managed-care firms
and large health systems voluntarily adopted aspects of the Consumer Bill
of Rights and Responsibilities.[90]

As payer-in-chief, the president also has significant leverage over the private health-care industry because it pays for large amounts of health care
and regulates hospitals, nursing homes, and many other health-care providers. Clinton established the Quality Interagency Coordination Task Force
to coordinate the efforts of twelve federal agencies to improve the quality of
health care.[91] Clinton issued a directive to improve patient safety and health-
care quality by addressing preventable medical errors. As Chris Jennings,

an assistant to the president for health policy, explained, the federal government "will try to use its leverage as the nation's biggest [payer] of health care to improve the quality of care for all Americans."[92] According to Clinton, the federal government would "help create an environment and a system in which providers, consumers, and private and public purchasers work to achieve the goal set by the Institute of Medicine (IOM) to cut preventable medical errors by 50 percent over five years."[93]

After Congress adopted the 1996 Health Insurance Portability and Accountability Act (HIPAA), which improved portability and continuity of health insurance coverage as well as required new privacy protections on health information, Clinton issued an executive order to address law enforcement use of protected health information (PHI).[94] HIPAA applied only to "covered entities," such as health-care plans, providers, and clearinghouses. HIPAA rules therefore did not apply to other organizations and individuals that gain access to protected health information, including federal officials who gain access to health records during health oversight activities. Clinton prohibited law enforcement from using PHI "except when the balance of relevant factors weighs clearly in favor of its use." In sum, protected health information could not be so used unless the public interest and the need for disclosure clearly outweighed the potential for injury to the patient, to the physician-patient relationship, and to the treatment services.[95]

George W. Bush, building on Clinton's precedent, acted in response to the rising budgetary cost of federal health programs. Bush established the Office of the National Coordinator for Health Information to develop a technology infrastructure aimed at improving the "quality and efficiency" of health care. Bush attempted to address the "longstanding problems of preventable errors, uneven quality, and rising costs in the health care system," adding, "As one of the largest [payers] of health care—in Medicare, Medicaid, the Community Health Centers program, the Federal Health Benefits program, Veterans medical care, and programs in the DOD—the federal government can create incentives and opportunities for health care providers to use electronic records, much like the private sector."[96] Bush also promoted more transparency in the health-care programs administered or sponsored by the federal government.[97] Bush directed federal agencies to maintain and update health information technology systems for use between federal agencies and nonfederal entities, to share information about the quality of care and prices paid to insurers, and to identify practices that foster efficient medical care.

Obama indicated that health-care reform would be "one of the biggest priorities for the first year of his presidency."[98] To advance this goal, he established the White House Office of Health Reform to "provide leadership to the executive branch in establishing policies, priorities, and objectives for the federal government's comprehensive effort to improve access to health care, the quality of such care, and the sustainability of the health care system."[99]

He appointed Nancy-Ann DeParle as his health policy "czar."[100] Such "czars"—an informal moniker for officials appointed by a president to oversee particular policy areas and who do not need Senate approval—are a distinctive feature of the modern presidency. Although FDR introduced the concept and appointed roughly eleven such figures—their informal role makes definitive counts difficult—most of his successors named only a handful. Until, that is, Bill Clinton, who named eight. George W. Bush named about thirty-three, Obama, thirty-eight. Obama's "proliferation of high-profile czars, in the case of health care reform, was his particular instantiation of a policy, common to all modern Presidents, of seeking to magnify his control over agency action in domestic policy."[101]

After Congress approved the Patient Protection and Affordable Care Act of 2014—informally called Obamacare—Obama issued an executive order to establish an enforcement mechanism for the federal statutory restriction on the federal funding of abortion known as the Hyde Amendment.[102] Obama agreed to issue an order in a political agreement with pro-life House Democrats who would not support the ACA without it.[103]

THE POWER OF THE PAYER AND NEW PROHIBITIONS AGAINST DISCRIMINATION

Obama, appealing to his LGBTQ supporters, directed HHS to issue rules for Medicare and Medicaid to empower enrollees in the programs the right to choose their own visitors during a hospital stay.[104] In the past, hospitals had barred visitors who were not related to an incapacitated patient by blood or marriage.[105] According to a story in the *Washington Post*, "Obama's mandate is the latest attempt to advance the agenda of a [political] constituency that strongly supported his presidential campaign."[106] Obama also mandated that hospitals receiving federal Medicare or Medicaid payments extend visitation rights to all domestic partners, including the partners of gay men and lesbians. Obama required hospitals to respect patients' choices regarding whom they authorized to make critical health-care decisions for them and to explain these rights to patients.[107]

Congress also delegated significant authority to Obama's HHS under the Affordable Care Act.[108] Under Section 1557 it formally prohibited discrimination in health-care programs or activities on the basis of race, color, national origin, sex, age, or disability.[109] Obama's HHS expanded this definition, also prohibiting the denial of health care or health coverage on the basis of pregnancy, gender identity, or sex stereotyping. Obama's rule also prohibited sex discrimination in health care by requiring that women must be treated equally with men in the health care they receive. In addition, Obama's HHS issued a directive prohibiting health insurers from denying transgender Americans coverage and services on the basis of gender identity. Although the Obama rule did not require health insurers to automatically approve all gender transitioning services, it suggested that they cannot categorically deny coverage to transgender individuals as they had in the past. The Obama rule, which applied to the antidiscrimination provisions of the ACA, was significant because it compelled insurers to apply the same standards to every plan they administered, including those in the private sector.[110] Obama's Veterans Health Administration also issued a directive to specify care available to transgender veterans through VA benefits.[111] Obama's DOD issued a directive that medically diagnosed issues related to gender, including gender-reassignment surgery, should be treated "in the same manner as other medical care and treatment."[112]

As he had done as the purchaser- and employer-in-chief, Obama used the power of the payer-in-chief to extend protections against sex discrimination within federal health programs to include medical treatment related to sexual orientation and gender identity.[113]

CONCLUSION

In 2020, the federal government is expected to spend $1.6 trillion on health care—6.9 percent of GDP. As health care has emerged as a national priority, presidents have sought to centralize control of domestic policy in the White House. The president sits atop a huge federal health program bureaucracy—Medicare, Medicaid, CHIP, VHA health programs, Defense Health Programs, and the FEHBP—that grew exponentially in the last half of the twentieth century and the first fifteen years of the twenty-first.

The payer-in-chiefs' orders and memos have rarely been reversed by their successors. More often than not, Congress has affirmed presidents' unilateral actions in formal legislation. For example, in 2014, Congress affirmed

Obama's effort when it approved the Veterans' Access to Care through Choice, Accountability, and Transparency Act, committing resources to improve access and quality of care for veterans.[114] Congress expanded mental health coverage under the 2008 Mental Health Parity and Addiction Equity Act. Congress approved Bush's EO dealing with health information technology within the Health Information Technology for Economic and Clinical Health Act, passed in 2009 as part of the American Recovery and Reinvestment Act.[115] Under the Affordable Care Act of 2010, Congress affirmed and expanded upon key aspects of Bill Clinton's EO on the patients' bill of rights by prohibiting the exclusion of preexisting conditions, limits on lifetime health insurance coverage, the restriction of annual coverage limits, and the limitation on rescissions, and adding provisions guaranteeing direct access to certain types of providers and to out-of-network emergency care.[116]

As CEO of the largest payer of health care in the United States, presidents have used executive power to dictate a range of "terms and conditions" in the relationship between the federal government and private sector health insurers and providers. Through this executive power, the president impacts the coverage, cost, and quality of health care not just for the beneficiaries offederal health programs, federal employees, but also for the broader, privately insured population. Consequently, as the nation's largest payer, the chief executive is able to significantly shape and move the health-care market.[117] As one recent report concluded, "Having one enormous payer can have outsize influence on players across the health care support chain."

Since the passage of the 1965 Social Security Amendments (Medicare) and the ACA in 2010, the president—through delegated authority, executive orders, and memoranda—has exercised more and more political control over these federal health programs and political influence on the private sector health-care industry. As the size and scope of the U.S. federal government increased dramatically during the twentieth century, the health-care arena became one more example of how, with the power of the purchaser, the power of the employer and power of the payer, the president calls the shots.

NINE

Impact of the President's Executive Powers on Politics and Policy

Calling the Shots has documented a fundamental phenomenon of modern American politics and policy: how the rapid increase in the size and scope of the federal government has transformed—and been transformed by—the presidency. This study broadens our understanding of presidential power in two ways. First, it focuses on the inherent power of the president as a chief executive officer of the federal bureaucracy. The president purchases billions of dollars' worth of goods and services, employs millions of federal employees, and pays trillions for federal health-care programs for seniors, active-duty military, veterans, and federal employees. Second, it conceptualizes these vast but underappreciated forms of executive power: the power of the purchaser, the power of the employer, and the power of the payer. Each of these executive powers must be viewed as a powerful weapon in the president's policymaking arsenal.

Presidents across time have sought to gain political control over federal procurement, personnel, and health payment rules and to exercise political influence over government and private sector policies that impact the lives of Americans. Barack Obama, too, used this unilateral authority to advance change. Through executive orders and memos, he increased the federal minimum wage on all federal contractors; institutionalized equal pay for equal and work; required all political appointees and federal employees to sign an ethics pledge; and mandated that all hospitals receiving Medicare or Medicaid payment extend visitation rights to the partners of gay men and lesbians and respect patients' choices regarding whom they have authorized to make health-care decisions for them. Obama's actions were not a radical break from the past but a continuation in the inexorable growth of presidential authority. They illustrate and provide several fresh insights into the institutional presidency illuminated in the previous chapters.

Calling the Shots urges us to see the president as the chief executive officer of a growing enterprise. The federal government is not a business, but the business metaphor is useful for understanding the challenges the United States has faced as it has grown and become more diverse. The range of constituent and interest group demands and responsive policies—the inputs and outputs of government—has increased rapidly since the dawn of the twentieth century. The federal bureaucracy that Obama commanded bears little resemblance to the one led by Theodore Roosevelt.

Especially since Franklin D. Roosevelt's administration, executive orders and memos have been a key tool for carrying out these new responsibilities and challenges. They have served not only a functional role—allowing presidents to define and direct the efficient operation of government—but also political and electoral roles. Presidents have often taken unilateral action to address the needs and concerns of important political constituencies before Congress was ready to act. In countless areas, from civil rights to health care, their directives were later codified through legislation. Presidents have led the way by calling the shots. Indeed, as the demands of the public seemed to outpace the ability of Congress to address them, presidential action has been essential to any policy movement. Over time, presidents from both parties have increasingly used these tools to achieve policy goals and, in many instances, to overcome political opposition.

These actions have transformed both the federal government and the private sector. As a purchaser, employer, and payer, presidents attempt to influence the private sector. They have accomplished this by stipulating the terms and conditions required of those who wish to do business with the federal government and by setting an example as a model employer and payer that others might follow. Their unilateral actions have also been symbolic. On many occasions, presidents have reiterated the previous declarations of their predecessors—especially regarding antidiscrimination policies—in order to plant their own flag. This expansive power, however, has been tempered and balanced by the fact that unilateral actions do not have the force of law. They can be overturned by newly elected leaders who do not share their predecessor's preferences or priorities.

As presidents rely on these executive powers to unilaterally shift the political and policy status quo, the question arises of how best to assess their impact on American politics and policy. Politically, how might other actors—voters and constituents, Congress, the courts, presidential successors, and the private sector or the market—respond? Voters may elect a new president who will repeal a prior executive order or memo, but they are unlikely to choose a candidate based on the fine details of these actions. A congressional majority may affirm an executive order by adopting a law. With greater difficulty—say, a majority in the House, sixty votes in the Senate and, if necessary, a two-thirds majority to override a presidential veto—Congress may repeal an order or pass a law nullifying it. Courts may declare an order unlawful or unconstitutional, but the record suggests they have been deferential to executive authority.[1] Successor presidents can affirm and expand upon their predecessors' orders; they can also reverse them. In some cases, presidents do not overturn prior orders for fear of paying a political price. For their part, private sector actors may choose not to contract with the federal government or receive payment from a federal health program. They can also emulate or reject the federal government's actions as a model employer.

These dynamics within the American system of shared powers will likely get more attention in the years ahead as it becomes increasingly clear to voters, Congress, and the courts that the president's authority as chief executive of the federal government has expanded tremendously over time, redefining the office and hence the governance of the nation. As part of that process, it is important to summarize the origins and evolution of this dynamic.

THE POWER OF THE PURCHASER AND PUBLIC POLICY

The evidence affirms that presidents have used the power of the purchaser to exercise political control over the federal procurement process and to influence policy in areas somewhat related to the efficient and economical purchase of goods and services.[2] This authority has either been specifically granted or accepted by Congress—which has recognized its functional or political necessity—and almost always upheld by the courts. Since the early twentieth century, presidents have used their political power to amend the terms and conditions of federal contracts and subcontracts to reflect independent executive policy decisions. Some procurement-related executive orders have been based on the president's powers under Article II of the Constitution. After FDR and Truman, most chief executives have invoked the congressional authority delegated under the 1949 Federal Property and Administrative Services Act (FPASA). In sum, Congress has authorized the executive to "prescribe policies and directives that the president considers necessary to provide the federal government with an economical and efficient system" for procurement.[3] The president is free to act.

If Congress preferred to limit the executive power of the purchaser, it could amend FPASA to clarify congressional intent or pass a law directed at specific requirements of procurement-related executive orders. Congress could also amend or repeal an executive order, terminate the underlying authority upon which it is based, or use its appropriations authority to limit its effect.[4] However, congressional repeal of an executive order has been relatively rare, primarily because such legislation runs counter to the president's preferences and requires a two-thirds congressional override of an expected presidential veto.[5]

Executive orders have come under legal challenge via multiple mechanisms: challenges to the president's power to promulgate an order; efforts to overturn the rules issued pursuant to an order; allegations that the order violates constitutional rights; arguments that the order has been improperly interpreted; or claims that resolution of a question of statutory interpretation ultimately hinges on the interpretation of an antecedent order.[6] The courts, however, have upheld the power of the purchaser under the FPASA as long as the "requisite nexus exists between the president's actions and goals of economy and efficiency in procurement."[7] Although the Supreme Court provided some parameters for the executive procurement power, a lower court has placed limits on the circumstances under which a president can intervene in labor-management relations. The one major case where the power of the purchaser was struck down involved Bill Clinton's executive order debarring federal contractors who hired permanent replacements for striking workers. Concluding that Clinton's executive order was "regulatory in nature because it imposed requirements on contractors rather than protected the federal government's interests as a purchaser," a district court invalidated it on the specific grounds that it was preempted by the 1935 National Labor Relations Act.[8] The court, however, did not conclude that the president's order exceeded the power of the purchaser and reaffirmed interpretations of the president's authority to act in pursuit of the goals of economy and efficiency—even those actions that "reach beyond any narrow concept of efficiency and economy in federal procurement."[9]

The power of the purchaser regarding immigration-related orders also has been challenged in the courts.[10] Upholding a George W. Bush order requiring federal contractors and subcontractors to use E-Verify to authorize all employees, the U.S. Court of Appeals for the Fourth Circuit ruled that "businesses can choose not to become a federal contractor if they wish to not use E-Verify, and thus the president is not required to justify the impact of the rule's efficiency for federal government contracts." Almost all executive orders based on the power of the purchaser have been upheld on the grounds that the president has authority to place conditions on federal contracts in "furtherance of his duty to promote an economic and efficient federal procurement system."[11]

Private sector businesses that do not want to play by the president's unilateral rules can choose not to contract or subcontract with the federal government, but this is often an unattractive, sometimes impossible, option. For many firms, such as defense contractors, the federal government is the largest, and sometimes the sole, purchaser of their goods and services.[12] Moreover, federal government contracts offer certain advantages. The risk of insolvency is vanishingly low, and the federal government, as a monopoly provider of many goods and services, can offer contracting parties access to monopoly profits not available in private markets. In reality, many private sector contractors simply pass the costs of additional procurement terms and conditions on to the federal government in the form of higher bids. Nevertheless, the central terms and conditions of the contract are still written by the federal government, with some added by the president as purchaser-in-chief. The government's superior bargaining power—if not the requirements of law—leaves federal contractors and subcontractors little choice with respect to the final terms and conditions. Appendix table 1 summarizes the actions of each president as purchaser-in-chief and the related policy outcomes.

Obama's use of the power of the purchaser in a range of new areas caused concern in the private sector federal contracting community.[13] For example, in a 2015 letter to the White House chief of staff, four industry groups expressed opposition to the dozen executive orders Obama had issued affecting federal government contractors. The industry groups wrote, "While we have openly expressed our support for some, suggested changes to others with which we agree on the intent, and raised major concerns about yet others, the net effect has been to significantly increase the costs of doing business with the [federal] government."[14] Obama's executive orders mattered because more than 20 percent of Americans were employed by private sector companies that did business with the federal government. Appendix table 2 highlights Obama's EOs and their policy-related outcomes.

THE POWER OF THE EMPLOYER, EQUAL EMPLOYMENT
OPPORTUNITY, AND PUBLIC POLICY

The evidence also affirms that presidents have used the power of the employer-in-chief to exercise political control over federal personnel and to influence the terms and conditions of the employment relationship between the federal government and its employees.[15] After Congress authorized the Office of Personnel Management to execute, administer, and enforce all civil service rules in 1978,[16] a president's executive order or memo to OPM has had a direct impact on federal employees, and at least an indirect effect on the private sector workers whose employers might emulate the federal government as a "model" employer.[17] In many cases Congress has codified presidential orders with a formal law. In some cases, presidents have acted once more in these same areas, pushing beyond the scope of the legislation. In yet other cases, especially highly partisan conflicts such as federal labor-management relations, recent presidents—George H. W. Bush, Bill Clinton, George W. Bush, and Barack Obama—have each overturned their predecessors' orders.

Historically, the concept of the federal government as a model employer has inspired chief executives to exert political control over the federal civil service system and political influence over federal personnel policy. Congress, affirming the power of the employer-in-chief with passage of the 1978 Federal Service Labor-Management Relations Act (FLSMRA), gave federal employees the right to organize and collectively bargain but prohibited them from bargaining over wages or striking. The president has retained the power to exclude a federal agency or one of its subdivisions from coverage under the FSLMRA if he determined that its primary work concerns national security.[18] For example, Congress affirmed George W. Bush's order to weaken collective bargaining and to allow the Department of Homeland Security to void collective bargaining contracts in the 2002 Department of Homeland Security Act.[19] Congress also affirmed a Clinton order by compensating current or former employees and their survivors whose ultra-hazardous work with nuclear weapons exposed them to dangers such as radiation (2000 Energy Employees Occupational Illness Compensation Program Act).[20]

After Jimmy Carter made early moves to establish the federal government as a flexible, family-friendly employer, Congress empowered federal agencies to experiment with flextime alternatives to the traditional five-day, forty-hour week (1978 Federal Employees Flexible and Compressed Work

Schedules Act).[21] Congress also affirmed prior executive orders by allowing federal agencies to increase part-time opportunities for federal employees (1978 Federal Employees Part-time Career Employment Act).[22] Congress extended the authority of federal agencies to allow employees more flexibility in scheduling their workweeks (1982 Federal Employees Flexible and Compressed Work Schedules Act).

Congress, affirming a Clinton executive order, provided federal employees the same and some expanded benefits as those offered to private sector employees under the 1993 Family Medical Leave Act (1994 Federal Employees Family Friendly Leave Act).[23] Moreover, Congress approved a 2008 FEMLA amendment to allow parents and spouses the opportunity to take up to six months of unpaid leave when their loved ones were seriously wounded in combat.[24]

Echoing language first used by Theodore Roosevelt, Obama's OPM stated its mission as follows: "We've set our sights on making the U.S. federal service America's model employer for the 21st century."[25] In 2015, Senate Democrats called on Obama to issue an executive order to make the federal government a "model employer" in various areas, including giving preference in federal government contracting to employers who pay a living wage; offering "fair" health-care and retirement benefits, granting paid leave for sickness and caregiving, providing full-time hours and stable schedules, and giving workers a voice through collective bargaining so they did not need to strike to be heard.[26] Appendix table 3 summarizes the employer-in-chief orders and policy-related outcomes.

Acting as the equal opportunity employer-in-chief, FDR and Harry S. Truman prohibited racial discrimination in the federal government. These orders were affirmed by their successors John F. Kennedy and Lyndon B. Johnson through equal employment opportunity policies for racial minorities and affirmative action policies that promoted the recruitment and hiring of minorities in the federal workforce. Later presidents used orders to extend equal employment opportunity to other categories.[27] Richard Nixon's Executive Order 11478 affirmed that the federal government would provide equal opportunity in federal employment on the basis of merit and fitness and without discrimination on the basis of race, color, religion, sex, or national origin.[28] Carter's executive order empowered the Equal Employment Opportunity Commission to enforce all federal equal employment opportunity laws and to coordinate and to lead the federal government's efforts to eradicate federal workplace discrimination.[29] Currently, the EEOC provides leadership and guidance to federal agencies on all aspects of the federal government's equal employment opportunity program.

Congress legislated that certain federal personnel actions cannot be based on attributes or conduct that do not adversely affect employee performance, such as marital status and political affiliation. Congress, under the 1978 Civil Service Reform Act (as amended), protected federal government applicants and employees from discrimination in personnel actions on the basis of race, color, sex, religion, national origin, age, disability, marital status, political affiliation, or of conduct that does not adversely affect the performance of the applicant or employee. This conduct can include sexual orientation or gender identity. In addition, the OPM has interpreted the prohibition of conduct-based sex discrimination to include discrimination based on sexual orientation and gender identity.[30]

Currently, with the employer-in-chief as the early mover, federal government policy reads:

> It is the policy of the federal government . . . to provide equal opportunity in federal employment for all persons, to prohibit discrimination in employment because of race, color, religion, sex, national origin, handicap, age, sexual orientation, gender identity or status as a parent, and to promote the realization of equal employment opportunity through a continuing affirmative program in each department and agency.[31]

Bill Clinton and Obama were the most recent chief executives to amend Nixon's original executive order and to extend the prohibition on discrimination to include sexual orientation and gender orientation. Congress has not affirmed this expansion to private sector employees under federal law. However, Congress has affirmed a number of executive prohibitions against discrimination and extended them to private sector employment, especially discrimination on the basis of race, color, national origin, religion, sex, age, or disability. These include the 1963 Equal Pay Act; Title VII of the 1964 Civil Rights Act; the 1964 Pregnancy Discrimination Act; the 1967 Age Discrimination in Employment Act; Sections 501 and 505 of the 1973 Rehabilitation Act; Title I and Title V of the 1990 Americans with Disabilities Act; the 1991 Civil Rights Act; and Title II of the 2008 Genetic Information Nondiscrimination Act (GINA).[32] Appendix table 4 summarizes executive orders relating to equal opportunity and their policy-related outcomes.

THE POWER OF THE ETHICAL EMPLOYER
AND PUBLIC POLICY

The evidence affirms that presidents rely on the power of the employer-in-chief to delimit basic principles of ethical conduct and dictate how high-ranking political appointees and executive branch employees should conduct themselves. Kennedy was the first chief executive to claim that ethics rules could be made without the cooperation of Congress—by "presidential order, memoranda or other form of action."[33] As the first employer-in-chief elected after the Watergate scandal, Carter proposed and Congress approved an Ethics in Government Act calling for financial disclosure, the creation of an Office of Ethics, and stronger restrictions on post-employment activities of government officials. Congress established the Office of Government Ethics (OGE) to provide overall leadership and oversight of ethics programs designed to prevent and resolve conflicts of interest in the executive branch (1977 Ethics in Government Act).[34] Presidents have empowered the Office of White House Counsel with political control over federal ethics rules and political influence over federal ethics policy.

Executive orders on ethics have typically stayed in effect unless modified by a successor. For example, George H. W. Bush declared fourteen basic principles of ethical conduct for executive branch employees.[35] Clinton extended these standards to include high-level political appointees.[36] George W. Bush asked all federal employees to become familiar with and faithfully observe existing federal ethics laws and rules, affirming the existing Standards of Ethical Conduct for Employees. Although presidents have imposed new ethics requirements, they have also allowed exemptions and waivers for political appointees from their very own ethics rules. Clinton, for example, suspended his ethics rules just before leaving the White House.

Obama promised "the strictest, most far-reaching ethics rules of any transition team in history."[37] His order barred "every appointee in every executive agency" from leaving employment with the federal government and then lobbying any executive branch official or senior appointee for the remainder of his administration.[38] However, the OGE, in consultation with the Office of White House Counsel, determined that certain categories of individuals were not required to sign the Ethics Pledge.[39] Moreover, as it only applied to political appointees, Obama's order did not restrict the post-employment actions of the vast majority of the 2.6 million federal employees, including even senior employees in the regulatory arena. As a result, many key officials moved freely in and out of the revolving door.[40] Appendix table 5 summarizes the power of the employer-in-chief ethics order and policy-related outcomes.

THE POWER OF THE PAYER AND PUBLIC POLICY

The evidence affirms that presidents use the power of the payer to dictate the terms and conditions of the relationship between the federal government and private sector health insurers and providers. Through executive orders or memoranda presidents have exercised political control over federal health program (Medicare, Medicaid, Defense, and the Veterans Health Administration) rulemaking and political influence on the quality and cost of health policy. Presidents have also exercised direct political influence and control on the Federal Employees Health Benefits Program by expanding health benefits as well as extending coverage for "temporary" federal employees as well as same-sex partners and their children. Through the power of the payer, presidents have shaped the coverage, cost, and quality of health care—not just for federal health program beneficiaries (veterans, military, federal employees, seniors, and working poor families), but also for the privately insured population. As one enormous payer, the president can have outsized influence on players across the health-care financing and delivery system.

More recently, under the 2010 Patient Protection and Affordable Care Act, Democrats in Congress delegated significant rulemaking authority to Obama's Department of Health and Human Services.[41] Without a formal executive order or memo, Obama's HHS defined individuals protected from discrimination in health care on the basis of sex to include prohibiting "denial of health care or health coverage based on pregnancy, gender identity, and sex stereotyping." Obama's HHS also prohibited health insurers from denying coverage and services to transgender Americans on the basis of their gender identity. The Obama rule, which applied to the antidiscrimination provisions of the Affordable Care Act, was significant because it compelled insurers to apply the same standards to every plan they administer, including those in the private sector.[42] Appendix table 6 summarizes payer-in-chief orders and their policy-related outcomes.

CONCLUSION

As the size of the federal government has increased, the scope of the presidency has widened. Regardless of partisan affiliation, presidents have sought to acquire and consolidate authority over the expanding federal bureaucracy. All have repeatedly used these executive powers—purchaser, employer, and payer—to shape the policy agenda, to secure political control over agency rulemaking, and to gain political influence over public policy. Except for a few notable exceptions, this has happened with the support of Congress and the blessing of the courts. By innovating new pathways of power that have met with little resistance, presidents have made unilateral action into an extremely effective tool to advance lasting reforms.

During the last several decades of increasing political polarization and gridlock in Congress, presidents have used these executive orders and memos in a wider range of controversial and contested policy areas. Indeed, as the possibility of legislative accomplishment has "grown dim in an era of divided government with high polarization between congressional parties," presidents have had an even greater incentive to go it alone.[43] The embedding of unilateral powers in the presidency is an enduring source of controversy. Critics claim that these executive orders and memorandum are an abuse of executive power; others conclude that the use of unilateral power is critical to the functioning of the federal government. Even though Todd Gaziano, a conservative legal scholar associated with the Heritage Foundation, acknowledges that an "aggressive use of this power is necessary for a modern president to manage the largest bureaucracy in the world," some of his former colleagues at the Heritage Foundation assert that "abusive, unlawful, and even potentially unconstitutional unilateral action has been a hallmark of the Obama presidency."[44] However, Eric Posner, writing in the *New Republic,* maintains that "Obama's assertion of unilateral executive authority is just routine stuff. He follows in the footsteps of his predecessors on a path set out by Congress."[45]

Finally, the rise of executive orders and memoranda has redefined American politics and raised the stakes of elections. Recent evidence suggests that when the new president is from the same party, an incumbent president has little incentive to issue last-minute changes. If Hillary Clinton had won the White House, most all of Obama's orders and memos would have survived. Clinton—facing the prospect of a Republican Congress—had also pledged to use executive orders to increase her clout in the White House to work around Congress and force Republicans to respond to her agenda.

However, there is evidence that when the incumbent's party loses, the successor president exercises "these powers with exceptional zeal, making final impressions on public policy in the short time before the opposition party assumes control."[46] Thus, we can predict that Trump's victory puts many of Obama's orders and memos at risk—given Trump's scattered ideological leanings, it is hard to say which ones. However, undoing a popular executive order (such as the increase in the federal minimum wage or an extension of civil rights protections) can become politically risky—if not impossible. Nevertheless, given that so much of Obama's legacy was rooted in policies he enacted with his phone and pen, it is likely he will see much of it undone, rather quickly.

In the long run, presidents of either party will almost certainly continue to seek to expand their influence and authority as a matter of bureaucratic necessity and political interest. The open question is whether other powers will rise up to limit them. Historically, Congress has had a difficult time enacting laws that amend or overturn orders issued by these presidents, but efforts to either codify in law or fund an executive order enjoy higher success rates. For the most part, by staying out of separation-of-powers issues, the courts have left it up to Congress to protect its own interests against any expansion of executive power. More broadly, executive orders have continued to grow in importance, and deferential court decisions have laid the foundation for further expansion of executive power. Courts have appeared willing to strike down a few executive orders, but the majority of such orders are never challenged.[47]

Voters have taken a greater interest in executive authority since Bill Clinton's presidency. During the presidential primaries, Obama's unilateral actions were a key punching bag for Republican candidates and an inspiration to the Democrats. One's view of this contentious debate is likely to depend less on principle than partisanship.

In sum, whoever wins, the *president will continue to Call the Shots*.

The Power of the Purchaser and Key Policy Outcomes

Policy Area/Federal Rules FAR[1]/DOL[2]	President's Order or Memo[3]
Labor-management relations *Subparts 22.5; 22.12; 22.16*	**G. H. W. Bush** EO 12800 (1992) EO 12818 (1992)
	Clinton EO 12836 (1993) revokes EO 12800; EO 12818 EO 12871 (1993) EO 12933 (1994) EO 12954 (1995)[4]
	G. W. Bush EO 13201 (2001) revokes EO 12836 EO 13202 (2001) revokes EO 12836 EO 13203 (2001)[5] revokes EO 12871 EO 13204 (2001) revokes EO 12933
	Obama EO 13494 (2009) EO 13495 (2009) revokes EO 13204 EO 13496 (2009) revokes EO 13201 EO 13502 (2009) revokes EO 13202 EO 13522 (2009)

Policy Area/Federal Rules FAR[1]/DOL[2]	President's Order or Memo[3]
Unemployment and inflation	**Nixon** EO 11158 (1971) EO 11627 (1971)[6] **Carter** EO 12092 (1978) EO 12161 (1979) **Reagan** EO 12288 (1981) revokes EO 12092 (1978) and EO 12161 (1979)
Poverty; empowerment contracting and HubZone *Subpart 19.3*	**Carter** EO 12073 (1978) **Clinton** EO 13005 (1996)
Small business set-aside *Subpart 19.5*	**Obama** Memo on Federal Contracting Opportunities for Small Business (2010)
Veteran-owned business/Service disabled veteran-owned business *Subpart 22.13; Subpart 19.4*	**Nixon** EO 11598 (1971) EO 11701 (1973) **G. W. Bush** EO 13360 (2004) **Obama** EO 13540 (2010) Veteran Small Business Development

Policy Area/Federal Rules FAR[1]/DOL[2]	President's Order or Memo[3]
Minority business enterprise development; women business enterprise; women-owned small business; economically disadvantaged women-owned small business; promoting procurement with small business owned and controlled by socially and economically disadvantaged individuals; HBCUs and minority institutions; Asian Americans and Pacific Islanders *Subpart 19.7* *Subpart 19.15* *Subpart 26.3*	**Nixon** EO 11458 (1969)[7] EO 11625 (1971) **Carter** EO 12007 (1977) EO 12138 (1979) **Reagan** EO 12432 (1983) **Clinton** EO 12928 (1994) Memo on Federal Procurement (1994) EO 13157 (2000) EO 13170 (2000) **G. W. Bush** EO 13339 (2004) Amended by **G. W. Bush** EO 13403 (2006) Superseded by **Obama** EO 13515 (2009)[8]
Immigration enforcement *Subpart 22.18*	**Clinton** EO 12989 (1996) **G. W. Bush** EO 13465 (2008)
Gun control	**Clinton** Memo on Child Safety Lock Devices for Handguns (1997)
Child labor *Subpart 22.15*	**Clinton** EO 13126 (1999)

Policy Area/Federal Rules FAR[1]/DOL[2]	President's Order or Memo[3]
Prohibition against discrimination based on race, creed, color, national origin; affirmative action and equal employment opportunity[9] *Subpart 22.8*	**FDR** EO 8802 (1941)[10] EO 8823 (1941) EO 9111 (1942) EO 9346 (1943)
	Truman EO 9664 (1945) EO 10210 (1951) EO 10308 (1951)
	Eisenhower EO 10479 (1953) EO 10482 (1953) EO 10577 (1954) EO 10733 (1957) superseded by EO 11246 (1965)[11]
	JFK EO 10925 (1961)[12] revokes EO 10479 (1953) EO 11114 (1963)
	LBJ EO 11246 (1965)[13]
	Nixon EO 11478 (1969)
	Carter EO 12067 (1978)
	Obama EO 13665 (2014)
	Obama EO 13672 (2014)[14] Adds sexual orientation and gender identity to EO 11246 (1965)

Policy Area/Federal Rules FAR[1]/DOL[2]	President's Order or Memo[3]
Antidiscrimination (housing)[15]	**JFK** EO 11063 (1962) **Carter** EO 12259 (1980) revises to apply to discrimination because of race, color, religion (creed), sex, or national origin[16] **Clinton** EO 12892 (1994) revokes EO 11063 (1962) (in part) EO 12259 (1980)
Antidiscrimination (age) *Subpart 22.9*	**LBJ** EO 11141 (1964)
Antidiscrimination (sex) Updated Rule (2015)[17]	**LBJ** EO 11375 (1967)
Antidiscrimination (disability) *Subpart 22.14*	
Faith-based contracting	**G. W. Bush** EO 13198 (2001) EO 13199 (2000) EO 13279 (2002) EO 13280 (2002) EO 13342 (2004) **Obama** EO 13498 (2009) EO 13559 (2010)[18]

Source: Author's compilation.

Notes
1. www.acquisition.gov/?q=browsefar.
2. Office of Federal Contract Compliance Programs (www.dol.gov/dol/cfr/Title_41 /Chapter_60.htm).
3. http://www.archives.gov/federal-register/executive-orders/disposition.html.
4. In *Chamber of Commerce of the United States, et al., v. Reich,* 74 F.3d 1322 (D.C. Cir. 1996), rehearing denied, 83 F.3d 442 (D.C. Cir. 1996), the U.S. Court of Appeals for the District of Columbia Circuit held that Clinton-EO 12954 is regulatory in nature, and is therefore preempted by the National Labor Relations Act. A petition for review on writ of certiorari was not filed with the Supreme Court.

5. Memorandum of October (1999).
6. Amends EO 11588 (1971); supersedes EO 11615 (1971); EO 11617 (1971); amended by EO 11630 (1971); EO 11632 (1971); superseded by EO 11640 (1972); revoked by EO 11788 (1974). See EO 11639 (1972); EO 11660 (1972); EO 11695 (1973); EO 11781 (1974); EO 11695 (1973).
7. Supersedes EO 11458 (1969); Advisory Council for Minority Enterprise continued by EO 11827 (1975); EO 11948 (1976); amended by EO 12007 (1977); council terminated by EO 11007 (1962).
8. Reaffirming Policy of Full Participation in the Defense Program by All Persons, Regardless of Race, Creed, Color, or National Origin.
9. The Office of Federal Contracts Compliance Programs (OFCCP) enforces the contractual promise of affirmative action and equal employment opportunity required of those who do business with the federal government. In addition to EO 11246, OFCCP enforces Section 503 of the Rehabilitation Act (1973) and the Vietnam Era Veterans' Readjustment Assistance Act (1974). Collectively, these three laws require contractors and subcontractors that do business with the federal government to prohibit discrimination and ensure equal opportunity in employment on the basis of race, color, religion, national origin, sex, disability, and status as a protected veteran (www.dol.gov/ofccp/aboutof.html).
10. http://docs.fdrlibrary.marist.edu/odex8802.html.
11. www.dol.gov/ofccp/regs/statutes/eo11246.htm.
12. Amended by EO 11114 (1963), EO 11162 (1964).
13. www.dol.gov/ofccp/regs/compliance/ca_11246.htm.
14. Amends EO 11246 (1965); EO 11478 (1969).
15. http://portal.hud.gov/hudportal/HUD?src=/program_offices/fair_housing_equal_opp/FHLaws.
16. http://portal.hud.gov/hudportal/HUD?src=/program_offices/fair_housing_equal_opp/FHLaws/EXO11063.
17. www.gpo.gov/fdsys/pkg/FR-2015-01-30/pdf/2015-01422.pdf.
18. http://ojp.gov/fbnp/pdfs/fbnprmpartnersfaq.pdf.

Obama, the Power of the Purchaser, and New Policy Areas

Policy Area/Federal Rules FAR[1]/DOL[2]	President Order or Memo
Transparency in federal contracting; Do-not-pay list	**Obama** Memo on Government Contracting (2009) **Obama** EO 13520 (2009) **Obama** Memo to Federal Agencies (2010)[3]
Human trafficking *Subpart 22.17*	**Obama** EO 13627 (2012)[4]
Minimum wage *Subpart 22.19*	**Obama** EO 13658 (2014)[5]
Non-retaliation for disclosure of pay *Final Rule (2015)*	**Obama** EO 13665 (2014)[6]
Paid sick leave *NPRM (2016)*	**Obama** EO 13706 (2014)[7]
Prohibit discrimination based on gender orientation *Final Rule (2014)*	**Obama** EO 13672 (2014)[8]

Policy Area/Federal Rules FAR[1]/DOL[2]	President Order or Memo
Fair pay and safe workplaces *DOL guidance[10]* *FAR proposed rule[11]*	**Obama** EO 13673 (2014)[9]

Source: Author's compilation.

Notes
1. https://www.acquisition.gov/?q=browsefar.
2. Office of Federal Contracts Compliance Programs (www.dol.gov/dol/cfr/Title_41 /Chapter_60.htm).
3. http://donotpay.treas.gov/Privacy.htm.
4. www.federalregister.gov/articles/2015/01/29/2015-01524/federal-acquisition-regu lation-ending-trafficking-in-persons.
5. www.dol.gov/whd/flsa/nprm-eo13658/factsheet.htm.
6. www.dol.gov/ofccp/regs/compliance/faqs/PayTransparencyFAQs.html#Q10.
7. www.dol.gov/whd/flsa/eo13706/faq.htm.
8. www.dol.gov/ofccp/lgbt/lgbt_faqs.html.
9. https://www.dol.gov/asp/fairpayandsafeworkplaces/.
10. www.federalregister.gov/articles/2015/05/28/2015-12562/guidance-for-executive -order-13673-fair-pay-and-safe-workplaces.
11. www.federalregister.gov/articles/2015/05/28/2015-12560/federal-acquisition-regu lation-fair-pay-and-safe-workplaces.

APPENDIX 3

The Power of Employer-in-Chief
and Policy Outcomes

Policy/Federal Rules	President's Order or Memo[1]
Labor-management in federal service; FLRA[2]	**FDR** EO 7916 (1938)
	Truman EO 9830 (1947)
	Truman EO 9922 (1948)
	Truman EO 10155 (1950)
	Eisenhower EO 10490 (1953)
	JFK Memo on Employee-Management Relations in the Federal Service (1961)
	JFK EO 10988 (1962)
	LBJ Memo on Employee Management Cooperation in the Federal Government (1967)
	Nixon EO 11491 (1969)
	Clinton EO 12871 (1993)
	Clinton EO 12871 amended by EO 12974 (1995); EO 12983 (1995); EO 13062 (1997); EO 13138 (1999); EO 13156 (2000)
	Bush EO 13203 (2001) revokes EO 12871
	Bush EO 13480 (2008)
	Obama EO 13522 (2009)[3]
	Obama EO 13522 continued by EO 13652 (2013); EO 13708 (2015)

Policy/Federal Rules	President's Order or Memo[1]
Pay freeze	**Obama** Memo on Pay Freeze (2009) **Obama** Memo on Freezing Federal Employee Pay Schedules and Rates That Are Set by Administrative Discretion (2010)
Long-term unemployed	**Obama** Memo on Long-Term Unemployed (2014)
Health and safety in federal workplace	**Wilson** EO 2455 (1916) **FDR** EO 8071 (1939) **Truman** EO 10194 (1950) revokes EO 8071 **Eisenhower** Memo on Occupational Safety in the Government Service (1954) **JFK** EO 10990 (1962) revokes EO 10194 **Nixon** Memo on ZERO IN on Federal Safety (1970) **Nixon** EO 11612 (1971)[4] **Ford** EO 11807 (1974) **Carter** EO 12196 (1980) **Reagan** Memo on an Occupational Safety and Health Program for Federal Employees (1982) **G. H. W. Bush** EO 12699 (1990) **G. W. Bush** Memo on the Safety, Health, and Return to Employment (SHARE) initiative (2004) **Obama** Memo on the Presidential POWER Initiative (2010)[5]
Providing compensation to America's nuclear weapons workers	**Clinton** EO 13179 (2000) Continued by **Obama** EO 13708 (2015)
Federal employee health and safety (Seat Belts)	**Reagan** EO 12566 (1986) **Clinton** EO 13043 (1996)
Drug-free workplace/drug testing	**Reagan** EO 12564 (1986), Drug-Free Federal Workplace/Drug Testing
AIDS in the federal workplace	**Reagan** EO 12601 (1987) **Reagan** Memo on AIDS (1988)[6]
Smoking in the federal workplace	**Clinton** EO 13058 (1997) **Clinton** Memo on Smoking Cessation Programs (2000)

Policy/Federal Rules	President's Order or Memo[1]
Health and fitness promotion in federal workplace	**G. W. Bush** EO 13266 (2002)
Flexible, family-friendly workplace (Child Support)	**Carter** EO 12105 (1978) **Clinton** EO 12953 (1995)
Flexible, family-friendly workplace (domestic violence)	**Obama** Memo on Addressing Domestic Violence (2012)
Flexible, family-friendly workplace (work and family balance)	**Carter** Memo on Part-time Federal Employment (1977) **Clinton** Memo on Expanding Family-Friendly Work Arrangements in the Executive Branch (1994) **Clinton** Memo on Family-Friendly Work Arrangements (1996) **Clinton** Memo on New Tools to Help Parents Balance Work and Family (1999) **G. W. Bush** EO 13426 (2007) **Obama** Memo on Enhancing Workplace Flexibilities and Work-Life Programs (2014) **Obama** Memo on Modernizing Federal Leave Policies for Childbirth, Adoption, and Foster Care to Recruit and Retain Talent and Improve Productivity (2015)

Source: Author's compilation.

Notes
1. www.archives.gov/federal-register/executive-orders/disposition.html.
2. Federal Labor Relations Authority (www.flra.gov/OGC_FLRA-FMCS_Joint_Train ing); https://www.flra.gov/resources-training/resources/statute-regulations/regulations.
3. www.whitehouse.gov/the-press-office/executive-order-creating-labor-management -forums-improve-delivery-government-servic.
4. Supersedes EO 10990, February 2, 1962; superseded by EO 11807, September 28, 1974; see EO 11654, March 13, 1972; EO 13585, September 30, 2011.
5. www.dol.gov/owcp/dfec/power/.
6. www.reaganlibrary.archives.gov/archives/speeches/1988/080588c.htm.

APPENDIX 4

Power of the Equal Opportunity Employer and Policy Outcomes

EEO Policy Area[1]/ Federal Law	President's Order or Memo
EEO (Race and ethnicity)[2]; Civil Rights Act (1964)	**FDR** EO 8802 (1941)
	Amended by **FDR** EO 8823 (1941); EO 9111 (1942); EO 9346 (1943)
	Truman EO 9644 (1945)
	Truman EO 9808 (1946)
	Truman EO 9980 (1948)
	Truman EO 9981 (1948)
	Clinton EO 13171 (2000)[3]
EEO (diversity and inclusion); Equal Employment Opportunity Act (1972)	**Eisenhower** EO 10590 (1955)
	JFK EO 10925 (1961)
	LBJ EO 11246 (1965); EO 11375 (1967)
	Nixon EO 11478 (1969)
	Amended by **Nixon** EO 11590 (1971)
	Carter EO 12106 (1978)
	Clinton EO 13087 (1998)
	Clinton EO 13152 (2000)
	Obama EO 13583 (2011)[4]

EEO Policy Area[1]/ Federal Law	President's Order or Memo
EEO (Sex)[5]; Equal Pay Act (1963), amending section 6(d) of Fair Labor Standards Act (1938)	JFK EO 10980 (1961) JFK Memo on Equal Opportunity for Women in the Federal Service (1962) LBJ EO 11375 (1967)[6] Nixon EO 11478 (1969) Nixon Memo about Women in Government (1971) Carter Memo on Federal Employment of Women (1977) Obama Memo on Advancing Pay Equality in the Federal Government and Learning from Successful Practices (2013)
EEO (Age)[7]; Age Discrimination in Employment Act (1967)	Hoover EO 5610 (1931) LBJ EO 11141 (1964) Nixon Memo about Age Discrimination in Federal Employment (1972)
EEO (Veterans)[8]; Veterans' Preference Act (1944) Vietnam Era Veterans' Readjustment Act (1974)	FDR EO 6203 (1933) FDR Letter on Preference for Veterans in Federal Employment (1944) Truman EO 9589 (1945) Truman EO 9644 (1945) EO 9662 (1945) Truman Memo on Veteran Preferences in Federal Agencies (1945); EO 9738 (1946) Eisenhower EO 10577 (1954) LBJ EO 11397 (1968) Nixon EO 11521 (1970) revokes EO 11397 (1968) Nixon EO 11598 (1971) Nixon Memo about Employment of Vietnam Veterans (1972) Carter EO 12107 (1978) amends EO 11521 G. H. W. Bush Memo on the Return of Desert Shield and Desert Storm Participants to Federal Civilian Employment (1991) Obama EO 13518 (2009)[9] Obama Memo on Uniformed Services Employment and Reemployment Rights Act Protections (2012)[10]

EEO Policy Area[1]/ Federal Law	President's Order or Memo
EEO (Disability)[11]; Vocational Rehabilitation Act (1973)	Eisenhower EO 10640 (1955) JFK Memo on Employment of the Mentally Retarded (1963) JFK EO 10994 (1962) LBJ Memo on Employment of Handicapped Persons by Federal Government (1964) Nixon EO 11478 (1969) Reagan EO 12640 (1988) G. H. W. Bush Memo on Access for People with Disabilities to Federal Programs and Employment (1991) Clinton EO 13078 (1998) Clinton EO 13124 (1999) Clinton Memo on Hiring People with Disabilities in the Federal Government (1999) Clinton EO 13163 (2000) Clinton EO 13164 (2000) Clinton EO 13187 (2001) Clinton EO 13078 amended by G. W. Bush EO 13172 (2000) G. W. Bush EO 13187 (2001) Obama EO 13548 (2010)[12] Obama EO 13583 (2011)
EEO (Sexual orientation)	Truman EO 9835 (1947) Truman EO 10001 (1948) Truman EO 10241 (1951) Eisenhower EO 10450 (1953) amends EO 9835 Clinton EO 12968 (1995)[13] amends EO 10450 (1953)
EEO (Sexual orientation)[14]	Clinton EO 13087 (1999) amends EO 11478 (1969) Clinton EO 13152 amends EO 11478 (2000)[15] Obama Memo on Extension of Benefits to Same-Sex Domestic Partners of Federal Employees (2010)
EEO (Status as a parent)	Clinton EO 13152 (2000)[16]
EEO (Genetic information)[17]; Genetic Information Non-Discrimination Act (2006)	Clinton EO 13145 (2000)

EEO Policy Area[1]/ Federal Law	President's Order or Memo
EEO (Gender identity)	**Obama** EO 13672 (2014)[18] amends EO 11246 (1965), EO 11478 (1969)

Source: Author's compilation.

Notes
1. www.eeoc.gov/laws/types/index.cfm.
2. www.eeoc.gov/laws/types/race_color.cfm.
3. www.chcoc.gov/content/executive-order-13171-hispanics-employment-federal -government.
4. See EO 13078 (1998); EO 13163 (2000); EO 13171 (2000); EO 13518 (2009); EO 13548 (2010) (www.opm.gov/policy-data-oversight/diversity-and-inclusion/reports /governmentwidedistrategicplan.pdf).
5. www.eeoc.gov/laws/types/equalcompensation.cfm.
6. Amends EO 11246 (1965).
7. www.eeoc.gov/laws/types/age.cfm.
8. www.opm.gov/policy-data-oversight/veterans-employment-initiative/vet-guide/.
9. www.opm.gov/news/releases/2014/04/veterans-employment-council-discusses -strategy-to-increase-employment-and-retention-of-veterans-in-federal-government/.
10. www.whitehouse.gov/the-press-office/2012/07/19/presidential-memorandum -uniformed-services-employment-and-reemployment-r.
11. www.eeoc.gov/laws/types/disability.cfm.
12. See EO 13163 (2000); EO 13583 (2011) (www.opm.gov/policy-data-oversight/diver sity-and-inclusion/reports/disability-report-fy2014.pdf).
13. See EO 12968 antidiscrimination statement, "The United States Government does not discriminate on the basis of race, color, religion, sex, national origin, disability, or sexual orientation in granting access to classified information" (www.gpo.gov /fdsys/pkg/FR-1995-08-07/pdf/95-19654.pdf).
14. www.eeoc.gov/federal/otherprotections.cfm.
15. This EO expands equal employment policy in the federal government by prohibiting discrimination based on sexual orientation.
16. www.dol.gov/oasam/programs/crc/eo013152.pdf.
17. www.eeoc.gov/laws/types/genetic.cfm.
18. This EO expands equal employment policy in the federal government by prohibiting discrimination based on gender identity.

APPENDIX 5

The Power of the Ethical
Employer-in-Chief and Policy Outcomes

Executive Ethics Policy[1]/ /Federal Law/Federal Regulation	President's Order or Memo[2]
Ethical conduct and conflict of interest	**JFK** EO 10939 (1961)
	JFK Memo on Preventing Conflicts of Interest on the Part of Special Government Employees (1962)
Code of Ethics for Government Service (1957–58)	**JFK** Memo on Conflicts of Interest and Ethical Standards of Conduct of Government Employees (1963)
Ethics in Government Act (1962)	**JFK** Memo on Preventing Conflicts of Interest on the Part of Special Government Employees (1963)
Ethics Reform Act (1978); 5 CFR Chapter XVI, Subchapter B	**JFK** memo (1963) revokes in part EO 10530 (1954)
	LBJ EO 11222 (1965)[3] revokes EO 10939 (1961); EO 11125 (1963)
	Nixon EO 11570 (1970)
	Nixon EO 11590 (1971)
	Reagan EO 12565 (1986)

Executive Ethics Policy[1]/ /Federal Law/Federal Regulation	President's Order or Memo[2]
To provide a guide on ethical standards to federal government officials; standards of ethical conduct for federal government officers and employees[1]; Ethics Reform Act (1989)[4] 5 C.F.R. part 2635[5]	**G. H. W. Bush** EO 12668 (1989) **G. H. W. Bush** EO 12674 (1989) revokes EO 11222 (1965) as modified by EO 12731 **G. H. W. Bush** EO 12731 (1990) **G. W. Bush** Memo on Standards of Official Conduct (2001)[6]
Ethics by executive branch appointees; ethics pledge for executive branch personnel	**Clinton** EO 12834 (1993) **Clinton** EO 13184 (2000) revokes EO 12834 (1993) **Obama** EO 13490 (2009)[7]

Source: Author's compilation.

Notes
1. https://www2.oge.gov/web/oge.nsf/Executive%20Orders.
2. http://www.archives.gov/federal-register/executive-orders/; http://www.archives.gov /federal-register/executive-orders/disposition.html
3. Revokes: EO 10939 (1961); EO 11125 (1963); Memorandum of May 2, 1963. Revokes in part: EO 10530 (1954). Amended by: EO 11590 (1971); EO 12107 (1978); EO 12565 (1986). Revoked by: EO 12674 (1989). See EO 11408 (1968) (according to Civil Service Commission EO 11222 supersedes orders revoked by EO 11408); EO 11560 (1970); EO 12731 (1990).
4. https://www.oge.gov/web/oge.nsf/Authorizing%20Legislation%20and%20Oversight /6FED47DB4CB9B89585257F1C00752BC7/$FILE/PL101-194.pdf?open.
5. https://www2.oge.gov/Web/oge.nsf/Resources/5+C.F.R.+Part+2635:++Standards+of +ethical+conduct+for+employees+of+the+executive+branch.
6. https://www.oge.gov/Web/OGE.nsf/All+Advisories/E61BD1F56A30128385257E96 005FBDA5/$FILE/DO-01-004.pdf?open.
7. https://www.whitehouse.gov/the-press-office/ethics-commitments-executive -branch-personnel; https://www.justice.gov/jmd/ethics-pledge-executive-order-13490.

The Power of the Payer-in-Chief
and Policy Outcomes

Health Policy Area/ Federal Law	President Order/Memo	Federal Agency Directive
Veterans; Agent Orange Act (1991); Veterans' Health Care Eligibility Reform Act (1996); Caregivers and Veterans Omnibus Health Services Act (2010);[1] Agent Orange Equity Act (2011)	**Hoover** EO 5398 (1930) **G. H. W. Bush** EO 12751 (1991) **Clinton** directive to expand Agent Orange benefits for Veterans (1996)[2] **G. W. Bush** EO 13214 (2001) **G. W. Bush** EO 13360 (2004) **G. W. Bush** EO 13426 (2007) **Obama** EO 13625 (2012)[3]	**Obama** VHA directive to specify care available to transgender and intersex veterans (2013)[4] **Obama** DOD directive that medically diagnosed issues related to gender (including reassignment surgery) should be treated the same as other medical care and treatment (2016)[5]
Federal Employees Health Benefits Plan (FEHBP): Drug Free; Mental Health Parity; Preventative Health Services; Mammography	**Reagan** EO 12564 (1986) **Reagan** Memo on Federal Initiatives for a Drug-Free America (1986) **Clinton** Memo on Mental Health Parity (1999) **Clinton** Memo on Preventive Health Services at the Federal Workplace (2001) **Clinton** Directive on Mammogram Screenings (1997)	

Health Policy Area/ Federal Law	President Order/Memo	Federal Agency Directive
FEHBP: Coverage regarding a diagnosis of Gender Identity Disorder/ Gender Dysphoria		**Obama** OPM Directive on Gender Identity Disorder/Gender Dysphoria (2014)[6]
FEHBP: Eligibility for Temporary Employees; Eligibility for Same-Sex Spouse		**Obama** OPM Directive on Federal Firefighters Access to Health Insurance (2012)[7] **Obama** OPM Directive on Same-Sex Spouse Benefits (2013)
Medicare and SCHIP	**Johnson** EO 11279 on Health Manpower (1966) **Clinton** Memo on Child Health Insurance Outreach and Enrollment (1997) **Clinton** Memo on Clinical Trials and Medicare Beneficiaries (2000) **Obama** Memo on SCHIP (2009)	**G. W. Bush** CMS Letter to State Officials on SCHIP Eligibility (2007)
Consumer Protection and Health Care Quality; Affordable Care Act (2010)	**Clinton** EO 13017 (1996) **Clinton** Memo on Federal Agency Compliance with the Patient Bill of Rights (1998)	

Health Policy Area/ Federal Law	President Order/Memo	Federal Agency Directive
Health Care Quality and Prevention of Medical Errors	**Clinton** Memo on Establishment of the Quality Interagency Coordination Task Force (1998) **Clinton** Memo on Improving Health Care Quality and Ensuring Patient Safety (1999)	
Health Information Privacy; Improved Quality, Efficiency and Information Technology; Health Insurance Portability and Accountability Act (1996); Health Information Technology for Economic and Clinical Health Act (2009); American Recovery and Reinvestment Act (2009)	**Clinton** EO 13181 (2000) **G. W. Bush** EO 13335 (2004) **G. W. Bush** EO 13410 (2006)	
AntiDiscrimination and Visiting Rights Regardless of Sexual Orientation	**Obama** Memo on Respecting the Rights of Hospital Patients to Receive Visitors and to Designate Surrogate Decision Makers for Medical Emergencies (2010)[8]	

Health Policy Area/ Federal Law	President Order/Memo	Federal Agency Directive
Health Care Reform; Affordable Care Act (2010)	**Obama** EO 13507 (2009)	**Obama** HHS directive defined individuals protected from discrimination in health care on the basis of "race, color, national origin, age, disability and sex, to include prohibiting denial of health care or health coverage based on pregnancy, gender identity, and sex stereotyping"[9]

Notes
1. http://www.military.com/benefits/veterans-health-care/veteran-benefits-caregiver programs-and-services.html.
2. http://www.benefits.va.gov/compensation/claims-postservice-agent_orange.asp.
3. https://www.whitehouse.gov/the-press-office/2012/08/31/executive-order-improving -access-mental-health-services-veterans-service.
4. http://www.va.gov/vhapublications/ViewPublication.asp?pub_ID=2863.
5. http://www.defense.gov/Portals/1/features/2016/0616_policy/DoD-Instruction-1300.28 .pdf.
6. https://www.opm.gov/healthcare-insurance/healthcare/carriers/2014/2014-17.pdf.
7. https://www.opm.gov/news/releases/2012/07/opm-announces-rule-change-to-allow -federal-firefighters-access-to-health-insurance/.
8. https://www.whitehouse.gov/the-press-office/presidential-memorandum-hospital -visitation.
9. http://www.hhs.gov/sites/default/files/Summary.pdf.

Notes

CHAPTER ONE

1. Megan Slack, "President Obama Holds the First Cabinet Meeting of 2014," January 14, 2014 (www.whitehouse.gov/blog/2014/01/14/president-obama-holds-first-cabinet-meeting-2014).

2. Gregory Korte, "Obama's Executive Orders You Never Hear About," *USA Today,* April 11, 2016.

3. Brad Plumer, "Obama Is Boosting the Minimum Wage for Federal Contractors. Here's How," *Washington Post,* January 28, 2014.

4. Mayer and Price (2002).

5. Moe and Wilson (1994).

6. Egerton (1980).

7. Gitterman (2013).

8. Steven Mufson and Juliet Eilperin, "Obama Expands Parental Leave for Federal Workers," *Washington Post,* January 15, 2015.

9. MacKenzie and Hafken (2002, p. 23).

10. United States Office of Government Ethics, "DO-09-003: Executive Order 13490, Ethics Pledge," January 2, 2009 (www.oge.gov/OGE-Advisories/Legal-Advisories/DO-09-003--Executive-Order-13490,-Ethics-Pledge/).

11. See Lin (2014, pp. 1353, 1365, 1367, 1370).

12. Ibid., p. 1365.

13. Stack (2005).

14. Newland (2015).

15. Mayer (1996, 1997); Cooper (1986, 1997); Cohen and Krause (1997); Krause and Cohen (1997, 2000); Deering and Maltzman (1999); Gomez and Shull (1995); Shanley (1983); Wigton (1991).

16. See Cooper (2001); Deering and Maltzman (1999); Howell and Lewis (2002); Krause and Cohen (1997); Mayer (1999); Mayer and Price (2002); Moe and Howell (1999a, 1999b).

17. See, for example, Edwards (2005); Rockman and Waterman (2007).

18. Moe and Wilson (1994).

19. See Moe and Howell (1999b, p. 850).

20. Lin (2014).

21. Moe and Howell (1999b).

22. Ibid.

23. As a practical matter, there is little legal difference between executive orders and presidential memoranda, as both are used by presidents to direct the actions of government officials and agencies. However, under the law, executive orders are required to be published in the *Federal Register* and are numbered; there is no such requirement for presidential memoranda. See Mayer (2001).

24. Kagan (2001).

25. Chu and Garvey (2014).

26. Krause and Cohen (1997); Moe and Howell (1999a); Mayer (1999, 2001); Deering and Maltzman (1999).

27. For more on the evolution of executive orders and presidential proclamations, see Contrubis (1999).

28. Mayer (1999). There are three recognized sources of presidential power: an express grant of power, an implied grant of power, and the power that is inherent in the office of the executive under the Constitution. See *Youngstown Sheet & Tube Co. v. Sawyer,* 343 U.S. 579, 635–37 (1952). It is clear that, if the president had authority to issue the order he did, it must be found in some provision of the Constitution. And it is not claimed that express constitutional language grants this power to the president. The contention is that presidential power should be implied from the aggregate of his powers under the Constitution. Particular reliance is placed on provisions in Article II, which say that "The executive Power shall be vested in a President . . ."; that "he shall take Care that the Laws be faithfully executed," and that he "shall be Commander in Chief of the Army and Navy of the United States."

29. A widely accepted description of executive orders and proclamations comes from a report issued in 1957 by the House Government Operations Committee:

Executive orders and proclamations are directives or actions by the President. When they are founded on the authority of the President de-

rived from the Constitution or statute, they may have the force and effect of law. . . . In the narrower sense Executive orders and proclamations are written documents denominated as such . . . Executive orders
are generally directed to, and govern actions by, Government officials
and agencies. They usually affect private individuals only indirectly.
Proclamations in most instances affect primarily the activities of private
individuals. Since the President has no power or authority over individual citizens and their rights except where he is granted such power and
authority by a provision in the Constitution or by statute, the President's proclamations are not legally binding and are at best hortatory
unless based on such grants of authority.

See Cooper (2001); Dodds (2013); U.S. Congress, House Committee on Government Operations, *Executive Orders and Proclamations: A Study of a Use of
Presidential Powers*, 85th Cong., 1st sess., 1957.

30. Cooper (1986, p. 234). On the court ruling, see *Lower Brule Sioux Tribe
v. Deer*, 911 F. Supp. 395 (D.S.D. 1995).

31. Chu and Garvey (2014).

32. Cooper (2002, p. 48).

33. Noah Feldman, "Obama and the Limits of Executive Power," *Bloom-
bergView*, December 28, 2015.

34. Deering and Maltzman (1999); Krause and Cohen (1997).

35. Lowande (2014); Gregory Korte, "Obama Issues 'Executive Orders by
Another Name,'" *USA Today*, December 17, 2014; Glenn Kessler, "Fact Checker:
Claims Regarding Obama's Use of Executive Orders and Presidential Memo-
randa," *Washington Post*, December 31, 2014.

36. Moe (1985).

37. Ibid.

38. Ibid.

39. Kagan (2001).

40. Ibid., p. 2248.

41. Moe and Wilson (1994).

42. Relyea (2008).

43. U.S. General Services Administration (2005); Jack Lew, "Turning the
Tide on Contract Spending," *OMBlog*, February 4, 2011 (www.whitehouse
.gov/blog/2011/02/04/turning-tide-contract-spending).

44. Danielle Ivory, "Federal Contracts Plunge, Squeezing Private Companies," *New York Times*, January 15, 2014.

45. Burrows and Manuel (2011).

46. Porter (2006, p. 7).

47. Alex Greer, "The Government Agencies That Employ the Most People,"
May 20, 2016 (http://federal-budget.insidegov.com/stories/13693/government

-agencies-most-employees); Henry Taylor, "Who Is the World's Biggest Employer? The Answer Might Not Be What You Expect," June 17, 2015 (https://www.weforum.org/agenda/2015/06/worlds-10-biggest-employers/).

48. U.S. Bureau of Labor Statistics, "Employment, Hours, and Earnings from the Current Employment Statistics Survey (National)" (http://data.bls.gov/timeseries/CES0000000001); U.S. Census Bureau, "Government Employment & Payroll: Historical Data: 2010" (www.census.gov//govs/apes/historical_data_2010.html); U.S. Office of Personnel Management, "Federal Employment Reports: Federal Civilian Employment" (www.opm.gov/policy-data-oversight/data-analysis-documentation/federal-employment-reports/reports-publications/federal-civilian-employment/).

49. U.S. Office of Personnel Management, "The Governmentwide Veterans' Recruitment and Employment Strategic Plan for FY 2010–FY 2012" (www.fedshirevets.gov/Blog/uploads/docs/FHVNews/2010/1/28/The-Governmentwide-Veterans-Recruitment/Vets_Initiative_Strategic_Plan.pdf).

50. MacKenzie and Hafken (2002).

51. United States Department of Justice, "Ethics Pledge, Executive Order 13490" (www.justice.gov/jmd/ethics-pledge-executive-order-13490); Robert I. Cusick to Agency Heads and Designated Agency Ethics Officials, memorandum, January 22, 2009, United States Office of Government Ethics (www2.oge.gov/Web/OGE.nsf/All%20Documents/912EE96BCFEC4A0185257E96005FBB85/$FILE/DO-09-003.pdf?open).

52. U.S. Department of Health and Human Services, Centers for Medicare and Medicaid Services, "Fiscal Year 2016: Justification of Estimates for Appropriations Committees" (www.cms.gov/About-CMS/Agency-Information/PerformanceBudget/Downloads/FY2016-CJ-Final.pdf).

53. Office of Management and Budget, "Table 15.1—Total Outlays for Health Programs: 1962–2021" (www.whitehouse.gov/omb/budget/Historicals).

54. Congressional Budget Office, "The 2015 Long-Term Budget Outlook," table 2.2, p. 43, June 2015 (www.cbo.gov/sites/default/files/114th-congress-2015-2016/reports/50250-LongTermBudgetOutlook-4.pdf).

55. U.S. Department of Health and Human Services, Centers for Medicare and Medicaid Services, "National Health Expenditure Projections 2014–2024 Forecast Summary" (www.cms.gov/Research-Statistics-Data-and-Systems/Statistics-Trends-and-Reports/NationalHealthExpendData/downloads/proj2014.pdf).

56. Newland (2015).

57. Ibid.; Stack (2005).

58. Phillip J. Cooper, "Playing Presidential Ping-Pong with Executive Orders," *Washington Post,* January 31, 2014.

CHAPTER TWO

1. Moe and Wilson (1994).

2. Kelman (2002). Federal procurement is the purchasing of goods and services by contract, purchase card, grant, intragovernmental transaction, or other means of sourcing. Federal agencies contract for products and services that their employees use, such as fighter aircraft, office supplies and computers, and for services they provide to others, such as collecting on delinquent student loans, running customer-service hotlines, and delivering job training.

3. U.S. Congress, *Federal Property and Administrative Services Act of 1949*, Pub. L. No. 81-152, 81st Cong., 1st sess. May 24, 1949.

4. The Federal Property and Administrative Services Act was passed in response to a report, in 1949, to the Commission on Organization of the Executive Branch of the Government (called the Hoover Commission for short), which concluded that the federal government's method of doing business must be modernized. See Reeves (1996, p. 11).

5. U.S. Congress, *Federal Property and Administrative Services Act of 1949*.

6. U.S. General Services Administration (2005).

7. The General Services Administration's original mission was to dispose of war surplus goods, manage and store government records, handle emergency preparedness, and stockpile strategic supplies for wartime. As the volume of federal purchasing increased, in 1969 Congress created the Commission on Government Procurement to recommend ways to "promote the economy, efficiency, and effectiveness" of federal procurement. The commission recommended the establishment of a strong, central office to provide leadership in procurement for all federal agencies within the Executive Office of the President. See Reeves (1996, p. 16).

8. Heifetz (1998). The Federal Acquisition Regulations Council, which was established in 1990, manages and oversees the Federal Acquisition Regulations (FAR), which are prepared through the coordinated action of the Defense Acquisition Regulations Council and the Civilian Agency Acquisition Council. The FAR system was established for the codification and publication of uniform policies and procedures for acquisition by all executive agencies. Prior to 1984, two sets of federal procurement regulations governed the purchase of all goods and services. Military-related purchasing was governed by the Armed Services Procurement Regulations, renamed the Defense Acquisition Regulations in 1978. Civilian-related purchasing was governed by the Federal Procurement Regulations. Under the 1984 Competition in Contracting Act, Congress established rules for choosing suppliers based on the policy of "full and open competition." For more information on FAR, see Federal Acquisition Regulations website, "Table

of Contents" (http://farsite.hill.af.mil/reghtml/regs/far2afmcfars/fardfars/far
/Far1toc.htm); Federation of American Scientists, "The Federal Acquisition
Regulation (FAR): Answers to Frequently Asked Questions" (www.fas.org/sgp
/crs/misc/R42826.pdf).

9. U.S. Congress, *Federal Procurement Policy Act of 1974*, Pub. L. No. 93-
400, 93rd Cong., 2nd sess. February 26, 1974. Congress insulated the Office
of Federal Procurement Policy from direct presidential political control after
Nixon's budget impoundments and the Office of Management and Budget's at-
tempts to exert political influence over administrative agencies. These protections included separate authorizations for the OFPP, a requirement that the
administrator report directly to Congress, and a provision vesting the OFPP's
authority in the administrator rather than in the director of the OMB. The OFPP
is headed by an administrator who is appointed by the president and confirmed
by the Senate. The OFPP sets procurement policies for all federal agencies and
coordinates the president's position on procurement-related legislation. Congress offered temporary authorization for the office in 1979 and renewed it in
1983 before making the office permanent in the 1988 OFPP Act Amendments.
See U.S. Congress, Pub. L. 100-679, 100th Cong., 2nd sess. November 17,
1988.

10. Ian Urbina, "The Shopping List as Policy Tool," *New York Times*, January 25, 2014.

11. The OFPP's primary focus is on the Federal Acquisition Regulations, the
federal-government-wide regulations governing agency acquisitions of goods
and services. See Office of Management and Budget, "Office of Federal Procurement Policy" (www.whitehouse.gov/omb/procurement_mission/).

12. George H. W. Bush, "Executive Order 12800: Notification of Employee
Rights Concerning Payment of Union Dues or Fees, April 13, 1992," American
Presidency Project (henceforth cited as APP). In *Communication Workers of
America v. Beck,* the Supreme Court ruled that workers were not obligated to
pay the portion of their union dues used for political advocacy. See *Communi-
cation Workers of America v. Beck*, 487 U.S. 735 (1988). The 1935 National
Labor Relations Act (NLRA) requires the payment of union dues for nonpoliti-
cal purposes only.

13. George H. W. Bush, "Executive Order 12800."

14. William J. Clinton, "Executive Order 12933: Nondisplacement of
Qualified Workers under Certain Contracts, October 20, 1994," APP. Under
the current law, when a service contract for maintenance of a public building
expired and a follow-up contract was awarded for the same service, the new contractor typically hired the majority of the predecessor's employees. Under the
Clinton order, all solicitations and service contracts for public buildings required
contractors performing similar services at the same building to offer employees
under the predecessor contract the right of first refusal of employment.

15. William J. Clinton, "Executive Order 12954: Ensuring the Economical and Efficient Administration and Completion of Federal Government Contracts, March 8, 1995," APP.

16. *NLRB v. Mackay Radio & Telegraph,* 304 U.S. 333 (1938).

17. Kimmett (1996).

18. Clinton, "Executive Order 12954."

19. Kimmett (1996).

20. George W. Bush, "Executive Order 13201: Notification of Employee Rights Concerning Payment of Union Dues or Fees, February 17, 2001," APP.

21. On "preservation of open competition and government neutrality": The order establishes the federal government's policy with regard to the use of project labor agreements (PLAs) in federal and federally funded construction projects. A PLA is a multi-employer, multi-union pre-hire agreement that governs labor relations at a construction site. See Mark W. Everson, "Memorandum for President's Management Council: OMB Guidance on Project Labor Agreement Executive Order," U.S. Office of Management and Budget, October 18, 2002 (www.whitehouse.gov/omb/grants_project_labor_agreements/). In 2002, the U.S. Court of Appeals for the D.C. Circuit upheld George W. Bush's EO 13202 in its decision in *Building and Construction Trades Dep't, AFL-CIO v. Allbaugh.* See George W. Bush, "Executive Order 13202: Preservation of Open Competition and Government Neutrality Towards Government Contractors Labor Relations on Federal and Federally Funded Construction Projects, February 17, 2001," APP; George W. Bush, "Executive Order 13204: Revocation of Executive Order on Nondisplacement of Qualified Workers Under Certain Contracts, February 17, 2001," APP.

22. Sky (1969).

23. Ibid., p. 1271. The Department of Defense implemented DMP-4 by setting aside up to 50 percent of procurement from general solicitation and offering it to firms operating in labor surplus areas.

24. Jimmy Carter, "Executive Order 12073: Federal Procurement in Labor Surplus Areas, August 16, 1978," APP.

25. William J. Clinton, "Executive Order 13005: Empowerment Contracting, May 21, 1996," APP.

26. Small Business Administration, "The HUBZone Maps" (www.sba.gov /content/hubzone-maps); Small Business Administration, "Understanding the HUBZone Program" (www.sba.gov/content/understanding-hubzone-program).

27. William J. Clinton, "Executive Order 13005: Empowerment Contracting, May 21, 1996," APP.

28. Quint (1984). Nixon, acting under the 1970 Economic Stabilization Act, imposed the first mandatory peacetime wage and price controls in the construction industry. In 1974 Congress enacted the Council on Wage and Price Stability Act, providing for an advisory body to monitor wage and price activity and

granting the president power to issue and monitor voluntary wage and price guidelines.

29. Richard M. Nixon, "Executive Order 11588: Providing for the Stabilization of Wages and Prices in the Construction Industry, March 29, 1971," APP.

30. Richard M. Nixon, "Executive Order 11627: Further Providing for the Stabilization of the Economy, October 15, 1971," APP.

31. Carter mandated that wage increases could total no more than 7 percent of a worker's salary and that price increases must be at least 0.5 percent less than the company's recent average price increases. Carter required all federal contractors to certify their compliance with the wage and price standards and directed the OFPP to implement sanctions against contractors who failed to comply.

32. Jimmy Carter, "Executive Order 12092: Federal Anti-Inflationary Procurement Practice, November 1, 1978," APP.

33. Ibid. Congress retained power in the area of wage and price controls, and it has only infrequently—and then within specific limitations—allowed the president to issue directives concerning this controversial area of the national economy. Congress has authorized the president to enforce wage and price controls only under conditions of specific grants of authority and firm expiration dates. These include the 1942 Emergency Price Control Act to regulate prices for government contracts; the 1942 Stabilization Act (amending the previous act) to limit wages and agricultural prices; and the 1950 Defense Production Act, again granting the president authority to control wages and prices—this act would later be amended to terminate that authority. In 1970, Congress approved the Economic Stabilization Act, thus authorizing the president to issue orders and regulations appropriate to stabilize prices, rents, wages, and salaries but stipulating that this authority would expire in 1974. See Rockoff (1984).

34. Ronald Reagan, "Executive Order 12288: Termination of the Wage and Price Regulatory Program, January 29, 1981," APP.

35. Clark, Moutray, and Saade (2006). See OFPP Policy Letter 79-1, "Implementation of Section 15(k) of the Small Business Act, as Amended: Office of Small and Disadvantaged Business," March 7, 1979; U.S. Department of Housing and Urban Development, "OSDBU Legislative Mandates," 2015 (www.hud.gov/offices/osdbu/policy/laws.cfm).

36. Richard M. Nixon, "Executive Order 11458: Prescribing Arrangements for Developing and Coordinating a National Program For Minority Business Enterprise, March 5, 1969," APP; Nixon, "Executive Order 11625: Prescribing Additional Arrangements for Developing and Coordinating a National Program for Minority Business Enterprise, October 13, 1971," APP.

37. Ronald Reagan, "Executive Order 12432: Minority Business Enterprise Development, July 14, 1983," APP.

38. William J. Clinton, "Executive Order 13170: Increasing Opportunities and Access for Disadvantaged Businesses, October 6, 2000," APP; U.S. Small Business Administration, "Social Disadvantage Eligibility" (www.sba.gov /contracting/government-contracting-programs/8a-business-development -program/eligibility-requirements/social-disadvantage-eligibility); U.S. Small Business Administration, "Economic Disadvantage Eligibility" (www.sba.gov /contracting/government-contracting-programs/8a-business-development -program/eligibility-requirements/economic-disadvantage-eligibility).

39. William J. Clinton, "Executive Order 12928: Promoting Procurement With Small Businesses Owned and Controlled by Socially and Economically Disadvantaged Individuals, Historically Black Colleges and Universities, and Minority Institutions, September 16, 1994," APP.

40. Congress, under the Small Business Reauthorization Act of 2000, created a Federal Contract Program for eligible women-owned small businesses in industries in which they were underrepresented or substantially underrepresented as determined by the SBA. See National Research Council (2005).

41. Jimmy Carter, "Executive Order 12138: Women's Business Enterprise, May 18, 1979," APP.

42. William J. Clinton, "Memorandum on Federal Procurement, October 13, 1994," APP.

43. William J. Clinton, "Executive Order 13157: Increasing Opportunities for Women-Owned Small Businesses, May 23, 2000," APP.

44. George W. Bush, "Executive Order 13339: Increasing Economic Opportunity and Business Participation of Asian Americans and Pacific Islanders, May 13, 2004," APP.

45. Richard M. Nixon, "Executive Order 11598: To Provide for the Listing of Certain Job Vacancies by Federal Agencies and Government Contractors and Subcontractors, June 16, 1971," APP; Richard Nixon, "Executive Order 11701: Employment of Veterans by Federal Agencies and Government Contractors and Subcontractors, January 24, 1973," APP; Richard Nixon, "Executive Order 11598: To Provide for the Listing of Certain Job Vacancies by Federal Agencies and Government Contractors and Subcontractors, June 16, 1971," APP; Richard Nixon, "Executive Order 11701: Employment of Veterans by Federal Agencies and Government Contractors and Subcontractors, January 24, 1973," APP.

46. George W. Bush, "Executive Order 13360: Providing Opportunities for Service-Disabled Veteran Businesses to Increase Their Federal Contracting and Subcontracting, October 20, 2004," APP.

47. U.S. Department of State, "United States Department of State Memorandum," *Stage.gov*, February 4, 2005 (www.state.gov/documents/organiza

tion/50115.pdf); Dina ElBoghdady, "Set-Aside Programs Fall Short of Goals," *Washington Post*, February 28, 2005.

48. Panoptic Enterprises, "'Blacklisting Regulations' Permanently Revoked, Called 'Unworkable and Defective' by FAR Council," "Federal Contracts Perspective," January 2002 (www.fedgovcontracts.com/newsltr/fcp3-1.htm). Under existing rules, Congress required federal agencies to award contracts only to "responsible" sources. See U.S. Congress, *Deficit Reduction Act of 1984*, Pub. L. No. 99-88, 99th Cong., 1st Sess. (August 15, 1985). An element of being a responsible contractor was to have a "satisfactory record of integrity and business ethics." See U.S. Code 41 (2015), §43(7)(D).

49. Clinton's order aimed to prevent taxpayers from subsidizing federal government contractors who consistently broke the law: chronic violators of labor, environmental, tax, antitrust, or employment laws would be denied the privilege of entering into contracts with the federal government. See Weissman (1999). Predictably, the directive was supported by labor and consumer groups and was opposed by business groups. Opponents—organized as the National Alliance Against Blacklisting—argued that Clinton's order would give unions inappropriate influence over contracting and could be used as a threatening tool during collective bargaining. For public interest groups, procurement provided an opportunity for the federal government to leverage its buying power to promote "more corporate respect for the law."

50. 65 Fed. Reg. 80256 (2000).

51. Elsbernd (2010).

52. Under the 2002 Homeland Security Act, Congress disbanded the Immigration and Naturalization Service to form three new federal agencies serving under the newly formed Department of Homeland Security: Customs and Border Patrol, Immigration and Customs Enforcement, and U.S. Citizenship and Immigration Services. See U.S. Immigration and Naturalization Services, "Post-9/11" (www.uscis.gov/history-and-genealogy/our-history/agency-history/post-911).

53. William J. Clinton, "Executive Order 12989: Economy and Efficiency in Government Procurement through Compliance with Certain Immigration and Naturalization Act Provisions, February 13, 1996," APP.

54. George W. Bush, "Executive Order 13465: Amending Executive Order 12989, as Amended, June 6, 2008," APP. Under Bush's order, contracting "only with providers that do not knowingly employ unauthorized alien workers and that have agreed to utilize the DHS electronic employment verification system to confirm the employment eligibility of their workforce will promote 'economy and efficiency' in procurement."

55. William J. Clinton, "Executive Order 13126: Prohibition of Acquisition of Products Produced by Forced or Indentured Child Labor, June 12,

1999," APP. All federal government agencies must consult the list before purchasing, and contractors must certify that child labor was not involved in their products.

56. For more information on EO 13126, see U.S. Department of Labor, "Frequently Asked Questions: Executive Order 13126 of 1999" (www.dol.gov /ilab/reports/pdf/2013EO_FAQ.pdf).

57. William J. Clinton, "Memorandum on Child Safety Lock Devices for Handguns, March 5, 1997," APP. The order initially covered only handguns but was expanded (1997) to cover all firearms issued to federal law enforcement officers.

58. Blumenauer, Lofgren, and Schumer (1998); Sipos (2002); Spitzer and Pope (2009).

59. U.S. Government Accountability Office, "Firearm Safety Locks: Federal Agency Implementation of the Presidential Directive," September 1998 (www .gao.gov/archive/1998/gg98201.pdf). In 1997, the manufacturers of most handguns in the United States announced that they would provide child-safety locks with their firearms. See James Bennet, "Gun Makers Agree on Safety Locks," *New York Times,* October 9, 1997. The gun manufacturers negotiated after Clinton threatened to press for legislation requiring child-safety locks on handguns and issued the executive order requiring locks on all handguns issued to federal law enforcement officers. See "Gunmakers, Clinton Forge Pact over Childproof Locks on Triggers," *Chicago Tribune,* October 10, 1997; William J. Clinton Presidential Library and Museum, "Crime Safety Locks," 1998 (http://clinton .presidentiallibraries.us/items/show/25963).

60. Mayer (1997).

61. Franklin D. Roosevelt, "Executive Order 8802: Reaffirming Policy of Full Participation in the Defense Program by All Persons, Regardless of Race, Creed, Color, or National Origin, and Directing Certain Action in Furtherance of Said Policy, June 25, 1941," APP; Franklin D. Roosevelt, "Executive Order 8823: Providing for an Additional Member of the Committee on Fair Employment Practice in the Office of Production Management, July 18, 1941," National Archives (www.archives.gov/federal-register/executive-orders/1941.html); Franklin D. Roosevelt, "Establishing Methods for Wartime Procurement, December 27, 1941," APP; Franklin D. Roosevelt, "Executive Order 9346: Establishing a Committee on Fair Employment Practice, May 27, 1943," APP.

62. Millenson (1999).

63. Roosevelt, "Executive Order 9346."

64. Roosevelt, "Executive Order 8802."

65. Mayer (1997).

66. Harry S. Truman, "Executive Order 9964: Creating a Board of Inquiry to Report on Certain Labor Disputes Affecting the Maritime Industry of the

United States, June 3, 1948," APP; Harry S. Truman, "Executive Order 10210: Authorizing the Department of Defense and the Department of Commerce to Exercise the Functions and Powers Set Forth in Title II of the First War Powers Act, 1941, February 2, 1951," APP; Harry S. Truman, "Executive Order 10308: Improving the Means for Obtaining Compliance with the Nondiscrimination Provisions of Federal Contracts, December 3, 1951," APP.

67. Dwight D. Eisenhower, "Executive Order 10479: Establishing the Government Contract Committee, August 13, 1953," APP; Dwight D. Eisenhower, "Executive Order 10577: Amending the Civil Service Rules and Authorizing a New Appointment System for the Competitive Service, November 22, 1954," APP.

68. Mayer (2001, p. 197).

69. John F. Kennedy, "Executive Order 10925: Establishing the President's Committee on Equal Employment Opportunity, March 6, 1961," APP.

70. John F. Kennedy, "Executive Order 11063: Equal Opportunity in Housing November 20, 1962," APP. Since the Great Depression, congressional policy helped build a two-tiered or "dual" housing market that actively segregated metropolitan regions and their material resources by race (Freund 2004, p. 3). Kennedy required nondiscrimination in new federally supported housing contracts. JFK required the Federal Housing Authority, the Public Housing Administration, the Urban Renewal Administration, and the Federal National Mortgage Association to commit themselves not only to "altering patterns of discrimination that the agencies had long sustained" but also to channeling resources to populations long denied the benefits of federal assistance (Freund 2004, p. 2). However, the scope of executive orders is shaped by politics. Kennedy prohibited racial discrimination in new, federally supported construction, but the order did not cover existing units. Kennedy's order did not apply to housing financed by private savings and loan associations, even those overseen and ultimately underwritten by the reserve and insurance functions of the Federal Home Loan Bank Board. The FHA decided to exclude from coverage all one- and two-family homes whose mortgages were insured by its agency. The fast-growing conventional market for home mortgages, while overseen and indirectly subsidized by regulatory agencies, including the bank board, was also exempt (ibid., p. 37).

71. John F. Kennedy, "Executive Order 11114: Extending the Authority of the President's Committee on Equal Employment Opportunity, June 22, 1963," APP. The PCEEO received broad authority to investigate employment practices and to punish contractors that failed to comply with regulations. Johnson transferred authority for enforcement of equal opportunity policy from the commission to a new Office of Federal Contract Compliance Programs, which the president empowered to require compliance reports on hiring practices before firms could bid on contracts. See MacLaury (2008).

72. Cooper (2002, p. 57); Lyndon B. Johnson, "Executive Order 11246: Equal Employment Opportunity, September 24, 1965," APP. Also see MacLaury (2008).

73. Lyndon B. Johnson, "Executive Order 11375: Amending Executive Order No. 11246, Relating to Equal Employment Opportunity, October 13, 1967," APP.

74. Fleishman and Aufes (1976); Johnson, "Executive Order 11375." Johnson charged the labor secretary with strong enforcement authority, with the responsibility of ensuring equal opportunity for minorities in federal contractors' recruitment, hiring, training, and other employment practices. Until that time, such efforts had been in the hands of various presidential committees.

75. According to one assessment of its impact, Johnson's order affected "some 225,000 contractors throughout the U.S. . . . building $30 billion worth of federally assisted construction projects, and directly or indirectly employing 20 million workers." See Graham (1992, p. 155).

76. Jimmy Carter, "Executive Order 12067: Equal Employment Opportunity Programs, June 30, 1978," APP. Under the Reorganization Plan No. 1 of 1978, the EEOC became responsible for coordinating all federal equal employment opportunity programs. Only three federal agencies—the EEOC, the Department of Justice, and the Department of Labor's Office of Federal Contract Compliance Programs—were left with significant responsibility for ensuring and overseeing equal employment opportunity. United States Department of Labor, Office of Federal Contract Compliance Programs, "OFCCP 50th Anniversary Celebration" (www.dol.gov/ofccp/about/50thAnniversary.html).

77. Ibid.; Millenson (1999).

78. Mayer (2001).

79. Gilman (2007).

80. Amy Sullivan, "Faith without Works," *Washington Monthly,* October 2004.

81. More specifically, "charitable choice" or "faith-based contracting" reforms aim to set specific rules for how religious organizations can contract with the federal government to operate social service programs without impairing their religious character. See Hoover (2002). Under the 1996 Personal Responsibility and Work Opportunity Reconciliation Act, Congress allowed the states to use federal funding to hire religious groups for the provision of social services. Under the Bush proposal, Congress would apply "charitable choice" to every federal social service program in addition to repealing any contrary statutory prohibitions. See "Faith-Based Charities Bill Idles," *CQ Almanac,* 2001 (http://library.cqpress.com/cqalmanac/document.php?id=l01-106-6379 -328305). For the first time, Congress had to address related employment issues as well (Title VII), including the question of whether religious organizations should be able to preempt civil rights laws that impinge upon the religious character

of the organization. This particular reform passed in the House, but the Senate refused to take it up.

82. In one of his first actions, Bush announced the formation of a White House Office of Faith-Based and Community Initiatives. See Tenpas (2002); George W. Bush, "Executive Order 13199: Establishment of White House Office of Faith-Based and Community Initiatives, January 29, 2001," APP. In follow-up orders, Bush established Centers for Faith-Based and Community Initiatives within various federal agencies. See George W. Bush, "Executive Order 13198: Agency Responsibilities With Respect to Faith-Based and Community Initiatives, January 29, 2001," APP; George W. Bush, "Executive Order 13280: Responsibilities of the Department of Agriculture and the Agency for International Development with Respect to Faith-Based and Community Initiatives, December 12, 2002," APP; George W. Bush, "Executive Order 13342: Responsibilities of the Departments of Commerce and Veterans Affairs and the Small Business Administration with Respect to Faith-Based and Community Initiatives, June 1, 2004," APP.

83. George W. Bush, "Executive Order 13279: Equal Protection of the Laws for Faith-Based and Community Organizations, December 12, 2002," APP.

84. Ibid.

85. Among these guidelines, designed to end what Bush perceived to be historic "discrimination" against religious groups, were provisions to "level the playing field" such that religious organizations could compete on an equal footing for grant money. See George W. Bush, "Executive Order 13279."

86. Johnson prohibited federal contractors from discriminating against any employee or applicant for employment on the basis of race, color, religion, sex, or national origin. See Lyndon B. Johnson, "Executive Order 11246: Equal Employment Opportunity, September 24, 1965," APP. The ability of religious groups to discriminate in hiring practices centers around whether the religious exemption in Title VII of the 1964 Civil Rights Act—which allows religious organizations to discriminate on religious grounds in their employment practices with *private* funds—should apply to religious organizations receiving federal (public) funds. Since Title VII is silent on the use of federal funds, there has been a great deal of debate about whether or not religious organizations otherwise covered by Title VII may use religion as a criterion in their employment practices, regardless of whether they only are engaged in secular activities funded by federal funding. See Sager, "Faith-Based Initiative."

87. The Bush order outlines how federal money can and cannot be used by any organization—including faith-based ones—in order to comply with constitutional requirements. For example, in 2004 the Department of Justice issued its Equal Treatment Regulations (28 CFR 38.1 and 38.2), which implemented Bush's order. The rules ensured that faith-based and other community organ-

izations can apply for appropriate DOJ grants and contracts on an equal basis with other nongovernmental organizations. See U.S. Department of Justice Archive, "Fact Sheet: Task Force for Faith-Based and Community Initiatives," 2015 (www.justice.gov/archive/fbci/about.html). Courts have ruled that the Bush faith-based order does not give employers free rein to violate Title VII's nondiscrimination protections, but rather it allows a limited carve-out for religiously affiliated employers. See Gilman (2007); White House Faith-Based and Community Initiatives, "Guidance to Faith-Based and Community Organizations on Partnering with the Federal Government," U.S. Department of Justice, Office of Justice Programs, 2008 (http://ojp.gov/fbnp/pdfs /GuidanceDocument.pdf); Wright (2009); Boden (2006); Goldenziel (2005); Carlson-Thies (2009).

88. U.S. Congress, *Federal Property and Administrative Services Act of 1949.*

89. Burrows and Manuel (2011).

90. Millenson (1999). Through the annual appropriations process, Congress subsequently approved substantial increases in funds for the Office of Federal Contracts Compliance Programs.

91. U.S. Department of Labor, Office of Federal Contract Compliance Programs, "Executive Order 11246, As Amended" (www.dol.gov/ofccp/regs/statutes /eo11246.htm). Currently, the OFCCP enforces three legal authorities that require equal employment opportunity: EO 11246, as amended; Section 503 of the 1973 Rehabilitation Act; and the Vietnam Era Veterans' Readjustment Assistance Act of 1974.

CHAPTER THREE

1. Michael Crowley, "Project Podesta," *New Republic,* November 12, 2008.

2. Jeff Zeleny, "Obama Weighs Quick Undoing of Bush Policy," *New York Times,* November 9, 2008.

3. Sam Stein, "Podesta Sketches Out Vision for Assertive Presidency," *New York Times,* December 13, 2008.

4. Mike Dorning, "Podesta's Push for Executive Power Raises Stakes on Obama Agenda," *Bloomberg* (website), December 20, 2013 (www.bloomberg .com/news/articles/2013-12-20/podesta-s-push-for-executive-power-raises -stakes-on-obama-agenda).

5. Sarah Rosen Wartell and John Podesta, "The Power of the President Recommendations to Advance Progressive Change," Center for American Progress, November 16, 2010 (www.americanprogress.org/issues/economy/report /2010/11/16/8658).

6. Jennifer Epstein, "Obama Calls for 'Year of Action,'" *Politico,* January 28, 2014 (www.politico.com/story/2014/01/state-of-the-union-2014-address-barack-obama-102752#ixzz4BfxiDVVL).

7. Carol E. Lee, "Obama to Bar Gay Discrimination," *Wall Street Journal,* June 16, 2014.

8. The Employee Free Choice Act would have given employees the option to choose how to form a union, either by ballot or by getting a majority of employees to sign a union-authorization card. See "The Employee Free Choice Act" (http://graphics8.nytimes.com/packages/pdf/politics/EFCA_Summary.pdf).

9. Barack Obama, "Remarks on Signing Executive Orders Regarding Labor and a Memorandum Creating the Middle Class Working Families Task Force, January 30, 2009," American Presidency Project (henceforth cited as APP).

10. Barack Obama, "Executive Order 13494: Economy in Government Contracting, January 30, 2009," APP; Barack Obama, "Executive Order 13495: Nondisplacement of Qualified Workers under Service Contracts, January 30, 2009," APP; Barack Obama, "Executive Order 13496: Notification of Employee Rights under Federal Labor Laws, January 30, 2009," APP; Barack Obama, "Executive Order 13502: Use of Project Labor Agreements for Federal Construction Projects, February 6, 2009," APP; Barack Obama, "Executive Order 13522: Creating Labor-Management Forums to Improve Delivery of Government Services, December 9, 2009," APP.

11. Sean P. McDevitt, "The Impact of President Obama's First 30 Days on the Labor and Employment Landscape," Pepper Hamilton LLP website, February 24, 2009 (www.pepperlaw.com/publications/the-impact-of-president-obamas-first-30-days-on-the-labor-and-employment-landscape-2009-02-24/); "Paving the High Road: Labor Standards and Procurement Policy in the Obama Era," *Berkeley Journal of Employment and Labor Law* 31, no. 2 (2010): 349–424; Zucker and Zucker (2009).

12. White House, "Supporting Small Businesses" (www.whitehouse.gov/economy/business/small-business).

13. Barack Obama, "Memorandum on Establishing an Interagency Task Force on Federal Contracting Opportunities for Small Businesses, April 26, 2010," APP.

14. Robert Brodsky, "White House Establishes Small Business Contracting Task Forces," *Government Executive,* April 26, 2010 (www.govexec.com/oversight/2010/04/white-house-establishes-small-business-contracting-task-forces/31372/); Small Business Administration website, "Report on Small Business Federal Contracting Opportunities," "Executive Summary Interagency Task Force on Federal Contracting Opportunities for Small Businesses," 2010 (www.sba.gov/sites/default/files/contracting_task_force_report_0.pdf). Under the Small Business Act of 1953, Congress created a federal-government-wide goal for

contracting to small businesses, which as of summer 2016 is 23 percent of all federal procurements. In order to meet the goals, each federal agency involved in procurement creates opportunities, called set-asides, for either all or a subset of small businesses to compete against a pool of like-size contractors. For more details on these programs, see Medina (2013).

15. Coglianese (2009).

16. "Agenda: Defense," Change.gov, The Office of the President Elect (http://change.gov/agenda/defense_agenda/).

17. "Restore Trust in Government and Improve Transparency," Obama '08 (website) (https://my.barackobama.com/page/-/Press/Restoring%20Trust%20 in%20Government%20Fact%20Sheet%20090407%20%282%29.pdf.pdf).

18. Jennifer LaFleur, "Has Obama Kept His Open-Government Pledge?," *ProPublica,* February 11, 2013 (www.propublica.org/article/has-obama-kept -his-open-government-pledge).

19. Coglianese (2009); "Campaign to Cut Waste: Reforming Government Contracting," White House website (www.whitehouse.gov/21stcenturygov /actions/reforming-government-contracting); Barack Obama, "Memorandum on Government Contracting, March 4, 2009," APP.

20. Barack Obama, "Executive Order 13520: Reducing Improper Payments, November 20, 2009," APP; Barack Obama, "Memorandum on Enhancing Payment Accuracy Through a 'Do Not Pay List,' June 18, 2010," APP; Jeffrey D. Zients, "Memorandum for the Heads of Departments and Agencies: Reducing Improper Payments through the 'Do Not Pay List,'" White House website, April 12, 2012 (www.whitehouse.gov/sites/default/files/omb /memoranda/2012/m-12-11_1.pdf). See also Gillian Brockell, "White House Unveils New Tool to Stop Improper Payments," Federal News Radio, April 12, 2012 (http://federalnewsradio.com/congress/2012/04/white-house-unveils-new -tool-to-stop-improper-payments/). Contracting officers also continue to use the Federal Awardee Performance and Integrity Information System. For further information, see U.S. Department of the Treasury, Bureau of the Fiscal Service, "The Do Not Pay (DNP) Business Center," 2015 (http://donotpay.treas .gov/); Jeffrey D. Zients, "Memorandum for the Heads of Executive Departments and Agencies: Reducing Improper Payments through the 'Do Not Pay List,'" April 12, 2012 (www.whitehouse.gov/sites/default/files/omb/memoranda /2012/m-12-11.pdf); Ed O' Keefe, "Obama to Order Federal Agencies to Compile 'Do Not Pay List,'" *Washington Post,* June 18, 2010. The Federal Acquisition Regulations require private sector companies to certify tax compliance before they can be awarded any federal contract. See White House, Office of the Press Secretary, "Memorandum for the Heads of Executive Departments and Agencies," January 20, 2010 (www.whitehouse.gov/the-press-office /memorandum-heads-executive-departments-and-agencies-1); U.S. Department of the Treasury, "Federal Guidelines Do Not Prohibit the Awarding of

Contracts to Contractors with Delinquent Tax Liabilities," September 28, 2010 (www.treasury.gov/tigta/auditreports/2010reports/201030120fr.pdf); C. Joël Van Over, "Recent Initiatives Increase Scrutiny of Federal Tax Compliance by Government Contractors," Pillsbury Law Advisory, February 24, 2010 (www .pillsburylaw.com/siteFiles/Publications/528D92A613F2F3B253A070C6D465 A19B.pdf).

21. Office of Management and Budget, "Memorandum for the Heads of Departments and Agencies: Verifying the Employment Eligibility of Federal Employees," August 10, 2007 (http://georgewbush-whitehouse.archives.gov/omb /memoranda/fy2007/m07-21.pdf); Marc Rosenblum and Lang Hoyt, "The Basics of E-Verify, the U.S. Employer Verification System," Migration Policy Institute, July 13, 2011 (www.migrationpolicy.org/article/basics-e-verify-us -employer-verification-system); U.S. Citizenship and Immigration Services, "What Is E-Verify?" (www.uscis.gov/e-verify/what-e-verify).

22. George W. Bush, "Executive Order 13465: Amending Executive Order 12989, as Amended, June 6, 2008," APP.

23. Julia Preston, "Judge Suspends Key Bush Effort in Immigration," *New York Times,* October 11, 2007.

24. Spencer S. Hsu, "Obama Revives Bush Idea of Using E-Verify to Catch Illegal Contract Workers," *Washington Post,* July 9, 2009; "Obama Administration to Begin E-Verify Enforcement for Certain Federal Contractors on September 8, 2009," Crowell Moring website, July 20, 2009 (www.crowell.com /NewsEvents/AlertsNewsletters/Labor-Employment-Law-Alert-US/Obama -Administration-to-Begin-E-Verify-Enforcement-For-Certain-Federal-Contractors -on-September-8-2009).

25. Bush, "Executive Order 13465."

26. Lory Stone and Jodi Avergun, "New Proposed Rules Increase Government Contractors' Responsibilities for Preventing Human Trafficking," American Bar Association website (www.americanbar.org/content/dam/aba/publications /criminaljustice/wcc2014_Stone.authcheckdam.pdf).

27. The Victims of Trafficking and Violence Protection Act of 2000, the Trafficking Victims Protection Reauthorization Act of 2003, the Trafficking Victims Protection Reauthorization Act of 2005, and the Trafficking Victims Protection Reauthorization Act of 2008 provide the tools to combat trafficking in persons both worldwide and domestically. The acts authorized the establishment of the Office to Monitor and Combat Trafficking in Persons (G/TIP) and the President's Interagency Task Force to Monitor and Combat Trafficking in Persons to assist in the coordination of anti-trafficking efforts. See U.S. Department of State, "U.S. Laws on Trafficking in Persons" (www.state.gov/j/tip /laws/).

28. Samuel Rubenfeld, "Obama Orders Government Contractors to Combat Human Trafficking," *Wall Street Journal,* September 25, 2012.

29. Council of Economic Advisors, "The Economics of Paid and Unpaid Leave," June 2014 (www.whitehouse.gov/sites/default/files/docs/leave_report _final.pdf).

30. White House, Office of the Press Secretary, "Fact Sheet: White House Unveils New Steps to Strengthen Working Families across America," January 14, 2015 (www.whitehouse.gov/the-press-office/2015/01/14/fact-sheet-white-house -unveils-new-steps-strengthen-working-families-acr); U.S. House of Representatives Committee on Education and the Workforce, "Providing Working Families Flexibility: Working Families Flexibility Act," 2015 (http://edworkforce .house.gov/yourtime/); Casey Leins, "Mixed Response to Obama's Paid Leave Legislation," *U.S. News and World Report,* January 21, 2015; Juliet Eilperin, "Perez, Jarrett to Take Paid-Leave Show on the Road Starting April 1," *Washington Post,* March 25, 2015.

31. Peter Baker, "Obama Orders Federal Contractors to Provide Workers Paid Sick Leave," *New York Times*, September 7, 2015; White House, Office of the Press Secretary, "Fact Sheet: Helping Middle-Class Families Get Ahead by Expanding Paid Sick Leave," September 7, 2015 (www.whitehouse.gov/the-press -office/2015/09/07/fact-sheet-helping-middle-class-families-get-ahead-expanding -paid-sick); Barack Obama, "Executive Order 13706: Establishing Paid Sick Leave for Federal Contractors, September 7, 2015," APP.

32. Peter Baker, "Obama Orders Federal Contractors to Provide Workers Paid Sick Leave," *New York Times,* September 7, 2015.

33. Greenhouse, "Plan to Seek Use of U.S. Contracts as a Wage Lever." Positive weight in the source selection process would be given to contract bidders based on the labor standards for their workforce. The criteria would include whether the contractor pays a livable wage and provides "quality, affordable health insurance," an employer-funded retirement plan, and paid sick leave. For more information, see Robert Brodsky, "High Road Contracting Policy Comes into Focus," *Government Executive,* April 2, 2010 (www.govexec.com /oversight/2010/04/high-road-contracting-policy-comes-into-focus/31208/); Gautham Nagesh, "White House Considers Pro-Labor Policy for Government Contractors," *The Daily Caller,* February 4, 2010 (http://dailycaller.com/2010 /02/04/white-house-considers-pro-labor-policy-for-government-contractors/).

34. Greenhouse, "Plan to Seek Use of U.S. Contracts as a Wage Lever."

35. Brodsky, "High Road Contracting Policy."

36. Matthew Weigelt, "Obama Administration May Give Better-Paying Contractors an Advantage; Move Considered as Part of Procurement Reform," *FCW: The Business of Federal Technology,* February 26, 2010 (https://fcw.com /articles/2010/02/26/high-road-labor-preference.aspx); Robert Brodsky, "OMB Not Moving to Implement 'High Road' Contracting Policy," *Government Executive,* March 8, 2011 (www.govexec.com/oversight/2011/03/omb-not-moving -to-implement-high-road-contracting-policy/33488/).

37. "Paving the High Road."

38. Obama required federal contractors to report any administrative merits determination, civil judgment, or arbitral award or decision rendered against them in the preceding three-year period for violations of any of fourteen identified federal labor laws and executive orders (or equivalent state laws). See White House, Office of the Press Secretary, "Fact Sheet: Fair Pay and Safe Workplaces Executive Order," July 31, 2014 (www.whitehouse.gov/the-press-office/2014/07/31/fact-sheet-fair-pay-and-safe-workplaces-executive-order). As part of Obama's order, businesses will have to self-report their labor violations and provide federal agencies with an update every six months. In addition, prime contractors will be responsible for confirming that subcontractors have "clean" records. See Amrita Jayakumar, "What Obama's New Executive Order Means for Federal Contractors," *Washington Post,* August 10, 2014.

39. Barack Obama, "Executive Order 13673: Fair Pay and Safe Workplaces, July 31, 2014," APP.

40. U.S. Department of Labor, "Memorandum for the Heads of Executive Departments and Agencies: Implementation of the President's Executive Order on Fair Pay and Safe Workplaces," March 6, 2015 (www.whitehouse.gov/sites/default/files/omb/memoranda/2015/m-15-08.pdf); Laura Mitchell, "Congress Members Ask U.S. Department of Labor and Federal Acquisition Regulatory Council to Withdraw Proposed Executive Order 13673 Proposals," *National Law Review,* July 20, 2015; John Kline and others, "Letter to Secretary Perez," July 15, 2015 (www.affirmativeactionlawadvisor.com/wp-content/uploads/sites/602/2015/07/letter_to_secretary_perez_7-14-15.pdf).

41. Jeff Zeleny and Michael Luo, "Obama Seeks Bigger Role for Religious Groups," *New York Times,* July 2, 2008.

42. Barack Obama, "Executive Order 13498: Amendments to Executive Order 13199 and Establishment of the President's Advisory Council for Faith-Based and Neighborhood Partnerships, February 5, 2009," APP; John J. DiIulio Jr. and Stephanie C. Boddie, "John DiIulio Previews How Faith-Based Initiatives Would Change If Barack Obama Is Elected President," Pew Research Center, September 23, 2008 (www.pewforum.org/2008/09/23/john-diiulio-previews-how-faith-based-initiatives-would-change-if-barack-obama-is-elected-president/).

43. Obama, "Executive Order 13498"; Center for Effective Government, "Questions Loom for President's Office of Faith-Based and Neighborhood Partnerships," February 24, 2009 (www.foreffectivegov.org/node/9731); Office of Management and Budget, "Memorandum for the Heads of Executive Departments and Agencies: Implementation of Executive Order 13559, 'Fundamental Principles and Policymaking Criteria for Partnerships With Faith-based and Other Neighborhood Organizations,'" August 2, 2013 (www.whitehouse.gov/sites/default/files/omb/memoranda/2013/m-13-19.pdf).

44. See Obama, "Executive Order 13559"; Melissa Rogers, "Continuity and Change: Faith-Based Partnerships under Obama and Bush," Brookings Institution website, December 13, 2010 (www.brookings.edu/research/opinions /2010/12/13-faith-based-rogers).

45. Obama's rule applied to nine federal agencies, and aimed to clarify that faith-based organizations were eligible to take part in federally funded programs "on the same basis as any other private organization." For more information on Obama's rule, see Office of Management and Budget, "Memorandum for the Heads of Executive Departments and Agencies: Implementation of Executive Order 13559"; U.S. Department of Health and Human Services, "Implementation of Executive Order 13559: Updating Participation in Department of Health and Human Services Programs by Faith-Based or Religious Organizations and Providing for Equal Treatment of Department of Health and Human Services Program Participants; Proposed Rule," *Federal Register,* Thursday, August 6, 2015.

46. U.S. President's Advisory Council on Faith-Based and Neighborhood Partnerships (2010).

47. Office of the President Elect, "Agenda: Poverty: The Obama-Biden Plan" (http://change.gov/agenda/poverty_agenda/).

48. Catherine Rampell and Steven Greenhouse, "$10 Minimum Wage Proposal Has Growing Support from White House," *New York Times,* November 7, 2013.

49. Bernie Sanders, United States Senator for Vermont (official website), "Senators Urge Obama to Set Minimum Wage for Federal Contract Workers," press release, September 25, 2013 (www.sanders.senate.gov/newsroom/press -releases/senators-urge-obama-to-set-minimum-wage-for-federal-contract -workers).

50. Barack Obama, "Address Before a Joint Session of the Congress on the State of the Union, January 28, 2014," APP.

51. Barack Obama, "Remarks on Signing an Executive Order Establishing a Minimum Wage for Contractors, February 12, 2014," APP.

52. Barack Obama, "Executive Order 13658: Establishing a Minimum Wage for Contractors, February 12, 2014," APP; Tom Shoop, "Obama Issues Order Boosting Minimum Wage for Contractors," *Government Executive,* February 12, 2014 (www.govexec.com/contracting/2014/02/obama-issues-order -boosting-minimum-wage-contractors/78725/); White House, Office of the Press Secretary, "Fact Sheet: Opportunity For All: Rewarding Hard Work," February 12, 2014 (www.whitehouse.gov/the-press-office/2014/02/12/fact -sheet-opportunity-all-rewarding-hard-work).

53. U.S. Department of Labor, "Final Rule: Executive Order 13658, Establishing a Minimum Wage for Contractors" (www.dol.gov/whd/flsa/eo13658/); U.S. Department of Labor, "Executive Order 13658 Frequently Asked Questions

(FAQs)" (www.dol.gov/whd/flsa/eo13658/faq.htm); U.S. Department of Labor, "US Labor Secretary Thomas E. Perez Announces Final Rule Raising the Minimum Wage for Federal Contract Workers," October 1, 2014 (www.dol.gov /whd/media/press/whdpressVB3.asp?pressdoc=national/20141001.xml).

54. Josh Hicks, "Obama Executive Order to Expand Overtime Pay," *Washington Post,* March 12, 2014; White House, Office of the Press Secretary, "Presidential Memorandum: Updating and Modernizing Overtime Regulations," March 13, 2014 (www.whitehouse.gov/the-press-office/2014/03/13/presidential -memorandum-updating-and-modernizing-overtime-regulations).

55. Since 1940, the Department of Labor's rules have generally required each of three tests to be met for one of the FLSA's white-collar exemptions to apply. See U.S. Department of Labor, "Fact Sheet: Proposed Rulemaking to Update the Regulations Defining and Delimiting the Exemptions for 'White Collar' Employees" (www.dol.gov/whd/overtime/NPRM2015/factsheet.htm); U.S. Department of Labor, "Notice of Proposed Rulemaking: Overtime" (www .dol.gov/whd/overtime/NPRM2015/). Paul Waldman, "Republicans Will Hate Obama's New Overtime Rule, But They Can't Do Anything about It," *Washington Post,* June 30, 2015.

56. U.S. Department of Labor, "Notice of Proposed Rulemaking: Overtime"; Lydia DePillis, "How to Make Sense of Obama's Big Changes to Overtime Policy," *Washington Post,* June 30, 2015.

57. Nia-Malika Henderson, "Obama, Democrats Put Spotlight on Gender Pay Gap. Will It Matter?" *Washington Post,* January 29, 2014.

58. Barack Obama, "Remarks on Signing an Executive Order on Non-Retaliation for Disclosure of Compensation Information and a Memorandum on Advancing Pay Equality through Compensation Data Collection, April 8, 2014," APP; Tom Risen, "Obama Seeks Wage Transparency with Executive Orders," *U.S. News and World Report,* April 7, 2014.

59. Barack Obama, "Executive Order 13665: Non-Retaliation for Disclosure of Compensation Information, April 8, 2014," APP; Mohana Ravindranath, "Executive Order: Contractors Must Allow Employees to Discuss Pay with Each Other," *Washington Post,* April 13, 2014. Obama required federal contractors and subcontractors to submit summary data on the compensation paid to their employees. See Barack Obama, "Memorandum on Advancing Pay Equality through Compensation Data Collection, April 8, 2014," APP. These data were to be organized according to sex and race. DOL would "use the data to encourage greater voluntary compliance by employers with federal pay laws and to identify and analyze industry trends." See U.S. Department of Labor, "Rule to Collect Summary Pay Data from Federal Contractors Proposed by US Labor Department," press release, August 6, 2014 (www.dol.gov/opa/media /press/ofccp/ofccp20141451.htm). See also Obama, "Memorandum on Advanc-

ing Pay Equality"; MaryBeth Shreiner, "OFCCP Issues Final Rule Promoting Pay Transparency," Federal Contractor Compliance Watch, September 15, 2015 (http://federalcontractorcompliancewatch.com/2015/09/15/ofccp-issues -final-rule-promoting-pay-transparency/).

60. Cooley LLP website, "EEOC and OFCCP Enter a New Memorandum of Understanding," Federal Contractor Compliance Watch, November 21, 2011 (http://federalcontractorcompliancewatch.com/2011/11/21/eeoc-and-ofccp -enter-a-new-memorandum-of-understanding/).

61. Tom Mason, "OFCCP Proposes New Sex Discrimination Guidelines for Contractors and Subcontractors," Federal Contractor Compliance Watch, January 30, 2015 (http://federalcontractorcompliancewatch.com/2015/01/30/ofccp -proposes-new-sex-discrimination-guidelines-for-contractors-and -subcontractors/). Obama issued additional rules that would require all private sector companies to report salary data based on race, gender, and ethnicity, setting up the federal government to "actively police pay disparities that have resisted other efforts at reform." Companies would report the salary data on a form they submit annually to the EEOC. On the updated form, employers would have to identify the race and gender of employees and report their W-2 earnings for a twelve-month period, including tips, taxable benefits, and bonuses. The pay data would provide the EEOC and the OFCCP with insight into pay disparities across industries and occupations and strengthen federal efforts to combat discrimination. See Danielle Paquette and Drew Harwell, "Obama Targets Gender Pay Gap with Plan to Collect Companies' Salary Data," *Washington Post,* January 29, 2016; Equal Employment Opportunity Commission, "EEOC Announces Proposed Addition of Pay Data to Annual EEO-1 Reports," January 29, 2016 (www.eeoc.gov/eeoc/newsroom/release/1-29-16.cfm).

62. White House, "Obama Administration Record for Veterans and Wounded Warriors" (www.whitehouse.gov/sites/default/files/docs/veterans_and_wounded _warriors_record_0.pdf).

63. Barack Obama, "Executive Order 13540: Interagency Task Force on Veterans Small Business Development, April 26, 2010," APP.

64. Interagency Task Force on Veterans Small Business Development (2011); McGann (2014).

65. Tom Mason, "OFCCP Unveils Its Game-Changing Final Rules for Veterans and Individuals with Disabilities," Federal Contractor Compliance Watch, August 28, 2013 (http://federalcontractorcompliancewatch.com/2013/08/28 /ofccp-unveils-its-game-changing-final-rules-for-veterans-and-individuals-with -disabilities/).

66. Josh Ulman and Christi Layman, "OFCCP in Overdrive," Higher Education Workplace, Spring 2012 (www.cupahr.org/diversity/files/OFCCP%20 in%20Overdrive.pdf).

67. Tom Mason, "OFCCP's Final Rules for Veterans and Disabled Become Effective," Federal Contractor Compliance Watch, March 26, 2014 (http://fede ralcontractorcompliancewatch.com/2014/03/26/ofccps-final-rules-for-veterans -and-disabled-become-effective/).

68. U.S. Department of Labor, "The New Regulations: Vietnam Era Veterans' Readjustment Assistance Act" (www.dol.gov/ofccp/regs/compliance/vevraa .htm). See also "Act Now Advisory: New Obligations Imposed on Federal Government Contractors with OFCCP's Issuance of Final Regulations Covering Veterans," Epstein Becker Green website, October 16, 2013 (www.ebglaw.com /news/act-now-advisory-new-obligations-imposed-on-federal-government -contractors-with-ofccps-issuance-of-final-regulations-covering-veterans/).

69. U.S. Department of Labor, "New Regulations: Section 503 of the Rehabilitation Act" (www.dol.gov/ofccp/regs/compliance/section503.htm). For more on Obama's rule, see Mason, "OFCCP Unveils Its Game-Changing Final Rules."

70. Zachary A. Goldfarb and Juliet Eilperin, "Obama to Sign Order Barring U.S. Contractors from Job Bias Based on Sexual Orientation," *Washington Post,* June 16, 2014; Lee, "Obama to Bar Gay Discrimination by Federal Contractors."

71. Barack Obama, "Executive Order 13672: Further Amendments to Executive Order 11478, Equal Employment Opportunity in the Federal Government, and Executive Order 11246, Equal Employment Opportunity, July 21, 2014," APP; Martin Lederman, "Why the Law Does Not (and Should Not) Allow Religiously Motivated Contractors to Discriminate against Their LGBT Employees," Religious Freedom Project, July 31, 2014 (http://berkleycenter.georgetown.edu /responses/why-the-law-does-not-and-should-not-allow-religiously-motivated -contractors-to-discriminate-against-their-lgbt-employees).

72. Barack Obama, "Remarks on Signing an Executive Order on Lesbian, Gay, Bisexual, and Transgender Employment Discrimination, July 21, 2014," APP.

73. Joel C. Hunter and others, "Letter to Obama from Faith Leaders," *Washington Post,* July 1, 2014; Michelle Boorstein, "Faith Leaders: Exempt Religious Groups from Order Barring LGBT Bias in Hiring," *Washington Post,* July 2, 2014; Esbeck (2015).

74. Elizabeth Dias, "Obama's Executive Order to Protect Gay Workers Will Have No Religious Exemption," *Time,* July 18, 2014.

75. See White House, Office of the Press Secretary, "Fact Sheet: Taking Action to Support LGBT Workplace Equality Is Good for Business," July 21, 2014 (www.whitehouse.gov/the-press-office/2014/07/21/fact-sheet-taking-action -support-lgbt-workplace-equality-good-business-0). Federal Contractor Compliance Watch summed up the changes as follows: "Under the final rule, con-

tractors are prohibited from discriminating on the basis of sexual orientation and gender identity. The new rules do not define 'sexual orientation' or 'gender identity', but the OFCCP notes that it uses the same definition used by the Equal Employment Opportunity Commission and in case law developed under Title VII." See Tom Mason, "OFCCP Opens LGBT Final Rules to Limited Notice and Comment While Lawmakers Protest," *Federal Contractor Compliance Watch,* December 13, 2014 (http://federalcontractorcompliancewatch.com /2014/12/13/ofccp-opens-lgbt-final-rules-to-notice-and-comment-in-response -to-pressure-from-lawmakers/). Obama's rules do provide an exception that permits religious organizations to prefer members of a particular religion in their employment decisions. See Griffin (2013).

76. T. W. Farnam, "House Democrats to Obama: Require Contractors to Disclose Political Donations," *Washington Post,* July 28, 2011.

77. Barack Obama, "Executive Order Draft 4/12/11; 4:00 pm: Disclosure of Political Spending by Government Contractors," *Politico,* April 12, 2011 (www.politico.com/pdf/PPM187_disclosure.pdf).

78. Amanda Becker and David M. Drucker, "Members Weigh In on Draft Disclosure," *Roll Call,* May 24, 2011 (www.rollcall.com/issues/56 _127/Congressional-Democrats-Contractor-Disclosure-205903-1.html). A series of Supreme Court decisions have freed corporations, labor unions, and other interest groups to participate in elections as long as they operate independently of candidates. As part of a broader effort to limit the influence of "super-PACs" (which played an expanded role in the 2010 midterm elections), some congressional Democrats attempted to address the problem of anonymous spending with the Democracy Is Strengthened by Casting Light on Spending in Elections (DISCLOSE) Act. Congress would have countered the influence of undisclosed contributions by requiring groups to show the names of top donors in campaign advertisements. Bidders on federal contracts have long been required to disclose contributions made directly through political action organizations.

79. Obama, "Executive Order Draft 4/12/11." Under Obama's draft order, required disclosures would include "any contributions or expenditures by the company, its officers, and directors and subsidiaries under its control to (or on behalf) of federal candidates, parties, party committees, or third party entities with the expectation that the contributions would be used for campaign purposes." See Jed Babbin, "Obama vs. the 'Undisclosed Donors,'" *American Spectator,* May 2, 2011. The disclosed information would be available through a searchable, downloadable database on Data.gov. Companies that won federal contracts would certify that they had disclosed the information as a condition of receiving the award. See Matthew Weigelt, "Contractors Required to Disclose Political Contributions: Draft Order," *Washington Technology,* April 20, 2011.

80. Robert Brodsky, "Administration Set to Order Contractors to Disclose Campaign Contributions," *Government Executive,* April 21, 2011. Greenhouse, "Plan to Seek Use of U.S. Contracts as a Wage Lever."

81. Brodsky, "Administration Set to Order Contractors to Disclose Campaign Contributions."

82. Perry Bacon Jr. and T. W. Farnam, "Obama Weighs Disclosure Order for Contractors," *Washington Post,* April 20, 2011; Megan R. Wilson, "Obama Urged to Impose Rules on Campaign Spending Disclosure," *The Hill,* March 3, 2015 (http://thehill.com/business-a-lobbying/234437-obama-urged-to-impose -rules-on-campaign-spending-disclosure); Julie Hirschfeld Davis, "President Obama May Require Federal Contractors to List Campaign Gifts," *New York Times,* January 19, 2016; Juliet Eilperin, "Obama Weighs Whether to Force Federal Contractors to Reveal Political Spending," *Washington Post,* January 20, 2016; Jordain Carney, "McConnell: Executive Order on Campaign Finance Would be Illegal," *The Hill,* January 20, 2016; Ed Kilgore, "The One Thing to Know About Obama's Philosophy on Executive Actions," *New York Magazine,* January 5, 2016.

83. Davis, "President Obama May Require Federal Contractors to List Campaign Gifts"; Eilperin, "Obama Weighs Whether to Force Federal Contractors to Reveal Political Spending."

84. Davis, "President Obama May Require Federal Contractors to List Campaign Gifts."

85. Sheldon Whitehouse, Senator from Rhode Island (official website), "Senators Urging Administration to Require Government Contractors to Disclose Political Spending," April 2, 2015 (www.whitehouse.senate.gov/news /release/senators-urging-administration-to-require-government-contractors-to -disclose-political-spending); Weiner, Norden, and Ferguson (2015).

86. Anne Gearan and Matea Gold, "Clinton Proposes New Caps on Political Donations," *Washington Post,* September 8, 2015.

CHAPTER FOUR

1. Blais, Blake, and Dion (1997, p. 51); Kellie Lunney, "Federal Employee Unions Back Obama in 2012 Election," *Government Executive,* November 5, 2012 (www.govexec.com/oversight/2012/11/federal-employee-unions-back -obama-2012-election/59273/); Daniel Schlozman, "The Alliance of U.S. Labor Unions and the Democratic Party," *Scholars Strategy Network,* October 2013 (www.scholarsstrategynetwork.org/brief/alliance-us-labor-unions-and -democratic-party).

2. Johnson and Libecap (1994, p. 17).

3. Ibid.

4. See Johnson and Libecap (1994).

5. U.S. Civil Service Commission (1889, p. 15).

6. By 1904, over 50 percent of the federal labor force was covered by merit provisions. See Johnson and Libecap (1994).

7. U.S. Office of Personnel Management (2003).

8. Moe (1985, 1993).

9. Franklin D. Roosevelt, "Executive Order 7916: Extending the Competitive Classified Civil Service, June 24, 1938," American Presidency Project (henceforth cited as APP).

10. Harry S. Truman, "Executive Order 9830: Amending the Civil Service Rules and Providing for Federal Personnel Administration, February 24, 1947," APP.

11. Ibid.

12. Moynihan (2004).

13. For more on the CSRA, see Ingraham and Ban (1984); Ingraham and Rosenbloom (1992). See also "The Civil Service Reform Act of 1978," Prentice Hall Documents (http://wps.prenhall.com/wps/media/objects/531/544609 /Documents_Library/civilser.htm). The OPM may not delegate its responsibility to conduct civil service exams.

14. United States Department of Labor, "The Coal Strike of 1902—Turning Point in U.S. Policy" (www.dol.gov/oasam/programs/history/coalstrike.htm).

15. Grossman (1975, p. 21); Harry S. Truman, "Executive Order 10155: Possession, Control, and Operation of Certain Railroads, August 25, 1950," APP. Truman had intervened in another railway dispute when union employees threatened to strike in 1948. He ordered the formation of an emergency board to negotiate a settlement between the railroad unions and owners. See Harry S. Truman, "Executive Order 9922: Creating an Emergency Board to Investigate a Dispute Between the Chicago, North Shore & Milwaukee Railway Company and Certain of Its Employees, January 13, 1948," APP.

16. Harry S. Truman, "Statement by the President upon Issuing Order Averting a Railroad Strike, July 8, 1950," APP. Dwight D. Eisenhower, "Executive Order 10490: Creating a Board of Inquiry To Report on Certain Labor Disputes Affecting the Maritime Industry of the United States, October 1, 1953," APP.

17. Mikusko and Miller (2014, p. 20).

18. Hampton (1972, p. 494).

19. For more on Congress and labor-management relations, see Hegji (2012).

20. Franklin D. Roosevelt, "Letter on the Resolution of Federation of Federal Employees against Strikes in Federal Service, August 16, 1937," APP.

21. Brian Friel, "Labor Pains," *Government Executive,* October 1, 2002 (www.govexec.com/magazine/2002/10/labor-pains/12518/); Terrence Scanlon, "Finding Common Cause in Fighting Public Sector Unions," *Washington*

Times, April 5, 2015; Thomas B. Edsall, "Republicans Sure Love to Hate Unions," *New York Times,* November 18, 2014; Joe Davidson, "GOP Hopefuls Spell Dread for Federal Employees," *Washington Post,* September 17, 2015; Jazz Shaw, "Government Employee Union President: 'God Help Us All' If the GOP Wins," *Hot Air,* February 9, 2016 (http://hotair.com/archives /2016/02/09/government-employee-union-president-god-help-us-all-if-the -gop-wins/).

22. Schlozman, "Alliance of U.S. Labor Unions and the Democratic Party."

23. Johnson and Libecap (1994, p. 100); Nesbitt (1976); Aaron, Najita, and Stern (1988).

24. John F. Kennedy, "Memorandum on Employee-Management Relations in the Federal Service, June 22, 1961," APP. Kennedy required federal agencies to develop procedures for processing employee grievances and to establish a labor-management program for federal employees. See John F. Kennedy, "Executive Order 10988: Employee-Management Cooperation in the Federal Service, January 17, 1962," APP. He established a three-tier system of recognition: exclusive representation, formal recognition, and informal recognition.

25. Johnson and Libecap (1994).

26. Masters (2004, p. 56). See Kearney and Mareschal (2008); Goldfield (1989).

27. Naff and Riccucci (2007); Masters, Albright, and Eplion (2003). See Moskow, Loewenberg, and Koziara (1970); Lyndon B. Johnson, "Memorandum on Employee-Management Cooperation in the Federal Government, September 8, 1967," APP.

28. Black (2007).

29. U.S. Federal Labor Relations Authority, "Study Committee Report and Recommendations, August 1969, which Led to the Issuance of Executive Order 11491" (www.flra.gov/webfm_send/568).

30. See "A Short History of the Statute," Federal Labor Relations Authority website (www.flra.gov/statute_history).

31. Richard M. Nixon, "Executive Order 11491: Labor-Management Relations in the Federal Service, October 29, 1969," APP.

32. Damon Stetson, "Nixon and the Unions; President Pins Hopes on Rank-and-File as the Split at the Top Becomes Clear," *New York Times,* August 21, 1971, p. 12. See Abarca (2001).

33. Hegji (2012).

34. Masters (2004, p. 57).

35. Federal Labor Relations Authority, "The Statute" (www.flra.gov/about /introduction-flra/statute).

36. Naff and Riccucci (2007).

37. Milkman and McCartin (2013). On work stoppages, see McCartin (2011); Andrew Glass, "Reagan Fires 11,000 Striking Air Traffic Controllers: Aug. 5, 1981," *Politico,* August 5, 2008 (www.politico.com/story/2008/08 /reagan-fires-11-000-striking-air-traffic-controllers-aug-5-1981-012292).

38. Masters, Albright, and Eplion (2003).

39. Ibid., p. 2.

40. Joseph A. McCartin, "The Strike That Busted Unions," *New York Times,* August 2, 2011.

41. Masters and Albright (1999).

42. William J. Clinton, "Executive Order 12871: Labor-Management Partnerships, October 1, 1993," APP.

43. Naff and Riccucci (2007).

44. Kearney and Mareschal (2014); Condrey (2010); George W. Bush, "Executive Order 13203: Revocation of Executive Order and Presidential Memorandum Concerning Labor-Management Partnerships, February 17, 2001," APP; William J. Clinton, "Executive Order 12871"; William J. Clinton, "Executive Order 13156: Amendment to Executive Order 12871 Regarding the National Partnership Council, May 17, 2000," APP.

45. George W. Bush, "Executive Order 13480: Exclusions from the Federal Labor-Management Relations Program, November 26, 2008," APP. Under the 1978 Civil Service Reform Act, Congress authorized the president to exclude any agency from the ability to bargain collectively if the agency or subdivision has a primary function of intelligence, counterintelligence, investigative, or national security work.

46. Kearney and Mareschal (2008). Pro-labor groups were critical of Bush's order and accused him of gutting employee rights in the public sector and weakening unions. In fact, the number of unions in the federal government decreased during the Bush presidency. Labor union membership in the federal sector fell 3.7 percent during Bush's terms.

47. Szymendera (2011).

48. Theodore Roosevelt, "Seventh Annual Message, December 3, 1907," APP.

49. Theodore Roosevelt, "Message to Congress on Worker's Compensation, January 31, 1908," APP.

50. Roosevelt, "Seventh Annual Message"; Fishback (2007).

51. Yarbrough (2012); Sidney Milkis, "Theodore Roosevelt: Impact and Legacy," University of Virginia, Miller Center, "American President" (http:// millercenter.org/president/biography/roosevelt-impact-and-legacy).

52. MacLaury (1981); Szymendera (2013).

53. Woodrow Wilson, "Executive Order 2455: Transferring to the Governor of the Panama Canal the Administration of the Act Approved September 7,

1916, So Far As Panama Canal and Panama Railroad Employees Are Concerned, September 15, 1916," Wikisource (https://en.wikisource.org/wiki/Executive _Order_2455).

54. Franklin D. Roosevelt, "Executive Order 8071: Establishing the Federal Interdepartmental Safety Council, March 21, 1939," National Archives (www .archives.gov/federal-register/executive-orders/1939.html); Bartrip (2006).

55. Ashford (1976); U.S. Department of Health and Human Services, "A Common Thread of Service: A Brief History of the Federal Security Agency, July 1, 1972" (https://aspe.hhs.gov/report/common-thread-service/brief-history -federal-security-agency).

56. Nordlund (1991). The Federal Security Agency was established under the Reorganization Act of 1939, P.L. 76-19.

57. See Harry S. Truman, "Executive Order 10194: Establishing the Federal Safety Council, December 19, 1950," APP.

58. Dwight D. Eisenhower, "Memorandum on Occupational Safety in the Government Service, October 14, 1954," APP.

59. Rosner and Markowitz (1989, pp. ix–xx); Lyndon B. Johnson, "Statement by the President Upon Issuing a New Safety Policy for the Federal Service, February 16, 1965," APP; Lyndon B. Johnson, "Statement by the President on the Government's Employee Safety Program, February 16, 1966," APP.

60. Lyndon B. Johnson, "Statement by the President on Accident Prevention in the Federal Government, June 13, 1967," APP; Lyndon B. Johnson, "Memorandum on the Federal Agency Program: Mission SAFETY-70, September 21, 1968," APP.

61. Richard M. Nixon, "Memorandum Announcing a New Program: 'ZERO IN on Federal Safety,' October 26, 1970," APP; Richard M. Nixon, "Memorandum About the 'Zero-In on Federal Safety' Program, November 15, 1972," APP.

62. U.S. Department of Labor, "Safety and Health Standards: Occupational Safety and Health," *Employment Law Guide* (www.dol.gov/elaws/elg /osha.htm).

63. Mason (2004); Richard M. Nixon, "Executive Order 11612: Occupational Safety and Health Programs for Federal Employees, July 26, 1971," APP; McCaffrey (1982); Zank (1996).

64. Richard M. Nixon, "Address to the Nation about Inflation and the Economy, July 25, 1974," APP.

65. Kaufman (1997); Gerald Ford, "Executive Order 11807: Occupational Safety and Health Programs for Federal Employees, September 28, 1974," APP.

66. Dark (1999); "Job Health and Safety," *CQ Researcher,* December 24, 1976. Other demands for action arose in response to the highly publicized death of a U.S. postal worker in 1978. For years USPS workers had complained of unsafe working conditions, and the death created a public crisis for the fed-

eral government. See Walsh and Mangum (1992). OSHA—which at the time only regulated private sector employers—was invited into USPS facilities to conduct inspections. Jimmy Carter, "Executive Order 12196: Occupational Safety and Health Programs for Federal Employees, February 26, 1980," APP.

67. Ronald Reagan, "Memorandum on an Occupational Safety and Health Program for Federal Employees, December 9, 1982," APP; Ronald Reagan, "Policy Statement on an Occupational Safety and Health Program for Federal Employees, December 9, 1982," APP; Ronald Reagan, "Memorandum on an Occupational Safety and Health Program for Federal Employees, December 9, 1982," Ronald Reagan Presidential Library and Museum (https://reaganlibrary .archives.gov/archives/speeches/1982/120982e.htm).

68. George H. W. Bush, "Executive Order 12699: Seismic Safety of Federal and Federally Assisted or Regulated New Building Construction, January 5, 1990," APP.

69. William J. Clinton, "The New OSHA Reinventing Worker Safety and Health, February 21, 1995" (http://govinfo.library.unt.edu/npr/initiati/common /reinvent-.htm); Gregory R. Watchman, "How the New OSHA Is Improving Safety and Health in Workplaces," June 24, 1997 (www.osha.gov/pls/oshaweb /owadisp.show_document?p_table=TESTIMONIES&p_id=88).

70. Watchman, "How the New OSHA Is Improving Safety and Health in Workplaces."

71. Kellough, Nigro, and Brewer (2010).

72. George W. Bush, "Executive Order 13225: Continuance of Certain Federal Advisory Committees, September 28, 2001," APP; George W. Bush, "Executive Order 13316: Continuance of Certain Federal Advisory Committees, September 17, 2003," APP; George W. Bush, "Executive Order 13385: Continuance of Certain Federal Advisory Committees and Amendments to and Revocation of Other Executive Orders, September 29, 2005," APP; George W. Bush, "Executive Order 13446: Continuance of Certain Federal Advisory Committees and Amendments to and Revocation of Other Executive Orders, September 28, 2007," APP.

73. George W. Bush, "Memorandum on the Safety, Health, and Return-to-Employment (SHARE) Initiative, January 9, 2004," APP; George W. Bush, "Memorandum on Extension of the Safety, Health, and Return-to-Employment (SHARE) Initiative, September 29, 2006," APP. Bush requested that OSHA and Office of Workers' Compensation Programs work with federal agencies to develop new strategies for promoting health and safety in work sites with high injury rates, improve the timeliness of reporting claims through electronic and other means, and provide suitable work and tools for injured and disabled employees.

74. U.S. Department of Labor, "Safety and Health Standards: Occupational Safety and Health," *Employment Law Guide* (www.dol.gov/elaws/elg/osha

.htm); U.S. Congress, Senate, S. Rep. No. 91-1282, 91st Cong., 2nd Sess. (1970), pp. 33, 42.

75. Congress aimed to avoid federal interagency disputes. It did not impose fines on federal agencies. Large agencies, such as the Departments of Defense and Agriculture did not have to comply with the safety recommendations, and there was no review commission in the federal government. Although OSHA did not account for self-enforcement or compliance mechanisms, its standards applied to all federal agencies. Congress made federal agency heads responsible for providing safe and healthful working conditions for their workers. OSHA could not fine federal agencies, but it could monitor these agencies and conduct federal workplace inspections in response to workers' reports of hazards. Jimmy Carter, "Executive Order 12196: Occupational Safety and Health Programs for Federal Employees, February 26, 1980," APP.

76. Ronald Reagan, "Executive Order 12566: Safety Belt Use Requirements for Federal Employees, September 26, 1986," APP; William J. Clinton, "Executive Order 13043: Increasing Seat Belt Use in the United States, April 16, 1997," APP.

77. Ronald Reagan, "Remarks Announcing the Campaign against Drug Abuse and a Question-and-Answer Session with Reporters, August 4, 1986," APP.

78. Ronald Reagan, "Executive Order 12564: Drug-Free Federal Workplace, September 15, 1986," APP.

79. Elwood (1994); Charles Mohr, "Drug Test Policy Caught in Snags," *New York Times*, December 18, 1988. For a full discussion, see Normand, Lempert, and O'Brien (1994).

80. Ronald Reagan, "Executive Order 12601: Presidential Commission on the Human Immunodeficiency Virus Epidemic, June 24, 1987," APP.

81. Ronald Reagan, "Statement Announcing a Human Immunodeficiency Virus Epidemic Action Plan, August 2, 1988," APP; Ronald Reagan, "Memorandums on the Human Immunodeficiency Virus Epidemic, August 5, 1988," APP.

82. Julie Johnson, "Reagan, Spurning Tougher Move, Orders Anti-Bias Rules on AIDS," *New York Times*, August 3, 1988.

83. Michael Bronski, "Rewriting the Script on Reagan: Why the President Ignored AIDS," *Forward*, November 14, 2003.

84. Cook and Bero (2009). Individual agencies took some action. For example, the Department of Health and Human Services banned smoking in all buildings in 1987, and in 1993, the U.S. Postal Service followed suit in all post offices.

85. William J. Clinton, "Executive Order 13058: Protecting Federal Employees and the Public from Exposure to Tobacco Smoke in the Federal Workplace, August 9, 1997," APP; Ronald J. Ostrow, "Clinton Prohibits Smoking in

Most Federal Buildings," *Los Angeles Times,* August 10, 1997; Bailey (2008); William J. Clinton, "Memorandum on Expanding Access to Smoking Cessation Programs, June 27, 2000," APP.

86. George W. Bush, "Executive Order 13266: Activities to Promote Personal Fitness, June 20, 2002," APP. Federal employees and OPM were not specifically addressed. See also the White House of President George W. Bush, "Healthier US: The President's Health and Fitness Initiative" (http://georgewbush-whitehouse .archives.gov/infocus/fitness/execsummary.html).

87. U.S. General Accounting Office (1992). For more information on workplace flexibility, see Georgetown University Law Center, "A Sampling of Government Reports on Workplace Flexibility," Spring 2008 (http://workplaceflexibility2010 .org/images/uploads/AppF-GovernmentReportsSampling.pdf).

88. U.S. Office of Personnel Management, "Work Arrangements and Quality of Work/Life," September 2005 (www.opm.gov/policy-data-oversight/human -capital-management/reference-materials/talent-management/qualityworklife .pdf).

89. Jimmy Carter, "White House Conference on Families Memorandum from the President, October 15, 1979," APP; Shane (1981); Jimmy Carter, "Federal Employees Flexible and Compressed Work Schedules Act of 1978: Statement on Signing H.R. 7814 Into Law, September 29, 1978," APP; Jimmy Carter, "Part-time Federal Employment Memorandum for the Heads of Executive Departments and Agencies, September 16, 1977," APP; Karlin Barker, " 'Flexi-time' for U.S. Workers May Bite Bureaucratic Dust," *Washington Post,* March 16, 1982 (www.washingtonpost.com/archive/politics/1982/03/16/flexitime-for-us -workers-may-bite-bureaucratic-dust/37877ab2-9700-4b31-8923-256bdb0 faac1/).

90. Barker, " 'Flexitime' for U.S. Workers May Bite Bureaucratic Dust."

91. George H. W. Bush, "Remarks at the California Chamber of Commerce Centennial Dinner in Los Angeles, March 1, 1990," APP.

92. Bush's OPM issued the first Federal Personnel Manual letter on Flexiplace. See U.S. Office of Personnel Management (1991, 1993); U.S. General Services Administration (2000); Liechty and Anderson (2007).

93. Jimmy Carter, "Executive Order 12105: Garnishment of Moneys Payable to Employees of Executive Agencies and the District of Columbia, December 19, 1978," APP; Carl M. Cannon, "Clinton to Unveil Reforms for Welfare, Child Support," *Baltimore Sun,* June 14, 1994 (http://articles.baltimoresun .com/1994-06-14/news/1994165074t); Hansen (1999); William J. Clinton, "Remarks on Signing the Executive Order to Facilitate Payment of Child Support and an Exchange with Reporters, February 27, 1995," APP. Clinton stated, "The Federal Government, through its civilian employees and Uniformed Services members, is the nation's largest single employer and as such

should set an example of leadership and encouragement in ensuring that all children are properly supported."

94. William J. Clinton, "Executive Order 12953: Actions Required of All Executive Agencies to Facilitate Payment of Child Support, February 27, 1995," APP. Under the FMLA, an employee is entitled to a total of twelve workweeks of unpaid leave during any twelve-month period for the birth, adoption, or foster care of a son or daughter; for the serious health condition of the employee; or to care for an employee's spouse, son or daughter, or parent with a serious health condition. An employee may substitute annual leave or sick leave, as appropriate, for unpaid leave under the FMLA.

95. William J. Clinton, "Memorandum on Expanding Family-Friendly Work Arrangements in the Executive Branch, July 11, 1994," APP; U.S. General Services Administration (2000). See William J. Clinton, "Memorandum on Family Friendly Work Arrangements, June 21, 1996," APP; U.S. Office of Personnel Management (1997); U.S. General Services Administration (2000). Clinton's OPM issued a 1995 publication, "Balancing Work and Family Demands Through Telecommuting," as well as a telework briefing tool called "The Telework Briefing Kit." See U.S. Office of Personnel Management, "Pay & Leave Reference Materials: Report to Congress on the 'Federal Employees Family Friendly Leave Act' (Public Law 103-388)," June 1997 (www.opm.gov /policy-data-oversight/pay-leave/reference-materials/reports/federal-employees -family-friendly-leave-act/).

96. William J. Clinton, "Memorandum on Expanded Family and Medical Leave Policies, April 11, 1997," APP.

97. William J. Clinton, "Executive Order 13163: Increasing the Opportunity for Individuals with Disabilities to Be Employed in the Federal Government, July 26, 2000," APP.

98. Cindy Romero, "'08 Bringing Progress on Family-Friendly Policies," National Partnership for Women and Families, May 1, 2008 (www.nationalpartnership .org/news-room/press-releases/08-bringing-progress.html).

99. See George W. Bush, "Executive Order 13426: Establishing a Commission on Care for America's Returning Wounded Warriors and a Task Force on Returning Global War on Terror Heroes, March 6, 2007," APP.

100. Jimmy Carter, "Federal Employees Part-Time Career Employment Act of 1978: Statement on Signing H.R. 10126 into Law, October 10, 1978," APP; U.S. Office of Personnel Management (1981).

101. Georgetown University Law Center, "The Federal Employees"; "Federal Leave Sharing," CQ Almanac 1988, 44th ed., 1989 (www.library.cqpress .com/cqalmanac/document.php?id=cqal88-1140757).

102. Wisensale (2001).

103. Clinton, "Memorandum on Expanded Family and Medical Leave Policies, April 11, 1997."

104. U.S. Department of Labor, "Military Family Leave Provisions of the FMLA (Family and Medical Leave Act) Frequently Asked Questions and Answers" (www.dol.gov/whd/fmla/finalrule/MilitaryFAQs.pdf).

105. Moffit, Nesterczuk, and Devine (2001).

106. Johnson and Libecap (1994, p. 126).

107. "Worker Voice in a Time of Rising Inequality," Council of Economic Advisers Issue Brief, October 2015 (www.whitehouse.gov/sites/default/files /page/files/worker_voice_issue_brief_cea.pdf).

108. Steven Greenhouse, "Most U.S. Union Members Are Working for the Government, New Data Shows," *New York Times*, January 22, 2010.

109. Kathryn Watson, "Federal Employee Union Membership Jumped in 2015," *The Daily Caller*, March 16, 2016 (http://dailycaller.com/2016/03/16 /federal-employee-union-membership-jumped-in-2015/).

110. Ralph Smith, "Proposals Emerging to Restrict Power and Influence of Federal Employee Unions," *FedSmith.com*, September 14, 2015 (www.fedsmith .com/2015/09/14/proposals-emerging-to-restrict-power-and-influence-of -federal-employee-unions/).

111. Michael Wald, "Despite Legal Threats, Membership in Federal Unions Shows Growth," *FedSmith.com*, March 15, 2016 (www.fedsmith.com/2016 /03/15/despite-legal-threats-membership-in-federal-unions-shows-growth/); U.S. Bureau of Labor Statistics, "Union Members—2015," press release, January 28, 2016 (www.bls.gov/news.release/pdf/union2.pdf).

CHAPTER FIVE

1. Public Broadcasting Service, "Segregation in the U.S. Government" (www.pbs.org/wnet/jimcrow/stories_events_segregation.html); Dick Lehr, "The Racist Legacy of Woodrow Wilson," *The Atlantic*, November 27, 2015 (www .theatlantic.com/politics/archive/2015/11/wilson-legacy-racism/417549/).

2. Franklin D. Roosevelt, "Executive Order 8802: Reaffirming Policy of Full Participation in the Defense Program By All Persons, Regardless of Race, Creed, Color, or National Origin, and Directing Certain Action in Furtherance of Said Policy, June 25, 1941," American Presidency Project (henceforth cited as APP); Franklin D. Roosevelt, "Executive Order 9346: Establishing a Committee on Fair Employment Practice, May 27, 1943," APP.

3. Gooding and Kazin (2013).

4. "Fair Employment Practices Committee," George Washington University, Eleanor Roosevelt Papers Project (www.gwu.edu/~erpapers/teachinger/glossary /fepc.cfm).

5. Roosevelt, "Executive Order 8802."

6. Ibid.

7. Roosevelt, "Executive Order 9346"; MacLaury (2008).

8. Collins (2001).

9. Roosevelt, "Executive Order 9346."

10. MacLaury (2008).

11. Collins (2001).

12. MacLaury (2008); Johnson and Libecap (1994).

13. Harry S. Truman, "Executive Order 9808: Establishing the President's Committee on Civil Rights, December 5, 1946," APP; Harry S. Truman, "Executive Order 9980: Regulations Governing Fair Employment Practices Within the Federal Establishment, July 26, 1948," APP; Harry S. Truman, "Executive Order 9981: Establishing the President's Committee on Equality of Treatment and Opportunity in the Armed Services, July 26, 1948," APP.

14. MacLaury (2008).

15. Truman, "Executive Order 9808."

16. Berman (1970).

17. President's Committee on Civil Rights (1947).

18. Truman, "Executive Order 9981."

19. Patrick Feng, "Executive Order 9981: Integration of the Armed Forces," National Museum of the United States Army (https://armyhistory.org/executive-order-9981-integration-of-the-armed-forces/).

20. Berman (1970).

21. Truman, "Executive Order 9980."

22. MacLaury (2008).

23. Ibid.

24. Ibid.

25. Ibid., p. 137.

26. Berman (1970).

27. Dwight D. Eisenhower, "Executive Order 10590: Establishing the President's Committee on Government Employment Policy, January 18, 1955," APP.

28. Ibid.

29. Pohlmann and Whisenhunt (2002).

30. MacLaury (2008).

31. John F. Kennedy, "Executive Order 10925: Establishing the President's Committee on Equal Employment Opportunity, March 6, 1961," APP.

32. Ibid.; U.S. Commission on Civil Rights (1961).

33. MacLaury (2008).

34. Kellough (1992).

35. Lyndon B. Johnson, "Executive Order 11141: Declaring a Public Policy Against Discrimination on the Basis of Age, February 12, 1964," APP; Lyndon B. Johnson, "Executive Order 11246: Equal Employment Opportunity, September 24, 1965," APP; Lyndon B. Johnson, "Executive Order 11375: Amending

Executive Order No. 11246, Relating to Equal Employment Opportunity, October 13, 1967," APP.

36. Johnson, "Executive Order 11246."

37. Goodwin (1976); Strober and Strober (1994).

38. Richard M. Nixon, "Executive Order 11478: Equal Employment Opportunity in the Federal Government, August 8, 1969," APP.

39. Ibid.

40. Ibid.; Johnson, "Executive Order 11246"; Johnson, "Executive Order 11375."

41. Dolan and Rosenbloom (2003).

42. Maxwell (2008).

43. Between 1969 and 1972, the percentage of African Americans represented in federal employment grew by 1.5 percent. In the year following the passage of the Equal Employment Opportunity Act, in 1972, the number of African Americans grew by the same percentage—indicating that the EEOA had a stronger effect than previous measures did upon federal agencies' efforts to hire and recruit minority candidates (Rose and Ping Chia 1978). By 1974, five years after Nixon's order and two years after the EEOA, the number of African Americans in the federal service had increased by about 2 percent.

44. Jimmy Carter, "Civil Service Reform Act of 1978: Remarks at the Bill Signing Ceremony, October 13, 1978," APP.

45. Nixon, "Executive Order 11478"; Jimmy Carter, "Executive Order 12106: Equal Employment Opportunity Enforcement, December 28, 1978," APP.

46. Maxwell (2008).

47. Raza, Anderson, and Custred (1999).

48. Warshaw (2004, p. 73).

49. B. Drummond Ayres Jr., "The Expanding Hispanic Vote Shakes Republican Strongholds," *New York Times,* November 10, 1996.

50. Pew Research Center, "Latino Voters in the 2012 Election," November 7, 2012 (www.pewhispanic.org/files/2012/11/2012_Latino_vote_exit_poll _analysis_final_11-07-12.pdf).

51. William J. Clinton, "Executive Order 13171: Hispanic Employment in the Federal Government, October 12, 2000," APP.

52. Ibid.

53. Ibid.

54. Ana Radelat, "No Excuses, No Results," *Latino Magazine,* Spring 2013 (http://latinomagazine.com/spring2013/features/federal.htm).

55. U.S. Civil Service Commission (1921); "Pendleton Act (1883)," *Our Documents,* 2015 (www.ourdocuments.gov/doc.php?flash=true&doc=48).

56. Rebecca Onion, "How to Employ Women in Government Jobs: Postwar Advice Drawn from the American Experience, *The Vault* (blog), *Slate*, December 1, 2014 (http://www.slate.com/blogs/the_vault/2014/12/01/history_of _women_s_employment_letter_from_american_civil_service_commission .html).

57. Rung (1997). See also McGuire (2008); Kessler-Harris (2001).

58. Harrison (1989).

59. Ibid.

60. Harrison (1980).

61. Dwight D. Eisenhower Presidential Library, Museum, and Boyhood Home, "Women in the 1950s" (www.eisenhower.archives.gov/research/online _documents/women_in_the_1950s.html).

62. Shauna Shames and Pamela O'Leary, "JFK, a Pioneer in the Women's Movement," *Los Angeles Times,* November 22, 2013.

63. John F. Kennedy, "Executive Order 10980: Establishing the President's Commission on the Status of Women, December 14, 1961," APP; John F. Kennedy, "Statement by the President on the Establishment of the President's Commission on the Status of Women, December 14, 1961," APP.

64. John F. Kennedy, "Memorandum on Equal Opportunity for Women in the Federal Service, July 24, 1962," APP.

65. Ibid.

66. Walker (2012); Jo Freeman, "How 'Sex' Got into Title VII: Persistent Opportunism as a Maker of Public Policy" (http://www.jofreeman.com/lawand policy/titlevii.htm).

67. Ibid.; Lyndon B. Johnson, "Executive Order 11375: Amending Executive Order No. 11246, Relating to Equal Employment Opportunity, October 13, 1967," APP.

68. Johnson, "Executive Order 11375."

69. Ibid.

70. Max Frankel, "Johnson Signs Order to Protect Women in U.S. Jobs from Bias," *New York Times,* October 14, 1967, p. 11.

71. Walker (2012).

72. Ibid.

73. Richard Nixon, "Executive Order 11478: Equal Employment Opportunity in the Federal Government, August 8, 1969," APP.

74. Jimmy Carter, "Federal Employment of Women Memorandum for Heads of Departments and Agencies, November 17, 1977," APP.

75. Ibid.

76. Ibid. Since the mid-1980s, the number of women in federal employment has stayed constant at just below 40 percent.

77. "Topics of the Time: Public Service and Private Business," *The Century Illustrated Monthly Magazine* 23, New Series, no. 1, April 1882.

78. Grover Cleveland, "Executive Order, February 2, 1888," APP; Grover Cleveland, "Executive Order: Civil Service Rules, May 6, 1896," APP; Dwight D. Eisenhower, "Executive Order 10577: Amending the Civil Service Rules and Authorizing a New Appointment System for the Competitive Service, November 22, 1954," APP.

79. David Stout, "Religion and Federal Worker: What Thou Shalt and Shalt Not Do," *New York Times*, August 14, 1997. The guidelines were drawn up by a committee that included the Union of Orthodox Jewish Congregations of America, the American Jewish Congress, the National Council of Churches, the Center for Law and Religious Freedom, and People for the American Way.

80. William J. Clinton, "Memorandum on Religious Exercise and Religious Expression in the Federal Workplace, August 14, 1997," APP.

81. Peter Steinfels, "Clinton Signs Law Protecting Religious Practices," *New York Times*, November 17, 1993. The new law overturned a 1990 Supreme Court ruling that set a looser standard for laws that restrict religious practices, *Employment Division v. Smith*, which abandoned a long-accepted principle of constitutional interpretation that required the government to demonstrate a "compelling state interest" to justify any measure restricting religious practices. Under the ruling, restrictions were acceptable as long as they were not aimed at religious groups alone. The new law restored the old standard, and even in cases where government concerns such as health or safety do justify infringements of religious practices, the new law required the use of whatever means would be least restrictive to religion. An unusual coalition of liberal, conservative, and religious groups supported the new law, including the National Association of Evangelicals, the Southern Baptist Convention, the National Council of Churches, the American Jewish Congress, the National Conference of Catholic Bishops, the Mormon Church, the Traditional Values Coalition, and the American Civil Liberties Union.

82. White House, Office of the Press Secretary, "Guidelines on Religious Exercise and Religious Expression in the Federal Workplace," press release, August 14, 1997 (http://clinton2.nara.gov/WH/New/html/19970819-3275 .html).

83. Ibid. Also see Al-Hibri, Elshtain, and Haynes (2001); Clinton, "Memorandum on Religious Exercise"; David Stout, "Religion and Federal Worker: What Thou Shalt and Shalt Not Do," *New York Times*, August 14, 1997.

84. U.S. Congress, Res. of Mar. 3, 1865, No. 27, 13 Stat. 571.

85. U.S. Civil Service Commission (1914, p. 47).

86. U.S. House of Representatives (1915, p. 1214).

87. U.S. Civil Service Commission (1895).

88. Stimson (2004).

89. Ibid.

90. U.S. Merit Systems Protection Board (2014b).

91. Benjamin Harrison, "Executive Order: Amendment of Civil Service Rules, September 23, 1892," APP.

92. U.S. Office of Personnel Management, "Veterans Services: Vet Guide," 2015 (www.opm.gov/policy-data-oversight/veterans-services/vet-guide/).

93. Theodore Roosevelt, "Executive Order, January 17, 1902," APP.

94. Skrentny (1996).

95. Herbert Hoover, "Executive Order 5610: Amendment of the Civil Service Rules Relating to Veterans' Preference, April 24, 1931," APP.

96. Franklin D. Roosevelt, "Executive Order 6203, Regarding Postmasters and Civil Service, July 12, 1933," APP.

97. Hoover, "Executive Order 5610."

98. Franklin D. Roosevelt, "Letter on Preference for Veterans in Federal Employment, February 26, 1944," APP.

99. Skrentny (1996).

100. Harry S. Truman, "Memorandum Concerning Veteran Preference in Federal Agencies, August 24, 1945," APP.

101. See the following EOs and memos by Harry S. Truman: "Executive Order 9589: Restricting Competition in Certain Civil Service Examinations to Veterans, July 16, 1945," APP; "Memorandum Concerning Veteran Preference"; "Executive Order 9644: Authorizing the Civil Service Commission to Confer a Competitive Classified Civil-Service Status Upon Certain Disabled Veterans, October 19, 1945," APP; "Executive Order 9662: Restricting Competition in Certain Civil-Service Examinations to Veterans, November 29, 1945," APP; "Executive Order 9738: Restricting Competition in Examination for the Position of Correctional Officer Under the Bureau of Prisons, Department of Justice, June 19, 1946," APP.

102. Truman, "Executive Order 9644."

103. Lyndon B. Johnson, "Executive Order 11397: Authorizing Transitional Appointments of Veterans Who Have Served During the Vietnam Era, February 9, 1968," APP.

104. See the following EOs and memos by Richard Nixon: "Executive Order 11521: Authorizing Veterans Readjustment Appointments for Veterans of the Vietnam Era, March 26, 1970," APP; "Executive Order 11598: To Provide for the Listing of Certain Job Vacancies by Federal Agencies and Government Contractors and Subcontractors, June 16, 1971," APP; "Memorandum About Employment of Vietnam Veterans, October 5, 1972," APP.

105. Ibid.

106. U.S. Senate (1970).

107. Nixon, "Executive Order 11598."

108. Jimmy Carter, "Veterans Readjustment and Career-Conditional Appointment Program Memorandum from the President, October 10, 1978," APP.

109. George H. W. Bush, "Memorandum on the Return of Desert Shield/ Desert Storm Participants to Federal Civilian Employment, March 8, 1991," APP.

110. Ibid.

111. Harry S. Truman, "Executive Order 9644: Authorizing the Civil Service Commission to Confer a Competitive Classified Civil-Service Status upon Certain Disabled Veterans, October 19, 1945," APP.

112. Harry S. Truman, "Statement by the President on Employment of Disabled Veterans and Other Handicapped Persons, September 12, 1946," APP. Truman later replaced EO 9644 with EO 9830, in which the preference for disabled veterans in employment was inserted among the president's broader instructions for competitive assignments under the civil service. See Harry S. Truman, "Executive Order 9830: Amending the Civil Service Rules and Providing for Federal Personnel Administration, February 24, 1947," APP.

113. Dwight D. Eisenhower, "Executive Order 10640: The President's Committee on Employment of the Physically Handicapped, October 10, 1955," APP; John F. Kennedy, "Executive Order 10994: The President's Committee on Employment of the Handicapped, February 14, 1962," APP.

114. Pelka (2012).

115. John F. Kennedy, "Memorandum on Employment of the Mentally Retarded, September 13, 1963," APP.

116. Ibid. See Lyndon B. Johnson, "Statement by the President on Federal Employment of Mentally Retarded Persons, March 28, 1965," APP.

117. U.S. Department of Labor, "Employment Rights: Who Has Them and Who Enforces Them" (www.dol.gov/odep/pubs/fact/rights.htm).

118. Equal Employment Opportunity Commission, "The Rehabilitation Act of 1973" (www.eeoc.gov/laws/statutes/rehab.cfm).

119. George H. W. Bush, "Memorandum on Access for People with Disabilities to Federal Programs and Employment, July 26, 1991," APP.

120. William J. Clinton, "Executive Order 13078: Increasing Employment of Adults with Disabilities, March 13, 1998," APP.

121. William J. Clinton, "Memorandum on Hiring People with Disabilities in the Federal Government, October 16, 1999," APP.

122. William J. Clinton, "Executive Order 13163: Increasing the Opportunity for Individuals with Disabilities to be Employed in the Federal Government, July 26, 2000," APP.

123. William J. Clinton, "Executive Order 13164: Requiring Federal Agencies to Establish Procedures To Facilitate the Provision of Reasonable Accommodation, July 26, 2000," APP.

124. William J. Clinton, "Executive Order 13124: Amending the Civil Service Rules Relating to Federal Employees with Psychiatric Disabilities, June 4, 1999," APP.

125. For more information on definitions of disability, see U.S. Equal Employment Opportunity Commission, "Disability Discrimination" (www.eeoc .gov/laws/types/disability.cfm).

126. Johnson (2004).

127. Harry S. Truman, "Executive Order 9835: Prescribing Procedures for the Administration of an Employees Loyalty Program in the Executive Branch of the Government, March 21, 1947," APP.

128. Ibid.

129. Johnson (2004); Goldstein (2006).

130. Miller (2008).

131. U.S. Merit Systems Protection Board (2014a).

132. Ibid.

133. Truman, "Executive Order 9835"; Johnson (2004).

134. Harry S. Truman, "Executive Order 10001: Prescribing or Amending Portions of the Selective Service Regulations and Directing the Selection of Persons for Induction into the Armed Forces and Their Induction, September 17, 1948," APP.

135. Harry S. Truman, "Executive Order 10241: Amending Executive Order No. 9835 Entitled 'Prescribing Procedures for the Administration of an Employees Loyalty Program in the Executive Branch of the Government,' April 28, 1951," APP.

136. Johnson (2004).

137. Truman, "Executive Order 9835."

138. Dwight D. Eisenhower, "Executive Order 10450: Security Requirements for Government Employment, April 27, 1953," APP.

139. U.S. Merit Systems Protection Board (2014b).

140. Dwight D. Eisenhower, "Executive Order 10450."

141. Ibid., p. 12. Employees began challenging these rules in federal court, and in 1969, the United States Court of Appeals for the District of Columbia Circuit ruled in *Norton v. Macy* that homosexuality could not be automatic grounds for dismissal.

142. Johnson (2004).

143. U.S. Merit Systems Protection Board (2014b). The CSC stated that the new rules were a change from past practice and had resulted from court decisions requiring that persons not be disqualified from federal employment solely because of their homosexual conduct. The new civil service rules established standards for evaluating sexual conduct regardless of whether it was heterosexual or homosexual in nature. Although applicants could no longer "be found unsuitable based on unsubstantiated conclusions concerning possible embarrassment for the federal service, a person may be dismissed or found unsuitable where the evidence exists that sexual conduct affects job fitness."

144. Ibid. PPPs are specific practices that conflict with merit systems principles.

145. Ibid., p. 19. Whereas the Subcommittee on Investigations had previously concluded that it was a "false premise that what a Government employee did outside of the office on his own time, particularly if his actions did not involve his fellow employees or his work, was his own business," the OPM rejected that conclusion and interpreted the PPPs as barring discrimination on the basis of sexual orientation.

146. Ibid., p. 20. The tenth PPP prohibits discrimination based on personal conduct that is not job related. See U.S. Merit Systems Protection Board (2010).

147. Ibid.

148. William J. Clinton, "Executive Order 12968: Access to Classified Information, August 2, 1995," APP.

149. Josh Hicks, "How Many Federal Workers Identify as LGBT?" *Washington Post,* March 27, 2013.

150. William J. Clinton, "Executive Order 13087: Further Amendment to Executive Order 11478, Equal Employment Opportunity in the Federal Government, May 28, 1998," APP; Blumenthal (2003).

151. Blumenthal (2003).

152. Ibid.

153. Neumark (2001).

154. John F. Kennedy, "Memorandum on Utilization of Older Workers in the Federal Service, March 14, 1963," APP.

155. Lyndon B. Johnson, "Executive Order 11141: Declaring a Public Policy against Discrimination on the Basis of Age, February 12, 1964," APP.

156. Richard M. Nixon, "Memorandum about Age Discrimination in Federal Employment, September 13, 1972," APP.

157. William J. Clinton, "Statement on Proposed Parental Antidiscrimination Legislation, November 11, 1999," APP; Christopher Dodd, speaking on S. 1907, November 10, 1999, 106th Cong., 1st sess., *Congressional Record* 145, pt. 20: 29451.

158. "White House Background Briefing on Genetic Discrimination Executive Order (1/2)," *U.S. Newswire,* February 8, 2000.

159. William J. Clinton, "Remarks on Signing an Executive Order to Prohibit Discrimination in Federal Employment Based on Genetic Information, February 8, 2000," APP.

160. William J. Clinton, "Executive Order 13087: Further Amendment to Executive Order 11478, Equal Employment Opportunity in the Federal Government, May 28, 1998," APP; William J. Clinton, "Executive Order 13152: Further Amendment to Executive Order 11478, Equal Employment Opportunity in Federal Government, May 2, 2000," APP.

161. Gregory (2001).

162. Naff and Riccucci (2008); Sargeant (2011); Richard Nixon, "298: Memorandum about Age Discrimination in Federal Employment, September 13, 1972," APP.

163. Ronald Reagan, "Statement on Signing the Age Discrimination in Employment Amendments of 1986, November 1, 1986," APP.

164. John Berry and Jacqueline Berrien, "Joint Memorandum on Equal Pay in the Federal Government," Equal Employment Opportunity Commission (www .eeoc.gov/federal/memo_epa.cfm); Equal Employment Opportunity Commission, "Facts About Equal Pay and Compensation Discrimination" (www.eeoc .gov/eeoc/publications/fs-epa.cfm).

165. Richard Nixon, "Executive Order 11478: Equal Employment Opportunity in the Federal Government, August 8, 1969," APP.

166. Quinn, de Paor, and Blanck (2014); Clinton, "Executive Order 13145."

167. Quinn, de Paor, and Blanck (2014, p. 19).

168. U.S. Merit Systems Protection Board (2014a).

CHAPTER SIX

1. Gregory Korte, "Obama Issues 'Executive Orders by Another Name,'" *USA Today,* December 17, 2014. Lowande (2014).

2. Justin Sink, "Obama: US Must 'Strengthen Unions,'" *The Hill,* June 17, 2014.

3. Joe Davidson, "Federal Diary," *Washington Post,* August 12, 2009.

4. U.S. Federal Labor Relations Authority, "50th Anniversary: Executive Order 10988," January 17, 2012 (www.flra.gov/50th_Anniversary_EO10988).

5. Barack Obama, "Executive Order 13522: Creating Labor-Management Forums to Improve Delivery of Government Services, December 9, 2009," American Presidency Project (henceforth cited as APP). Obama continued the existence of the National Council on Federal Labor-Management Relations until September 2013, until September 2015, and until September 2017. See National Council on Labor-Management Relations, "About the Council," 2016 (www.lmrcouncil.gov/about/index.aspx); Joe Davidson, "Federal Diary," *Washington Post,* August 12, 2009; White House, Office of the Press Secretary, "President Obama Announces Members of the National Council on Federal Labor-Management Relations," July 15, 2014 (www.whitehouse.gov/the-press -office/2014/07/15/president-obama-announces-members-national-council -federal-labor-managem).

6. National Council on Federal Labor-Management Relations, "Agency Implementation Plans" (www.lmrcouncil.gov/plans/index.aspx).

7. Barack Obama, "Memorandum on Pay Freeze, January 21, 2009," APP.

8. Obama's memorandum did not affect payments or salary adjustments for federal civilian employees who were not political appointees. See Barack Obama, "Memorandum on the Freeze on Discretionary Awards, Bonuses, and Similar Payments for Federal Political Appointees, August 3, 2010," APP.

9. Barack Obama, "Memorandum on Freezing Federal Employee Pay Schedules and Rates That Are Set by Administrative Discretion, December 22, 2010," APP; Scott Wilson, "Obama Orders Freeze on Bonuses, Monetary Rewards for Federal Political Appointees," *Washington Post,* August 4, 2010; Lisa Rein, "Federal Workers Becoming a Flash Point in Midterm Elections," *Washington Post,* September 25, 2010. Obama's memo applied to all civilian employees of the federal government, including those in various alternative pay plans and those working at the Department of Defense. See White House, Office of the Press Secretary, "Fact Sheet: Cutting the Deficit by Freezing Federal Employee Pay," November 29, 2010 (www.whitehouse.gov/the-press-office/2010/11/29/fact-sheet-cutting-deficit-freezing-federal-employee-pay); Obama, "Memorandum on Freezing Federal Employee Pay Schedules."

10. U.S. Office of Personnel Management, "Senior Executive Service—Compensation" (www.opm.gov/policy-data-oversight/senior-executive-service/compensation/); Eric Yoder, "No Raise for You, Guidance Reminds Appointees," *Washington Post,* December 23, 2014; Ian Smith, "House Committee Fires Off Letters Demanding Data on Federal Employees' Use of 'Official Time,'" *FedSmith.com,* February 16, 2016 (http://blogs.fedsmith.com/2015/12/22/pay-freeze-continues-for-vice-president-and-other-senior-officials/).

11. U.S. Office of Personnel Management, "Senior Executive Service Overview & History" (www.opm.gov/policy-data-oversight/senior-executive-service/overview-history/).

12. U.S. Office of Personnel Management, "Senior Executive Service: Leading America's Workforce" (www.opm.gov/policy-data-oversight/senior-executive-service/).

13. The new cap—equal to the average agency percentage spent in 2010 before the White House and OPM lowered the cap in 2010—is equal to the average federal agency percentage spent in 2010 before it was lowered.

14. Barack Obama, "Executive Order 13714: Strengthening the Senior Executive Service, December 15, 2015," APP; Joe Davidson, "Obama Adds Muscle to Plan for Senior Feds' Pay Raise as Administration Honors Workforce," *Washington Post,* December 15, 2015; Joe Davidson, "White House Eyes Better Pay for Top Civil Servants," *Washington Post,* November 29, 2015; Charles S. Clark, "Obama Increases SES Performance Award Spending Cap," *Government Executive,* December 15, 2015.

15. Barack Obama, "Memorandum on the Presidential POWER Initiative: Protecting Our Workers and Ensuring Reemployment, July 19, 2010," APP.

16. Barack Obama, "Executive Order 13548: Increasing Federal Employment of Individuals with Disabilities, July 26, 2010," APP; Szymendera (2013).

17. Maxwell and others (2013); U.S. Department of Labor, "Best Practices in Return to Work for Federal Employees Who Sustain Workplace Injury or Illness: A Guide for Agencies," 2013 (www.dol.gov/owcp/dfec/power/Best _Practices_FECA_Return_to_Work.pdf). Three years later, in 2013, Obama's budget proposal included cuts to workers' compensation benefits under FECA, but these changes were not well received by congressional Democrats, labor leaders, and many other groups, and these specific cuts did not pass. Obama tried again in 2015 and proposed changes to FECA, including a major cut in his budget for federal employees' workers' compensation benefits. See Louis C. LaBrecque, "Public Sector Roundup: Obama Plan for Modifying Federal Employees' Compensation Act Benefits Aired at Hearing," Bloomberg, *Labor and Employment Blog,* July 17, 2013 (www.bna.com/public-sector-roundup -b17179875234/); Joe Davidson, "Obama Administration Clashes with Friends over Workers' Comp," *Washington Post,* May 31, 2015; "Administration Details Its Proposed FECA Reforms," *FEDweek,* May 27, 2015 (www.fedweek .com/issue-briefs/administration-details-its-proposed-feca-reforms/).

18. Chase (2014); Katie Stanton, "The Distracted Driving Summit Begins," October 1, 2009 (www.whitehouse.gov/blog/2009/10/01/distracted-driving -summit-begins).

19. Barack Obama, "Executive Order 13513: Federal Leadership on Reducing Text Messaging While Driving, October 1, 2009," APP; Ashley Halsey III, "Obama Bans Federal Employees from Texting While Driving," *Washington Post,* October 2, 2009.

20. See Obama, "Executive Order 13513"; U.S. Department of Transportation, "Distracted Driving Campaign," January 31, 2013 (www.transportation .gov/mission/performance/distracted-driving-campaign); Chase (2014).

21. Barack Obama, "Memorandum Establishing Policies for Addressing Domestic Violence in the Federal Workforce, April 18, 2012," APP.

22. U.S. Office of Personnel Management, "Guidance for Agency-Specific Domestic Violence, Sexual Assault, and Stalking Policies," February 2013 (www.opm.gov/policy-data-oversight/worklife/reference-materials/guidance -for-agency-specific-dvsas-policies.pdf).

23. Jeffrey M. Jones, "Gender Gap in 2012 Vote Is Largest in Gallup's History," *Gallup,* November 9, 2012 (www.gallup.com/poll/158588/gender-gap -2012-vote-largest-gallup-history.aspx).

24. Congress expanded the time period for filing complaints of employment discrimination concerning compensation. The Equal Pay Act prohibited gender-based wage discrimination between men and women in the same establishment who perform jobs that require substantially equal skill, effort, and responsibility under similar working conditions. See Peter Baker, "Obama Signs Measures

to Help Close Gender Gap in Pay," *New York Times*, April 8, 2014; Sheryl Gay Stolberg, "Obama Signs Equal-Pay Legislation," *New York Times*, January 29, 2009; "National Equal Pay Enforcement Task Force" (www.whitehouse.gov /sites/default/files/rss_viewer/equal_pay_task_force.pdf). Barack Obama, "Memorandum on Advancing Pay Equality in the Federal Government and Learning from Successful Practices, May 10, 2013," APP.

25. U.S. Office of Personnel Management, "Governmentwide Strategy on Advancing Pay Equality in the Federal Government," April 2014 (www.opm .gov/policy-data-oversight/pay-leave/reference-materials/reports/governmentwide -strategy-on-advancing-pay-equality-in-the-federal-government.pdf).

26. White House, "Obama Administration Initiatives to Help Americans Meet Work and Family Responsibilities" (www.whitehouse.gov/sites/default /files/rss_viewer/Work-Family-fact-sheet.pdf). This view was bolstered by the Council of Economic Advisors, which released a report on the economic value of workplace flexibility. See "Work-Life Balance and the Economics of Workplace Flexibility," March 2010 (www.whitehouse.gov/files/documents/100331 -cea-economics-workplace-flexibility.pdf).

27. Barack Obama, "Remarks at the Closing Session of the Workplace Flexibility Forum, March 31, 2010," APP.

28. Barack Obama, "Memorandum on Enhancing Workplace Flexibilities and Work-Life Programs, June 23, 2014," APP; Council of Economic Advisors, "Work-Life Balance and the Economics of Workplace Flexibility"; White House, Office of the Press Secretary, "President and First Lady Host White House Forum on Workplace Flexibility," *WhiteHouse.gov*, March 31, 2010 (www.whitehouse.gov/the-press-office/president-and-first-lady-host-white -house-forum-workplace-flexibility); Alyssa Rosenberg, "OPM Will Test New Work Flexibility Program," *Government Executive*, March 31, 2010 (www .govexec.com/pay-benefits/2010/03/opm-will-test-new-work-flexibility -program/31199/).

29. Barack Obama, "Memorandum on an Emergency Leave Transfer Program for Federal Employees Adversely Affected by Hurricane Sandy, November 9, 2012," APP; Barack Obama, "Memorandum on Emergency Leave Transfer Program for Federal Employees Adversely Affected by Severe Storms and Tornadoes in Oklahoma, June 3, 2013," APP.

30. Executive Office of the President, Council of Economic Advisors, "The Economics of Paid and Unpaid Leave," 2014 (www.whitehouse.gov/sites /default/files/docs/leave_report_final.pdf); Obama's proposal would provide federal employees with six weeks of paid administrative leave for the birth, adoption, or foster placement of a child. In addition, the reform would allow parents to use sick days to care for a healthy child following either an adoption or a birth mother's period of incapacitation. See White House, Office of the Press Secretary, "Fact Sheet: White House Unveils New Steps to Strengthen

Working Families across America," January 14, 2015 (www.whitehouse.gov/the
-press-office/2015/01/14/fact-sheet-white-house-unveils-new-steps-strengthen
-working-families-acr).

31. Eric Yoder, "Democrat Bill Would Give Federal Workers Paid Parental
Leave," *Washington Post,* January 26, 2015.

32. White House, Office of the Press Secretary, "Presidential Memorandum—
Modernizing Federal Leave Policies for Childbirth, Adoption and Foster Care
to Recruit and Retain Talent and Improve Productivity," January 15, 2015
(www.whitehouse.gov/the-press-office/2015/01/15/presidential-memorandum
-modernizing-federal-leave-policies-childbirth-ad).

33. Rebecca J. Rosen, "Netflix's New Parental-Leave Policy: 'Just About
Ideal,'" *The Atlantic,* August 5, 2015; Heather Kelly, "Microsoft Bumps Up Its
Parental Leave Benefits," *CNN Money,* August 6, 2015 (http://money.cnn
.com/2015/08/05/technology/microsoft-maternity-leave/).

34. Adam Nagourney, "Obama Elected President as Racial Barrier Falls,"
New York Times, November 4, 2008.

35. Barack Obama, "Executive Order 13583: Establishing a Coordinated
Government-Wide Initiative to Promote Diversity and Inclusion in the Federal
Workforce, August 18, 2011," APP. Latinos constituted only 4.1 percent of
employees at senior pay levels in fiscal 2010; African Americans, 6.7 percent;
and women, 31.2 percent. See Joe Davidson, "Workplace Diversity Order Is
Just the First Step in Effort," *Washington Post,* August 22, 2011.

36. Obama, "Executive Order 13583."

37. White House, Office of the Press Secretary, "Fact Sheet: Presidential
Memorandum Supporting Veterans' Employment and Reemployment across the
Federal Workforce," July 19, 2012 (www.whitehouse.gov/the-press-office
/2012/07/19/fact-sheet-presidential-memorandum-supporting-veterans
-employment-and-re); White House, Office of the Press Secretary, "President
Obama's Plan to Put Veterans Back to Work," February 3, 2012 (www.whitehouse
.gov/the-press-office/2012/02/03/president-obama-s-plan-put-veterans-back
-work).

38. Steve Vogel, "Returning Military Members Allege Job Discrimination—By
Federal Government," *Washington Post,* February 19, 2012.

39. U.S. Department of Labor, "e-Laws: USERRA Advisor: Overview of
USERRA" (http://webapps.dol.gov/elaws/vets/userra/userra.asp). Obama directed OPM to develop a federal-government-wide Veterans Recruitment and
Employment Strategic Plan every three years to address barriers to the employment of veterans in the executive branch. See Barack Obama, "Executive Order
13518: Employment of Veterans in the Federal Government, November 9,
2009," APP.

40. Joe Davidson, "Veterans Praise Obama Executive Order on Hiring Veterans," *Washington Post,* November 11, 2009; Barack Obama, "Memoran-

dum on Uniformed Services Employment and Reemployment Rights Act Protections, July 19, 2012," APP; White House, Office of the Press Secretary, "President Obama Calls on Congress to Act on Veterans Job Corps in 'To Do List' and Launches New Military Credentialing Initiative to Fill Workforce Needs," May 31, 2012 (www.whitehouse.gov/the-press-office/2012/05/31 /president-obama-calls-congress-act-veterans-job-corps-do-list-and-launch); Executive Office of the President, "Military Skills for America's Future: Leveraging Military Service and Experience to Put Veterans and Military Spouses Back to Work," May 31, 2012 (www.whitehouse.gov/sites/default/files/docs /veterans_report_5-31-2012.pdf); Executive Office of the President, "The Fast Track to Civilian Employment: Streamlining Credentialing and Licensing for Service Members, Veterans, and Their Spouses," February 2013 (www .whitehouse.gov/sites/default/files/docs/military_credentialing_and_licensing _report_2-24-2013_final.pdf); U.S. Army Training and Doctrine Command Public Affairs, "Military Credentialing Initiatives a Top Priority for TRA-DOC," U.S. Army website, September 21, 2012 (www.army.mil/mobile/article /?p=87767).

41. Barack Obama, "Memorandum on Uniformed Services Employment and Reemployment Rights Act Protections, July 19, 2012," APP. Obama expanded upon his earlier executive order for federal agencies to take steps to enhance recruitment of and promote employment opportunities for veterans within the executive branch. See Obama, "Executive Order 13518"; Ed O'Keefe, "Obama Signs Order on Veterans Employment," *Washington Post,* November 9, 2009; Joe Davidson, "Federal Diary: Veterans Praise Obama Executive Order on Hiring Veterans," *Washington Post,* November 11, 2009.

42. William J. Clinton, "Executive Order 13163: Increasing the Opportunity for Individuals with Disabilities to Be Employed in the Federal Government, July 26, 2000," APP. In 2010, individuals with disabilities represented less than 5 percent of the 2.5 million people in the federal workforce, even though they represented 19 percent of the overall population. See Barack Obama, "Executive Order 13548: Increasing Federal Employment of Individuals with Disabilities, July 26, 2010," APP.

43. Obama, "Executive Order 13548."

44. See Hilda L. Solis and John Berry, "Memorandum for Heads of Executive Departments and Agencies: Increasing the Federal Employment of People with Disabilities—Resources for Implementing Executive Order 13548," U.S. Department of Labor, January 12, 2012 (www.dol.gov/odep/wrp/DOLOPM .pdf); U.S. Office of Personnel Management, "Disability Employment Reference Materials: Federal Agencies" (www.opm.gov/policy-data-oversight/disability -employment/reference-materials/). Targeted disabilities included blindness, deafness, partial and full paralysis, missing extremities, dwarfism, epilepsy, intellectual disabilities, and psychiatric disabilities.

45. Barack Obama, "Memorandum on Enhancing Safeguards to Prevent the Undue Denial of Federal Employment Opportunities to the Unemployed and Those Facing Financial Difficulty through No Fault of Their Own, January 31, 2014," APP; White House, Office of the Press Secretary, "Fact Sheet: Getting Long-Term Unemployed Americans Back to Work," October 15, 2014 (www .whitehouse.gov/the-press-office/2014/10/15/fact-sheet-getting-long-term -unemployed-americans-back-work); Gene Sperling and Valerie Jarrett, "Helping the Long-Term Unemployed Get Back to Work," February 10, 2014 (www .whitehouse.gov/blog/2014/02/10/helping-long-term-unemployed-get-back -work); Roger Runningen and Mike Dorning, "CEOs Pledge Help to White House for Long-Term Unemployed," *Bloomberg Business,* January 31, 2014 (www.bloomberg.com/news/articles/2014-01-31/ceos-pledge-help-to-white -house-for-long-term-unemployed); Sperling and Jarrett, "Helping the Long-Term Unemployed."

46. Barack Obama, "Executive Order 13562: Recruiting and Hiring Students and Recent Graduates, December 27, 2010," APP.

47. Martin Longman, "Obama Created the Pathway Programs for Applicants without Prior Work Experience," *Washington Monthly,* September 8, 2014; U.S. Office of Personnel Management, "Hiring Authorities: Students & Recent Graduates," 2012 (www.opm.gov/policy-data-oversight/hiring-authorities /students-recent-graduates/).

48. When the Defense of Marriage Act was passed, a House report stated that a primary goal was to "preserve scarce government resources." See Ginsberg and Topoleski (2013).

49. Brad Knickerbocker, "Is Obama the 'First Gay President' as *Newsweek* Proclaims?," *Christian Science Monitor,* May 13, 2012; Emma Margolin, "The Political Perks of Being 'The First Gay President,'" *MSNBC,* July 6, 2014 (www.msnbc.com/msnbc/the-political-perks-being-the-first-gay-president).

50. "111th Congress (2009–2010); Statement of John Berry, Director U.S. Management, Before the Subcommittee on Federal Workforce, Postal Service and the District of Columbia Committee on Oversight and Government Reform, U.S. House of Representatives, on H.R. 2517, The 'Domestic Partnership Benefits and Obligations Act of 2009,'" July 8, 2009 (www.opm.gov/news /testimony/111th-congress/hr-2517-the-domestic-partnership-benefits-and -obligations-act-of-2009/).

51. Barack Obama, "Memorandum on Federal Benefits and Non-Discrimination, June 17, 2009," APP; Barack Obama, "Statement on Signing a Memorandum on Federal Benefits and Non-Discrimination and Support of Domestic Partners Benefits and Obligations Legislation"; Barack Obama, "Remarks on Signing a Memorandum on Federal Benefits and Non-Discrimination, June 17, 2009," APP.

52. See John Berry, "Federal Benefits for Same-Sex Domestic Partner," Memorandum for Heads of Executive Departments and Agencies, Chief Human Capital Officers Council website, July 10, 2009 (www.chcoc.gov/content/federal-benefits-same-sex-domestic-partner).

53. Barack Obama, "Memorandum on Extension of Benefits to Same-Sex Domestic Partners of Federal Employees, June 2, 2010," APP. Same-sex partners were ineligible for health insurance benefits under the Federal Employee Health Benefit Program, and they could not be listed as beneficiaries for compensation if their partners were injured or disabled while performing their jobs. However, for certain federal employee benefits, the term "spouse" was either not found in the benefit's authorizing language, or the authorizing language widened the scope of eligibility. See Ginsberg and Topoleski (2013); U.S. Office of Personnel Management, "Office of Personnel Management Plan for Retrospective Analysis of Existing Rules," August 22, 2011 (www.whitehouse.gov/sites/default/files/other/2011-regulatory-action-plans/officeofpersonnelmanag ementregulatoryreformplanaugust2011.pdf).

54. U.S. Department of Defense, "Memorandum for Secretaries of the Military Departments Acting Under Secretary of Defense for Personnel and Readiness, Subject: Extending Benefits to Same-Sex Domestic Partners of Military Members," February 11, 2013 (http://archive.defense.gov/news/Same-SexBenefitsMemo.pdf); U.S. Department of Defense, "Memorandum: Changes to Department of Defense Issuances Regarding Benefits to Same-Sex Domestic Partners of Military Members," April 11, 2013 (http://militarypartners.org/wp-content/uploads/2009/12/Changes-to-DoD-Regulations.pdf).

55. See Amelia Gruber, "Personnel Agency Opens Long-Term Care to Same-Sex Partners," *Government Executive,* June 1, 2010 (www.govexec.com/pay-benefits/2010/06/personnel-agency-opens-long-term-care-to-same-sex-partners/31638/); U.S. Office of Personnel Management, "Federal Long Term Care Insurance Program Eligibility Changes: A Proposed Rule," *Federal Register,* November 13, 2014 (www.federalregister.gov/articles/2014/11/13/2014-26779/federal-long-term-care-insurance-program-eligibility-changes); "OPM Rule Would Expand FLTCIP Eligibility," *Federal Soup,* November 18, 2014 (http://federalsoup.com/articles/2014/11/18/opm-expands-fltcip-eligibility.aspx).

56. *United States v. Windsor,* 570 U.S. 133 S. Ct. 2675; 186 L.Ed.2d 808.

57. Barack Obama, "Statement on the United States Supreme Court Ruling on the Defense of Marriage Act, June 26, 2013," APP; U.S. Office of Personnel Management, "Statement by Acting Director Elaine Kaplan on the Supreme Court Decision in *United States v. Windsor*," press release, June 26, 2013 (www.opm.gov/news/releases/2013/06/statement-by-acting-director-elaine-kaplan-on-the-supreme-court-decision-in-united-states-v-windsor/); Eric Holder,

"Memorandum to the President: Implementation of *United States v. Windsor*," Department of Justice, Office of the Attorney General, June 20, 2014 (www .justice.gov/iso/opa/resources/972201462010393094785.pdf). The attorney general's memo summarized the OPM's additional efforts to implement *United States v. Windsor*.

58. Michael D. Shear, "Obama Extends Marriage Benefits to Gay Couples," *New York Times,* June 20, 2014.

59. Jennifer Bendery, "Obama Signs Executive Order on LGBT Job Discrimination," *Huffington Post,* July 21, 2014 (www.huffingtonpost.com/2014 /07/21/obama-gay-rights_n_5605482.html?).

60. Gautam Raghavan, "What Is the Employment Non-Discrimination Act? (ENDA)," November 6, 2013 (www.whitehouse.gov/blog/2013/11/06 /what-employment-non-discrimination-act-enda); Valerie Jarrett, "President Obama Speaks Out in Support of ENDA," November 4, 2013 (www.whitehouse .gov/blog/2013/11/04/president-obama-speaks-out-support-enda).

61. The White House, "Presidential Appointment Application; Apply for Presidential Appointments with the Obama Administration" (https://apply.white house.gov/content/getting-started).

62. William J. Clinton, "Statement on Signing an Executive Order on Equal Employment Opportunity in the Federal Government, May 28, 1998," APP; Barack Obama, "Executive Order 13672: Further Amendments to Executive Order 11478, Equal Employment Opportunity in the Federal Government, and Executive Order 11246, Equal Employment Opportunity, July 21, 2014," APP; Christopher Ingraham, "Obama's LGBT Order Is Both Narrower and More Sweeping Than the Employee Non-Discrimination Act," *Washington Post,* July 21, 2014.

63. Barack Obama, "Remarks on Signing an Executive Order on Lesbian, Gay, Bisexual, and Transgender Employment Discrimination, July 21, 2014," APP. According to guidelines released by the OPM, "Gender identity means one's inner sense of one's own gender, which may or may not match the sex assigned at birth." See U.S. Office of Personnel Management, "Addressing Sexual Orientation and Gender Identity Discrimination in Federal Civilian Employment: A Guide to Employment Rights, Protections, and Responsibilities," June 2015 (www.opm.gov/policy-data-oversight/diversity-and-inclusion/reference -materials/addressing-sexual-orientation-and-gender-identity-discrimination -in-federal-civilian-employment.pdf); Juliet Eilperin, "Obama's Quiet Transgender Revolution," *Washington Post,* December 1, 2015.

64. Katherine Archuleta, "Celebrating Every Member of Our Federal Family," U.S. Office of Personnel Management, *Director's Blog,* June 3, 2015 (www.opm.gov/blogs/Director/2015/6/3/Celebrating-Every-Member-of-our -Federal-Family). See also Equal Employment Opportunity Commission, "Agencies Release Guide on LGBT Discrimination Protections for Federal Workers,"

press release, June 3, 2015 (www.eeoc.gov/eeoc/newsroom/release/6-3-15.cfm); U.S. Office of Personnel Management, "Addressing Sexual Orientation and Gender Identity Discrimination in Federal Civilian Employment" (www.opm .gov/policy-data-oversight/diversity-and-inclusion/reference-materials /addressing-sexual-orientation-and-gender-identity-discrimination-in-federal -civilian-employment.pdf).

65. Human Rights Campaign, "U.S. Federal Government Employment Policies" (www.hrc.org/resources/u.s.-federal-government-employment-policies).

66. Andrew Sullivan, "Andrew Sullivan on Barack Obama's Gay Marriage Evolution," *Newsweek*, May 13, 2012. Obama identified a number of motivations for issuing the memoranda: he wanted to help "achiev[e] equality" for "LGBT Americans," and believed that "sound economic policy" would attract top talent to the federal workforce, since many private sector employers had already extended such benefits. See Barack Obama, "Statement on Signing a Memorandum on Federal Benefits and Non-Discrimination and Support of Domestic Partners Benefits and Obligations Legislation, June 17, 2009," APP.

67. Peter Overby, "Explainer: What Is a Bundler," September 14, 2007 (www.npr.org/templates/story/story.php?storyId=14434721).

68. Margolin, "The Political Perks of Being 'The First Gay President.'"

69. Congress, under the Consolidated Appropriations Act, continued the freeze on pay for the vice president and certain senior political appointees. See Beth F. Cobert, "January 2016 Pay Adjustments," December 18, 2015 (www .chcoc.gov/content/january-2016-pay-adjustments-0); U.S. Office of Personnel Management, "Pay & Leave Salaries & Wages" (www.opm.gov/policy-data -oversight/pay-leave/salaries-wages/#url=2016). Congress approved the pay freeze in 2012 and 2013. Statutory pay adjustments for all executive branch pay schedules were frozen for a two-year period. Congress also prohibited agencies from providing any base salary increases at all to senior executives or senior-level employees, including performance-based increases. See Chief Human Capital Officers Council, "Continued Freeze on Pay Adjustments for Federal Civilian Employees," April 5, 2013 (www.chcoc.gov/content/continued-freeze -pay-adjustments-federal-civilian-employees).

70. The 1994 Violence Against Women Act had expired in 2011, and Congress did not pass the Violence Against Women Reauthorization Act until 2013. Republicans opposed provisions that made federal grants available to organizations combating domestic violence contingent on nondiscrimination against gay, lesbian, and transgender victims; rules extending the authority of tribal courts over domestic violence matters; and the provision of more visas for abused undocumented women who agree to cooperate with law enforcement. Under the renewed legislation, Congress did expand federal protections to gay, lesbian, transgender, Native American, and immigrant individuals. See Kate Pickert, "What's Wrong with the Violence Against Women Act?" *Time*, February 27, 2013.

CHAPTER SEVEN

1. United States Office of Government Ethics, "Political Appointees," February 26, 2016 (www2.oge.gov/Web/oge.nsf/Resources/Political+Appointees).

2. MacKenzie and Hafken (2002); Gilman (1995).

3. White House, "Presidential Department Descriptions" (www.whitehouse .gov/participate/internships/departments).

4. Roberts (1988).

5. Under this rule, federal employees had to wait two years before serving as an "attorney or agent" in prosecuting claims related to their former depart-ment. See Cooper (2012).

6. See Handlin (2014); Cooper (2012); Stathis (2003); MacKenzie and Hafken (2002).

7. See MacKenzie and Hafken (2002).

8. Straus (2011a); Handlin (2014); Donald G. Schweitzer, "Government Ethical Standards Are Toothless, Unenforced," *Truthout,* December 8, 2012 (www.truth-out.org/opinion/item/13169-government-ethical-standards-are -toothless-unenforced).

9. MacKenzie and Hafken (2002); Gilman (1995).

10. Cooper (2012); Amos Kendall, "Duties of Public Officers: The Rules of Conduct for Federal Employees," Illinois Institute of Technology, Ethics Codes Collection, "Duties of Public Officers (1829)" (http://ethics-t.iit.edu/ecodes /node/4164).

11. Roberts (1988).

12. MacKenzie and Hafken (2002). In the Eighty-Second Congress (1951– 52), hearings were held on a proposal to create a Commission on Ethics in Gov-ernment. See Straus (2013); Douglas (1952).

13. Roberts (1988); Harry S. Truman, "Special Message to the Congress Recommending Conflict-of-Interest Legislation, September 27, 1951," Ameri-can Presidency Project (henceforth cited as APP); Straus (2011a).

14. MacKenzie and Hafken (2002).

15. Ibid.

16. Robert J. Garrity Jr., "Testimony before House of Representatives Committee on Government Reform: The FBI's Visa Name Check Pro-cess," July 10, 2003 (www.fbi.gov/news/testimony/the-fbis-visa-name-check -process).

17. John F. Kennedy, "Special Message to the Congress on Conflict-of-Interest Legislation and on Problems of Ethics in Government, April 27, 1961," APP; John F. Kennedy, "Memorandum on Conflicts of Interest and Ethical Standards of Conduct of Government Employees, January 22, 1963," APP.

18. John F. Kennedy, "Executive Order 10939: To Provide a Guide on Ethical Standards to Government Officials, May 5, 1961," APP. The order applied to all heads and assistant heads of agencies, full-time members of boards and commissions appointed by the president, and members of the White House staff.

19. John F. Kennedy, "Memorandum on Preventing Conflicts of Interest on the Part of Special Government Employees," *Federal Register*, May 7, 1962. Kennedy required each agency "to review its regulations covering conflicts of interest and ethical conduct to ensure that they are consistent with the new law." See John F. Kennedy, "Memorandum on Conflicts of Interest and Ethical Standards of Conduct of Government Employees, January 22, 1963," APP; John F. Kennedy, "Memorandum on Preventing Conflicts of Interest on the Part of Special Government Employees, May 2, 1963," *Archives.gov* (www .archives.gov/federal-register/codification/executive-order/11222.html); Steven G. Bradbury, "Days of Service by Special Government Employees," January 26, 2007 (www.justice.gov/sites/default/files/olc/opinions/attachments/2015/05/29 /op-olc-v031-p0013.pdf).

20. "House Revises Conflict-of-Interest Laws," *CQ Almanac 1961* (http:// library.cqpress.com.libproxy.lib.unc.edu/cqalmanac/cqal61-1373531); John F. Kennedy, "Memorandum on Conflicts of Interest"; Gilman (1995); Morgan (1980); "House Revises Conflict-of-Interest Laws"; Lyndon B. Johnson, "Executive Order 11222: Prescribing Standards of Ethical Conduct for Government Officers and Employees, May 8, 1965," APP; Scott H. Amey, "The Politics of Contracting," Project on Government Oversight, June 29, 2004 (www.pogo.org /our-work/reports/2004/gc-rd-20040629.html); Office of Government Ethics, "Special Government Employees," 2015 (www.oge.gov/Topics/Selected-Employee -Categories/Special-Government-Employees/).

21. Lyndon B. Johnson, "Executive Order 11222: Prescribing Standards of Ethical Conduct for Government Officers and Employees, May 8, 1965," APP.

22. Richard Nixon, "Executive Order 11570: Providing for the Regulation of Conduct for the Postal Rate Commission and its Employees, November 24, 1970," APP; Richard Nixon, "Executive Order 11590: Applicability of Executive Order No. 11222 and Executive Order 11478 to the United States Postal Service and of Executive Order No. 11478 to the Postal Rate Commission, April 23, 1971," APP.

23. MacKenzie and Hafken (2002); White House, Office of the Press Secretary, "Obama Announces Key Additions to the Office of the White House Counsel," January 28, 2009 (www.whitehouse.gov/the-press-office /obama-announces-key-additions-office-white-house-counsel); Bruce Ackerman, "Abolish the White House Counsel," *Slate*, April 22, 2009 (www.slate .com/articles/news_and_politics/jurisprudence/2009/04/abolish_the_white _house_counsel.html).

24. Roberts (1988).

25. Cooper (2012).

26. Jimmy Carter, "Report to the American People: Remarks from the White House Library, February 2, 1977," APP.

27. Ibid.

28. Jimmy Carter, "Conflict of Interest and Financial Guidelines Announcement of Two Exceptions Published by the Carter-Mondale Transition Group, with the President's Letters to the Two Nominees, February 9, 1977," APP.

29. Carter proposed an Ethics in Government Act calling for a three-part program of financial disclosure, the creation of an Office of Ethics in the Civil Service Commission, and stronger restrictions on post-employment activities of government officials. See Jimmy Carter, "Ethics in Government Message to the Congress, May 3, 1977," APP; U.S. Civil Service Commission (1977).

30. Jimmy Carter, "Ethics in Government Message to the Congress."

31. See Office of Government Ethics, "Legal Advisories" (www.oge.gov /OGE-Advisories/Legal-Advisories/Legal-Advisories/); Office of Government Ethics, "106th Congress, Testimony, Statement of Stephen D. Potts, Reauthorization of the Office of Government Ethics, August 4, 1999" (https://www2.oge .gov/Web/OGE.nsf/Resources/Statement+of+Stephen+D.+Potts,+Reauthorization +of+the+Office+of+Government+Ethics).

32. Gilman (1995).

33. *Code of Federal Regulations*, "Organization and Functions of the Office of Government Ethics," title 5, sec. 2600.

34. Jimmy Carter, "Ethics in Government Act of 1978, Remarks on Signing S. 555 Into Law, October 26, 1978," APP.

35. Ronald Reagan, "Executive Order 12565: Prescribing a Comprehensive System of Financial Reporting for Officers and Employees in the Executive Branch, September 25, 1986," APP. This system would complement the financial disclosure system established by the 1978 Ethics in Government Act.

36. Handlin (2014).

37. The congressional rationale supporting the OGE's independence was "to not only promote its visibility and heighten awareness of ethics but to also promote administrative efficiency." See U.S. Congress, House of Representatives, Committee on Government Reform, *The Reauthorization of the Office of Government Ethics: Hearing before the Subcommittee on the Federal Workforce and Agency Organization*, 109th Cong., 2nd sess., 2006 (www .gpo.gov/fdsys/pkg/CHRG-109hhrg32968/html/CHRG-109hhrg32968.htm). Over the years, the OGE's status has been reviewed and reauthorized by Congress. Congress clarified, but did not expand, the authority of the OGE to order corrective action by agencies and individuals. See "Government

Ethics Unit Reauthorized," *CQ Weekly,* October 22, 1988 (http://library
.cqpress.com/cqweekly/WR100404880); "Ethics Office Reauthorized," *CQ
Almanac 1998* (http://library.cqpress.com/cqalmanac/document.php?id=cqal88
-1140770).

38. James Gerstenzang, "Bush Appoints Panel on Federal Code of Ethics,"
Los Angeles Times, January 26, 1989.

39. George H. W. Bush, "Executive Order 12668: President's Commission
on Federal Ethics Law Reform, January 25, 1989," APP; Dana Priest, "Sud-
denly 'Being Taken Seriously' at Office of Government Ethics," *Washington
Post,* January 15, 1992; MacKenzie and Hafken (2002).

40. George H. W. Bush, "Executive Order 12674: Principles of Ethical
Conduct for Government Officers and Employees, April 12, 1989," APP.
Bush's orders replaced Johnson's EO 11222 (1965) and Reagan's EO 12565
(1986). See "Organization and Functions of the Office of Government Ethics,"
Code of Federal Regulations, Title V, 2003 (www.gpo.gov/fdsys/pkg/CFR
-2003-title5-vol3/xml/CFR-2003-title5-vol3-part2600.xml); George H. W.
Bush, "Executive Order 12731: Principles of Ethical Conduct for Government
Officers and Employees, October 17, 1990," APP. See also Office of Government Ethics, "5 C.F.R. Part 2635: Standards of Ethical Conduct for Employees
of the Executive Branch," 1992 (www.oge.gov/Laws-and-Regulations/OGE
-Regulations/5-C-F-R--Part-2635---Standards-of-ethical-conduct-for
-employees-of-the-executive-branch/); Office of Government Ethics, "14 General Principles: Principles of Ethical Conduct," 2003 (www.oge.gov/uploadedFiles
/Education/Education_Resources_for_Ethics_Officials/Resources/14_general
_principles_card.pdf).

41. In 1993 the OGE issued the Standards of Ethical Conduct for Employees of the Executive Branch, replacing the many individual agency standards of
conduct regulations with a uniform set of standards applicable to all employees
of the executive branch. See George H. W. Bush, "Statement on Executive
Branch Revised Standards of Conduct, August 6, 1992," APP.

42. George H. W. Bush, "Statement on Signing the Ethics Reform Act of
1989, November 30, 1989," APP.

43. Michael Wines, "Ethical Issues Facing the White House," *New York
Times,* November 3, 1996.

44. Douglas Jehl and Sara Fritz, "Clinton Team Issues Ethics Rules for Top
Appointees: Strictest-Ever Standards Are Meant to Close the Revolving Door
between Public Service, Lobbying Activities," *Los Angeles Times,* December 10, 1992.

45. William J. Clinton, "Executive Order 12834: Ethics Commitments by
Executive Branch Appointees, January 20, 1993," APP.

46. "Clinton Announces New Ethics Standards," *CQ Almanac 1992*
(http://library.cqpress.com.libproxy.lib.unc.edu/cqalmanac/cqal92-1106991).

47. George W. Bush, "Memorandum on Standards of Official Conduct, January 20, 2001," APP; Amy L. Comstock, "Memorandum to Designated Agency Ethics Officials: Presidential Memorandum on Ethical Conduct," January 22, 2001 (www.oge.gov/Web/OGE.nsf/All+Advisories/E61BD1F56A3012838525 7E96005FBDA5/$FILE/DO-01-004.pdf).

48. Overall, there are four main categories of politically appointed positions: presidential appointments with Senate confirmation (PAS), presidential appointments without Senate confirmation, political appointees to the Senior Executive Service, and Schedule C political appointees. Bush addressed the procedures under which a "potential future PAS" appointee for a subcabinet position could be employed as "an advisor or counselor" to the secretary or agency head of a federal agency. Certain "standards of behavior" were established for potential PAS appointees hired as advisers or counselors, and among these standards was the requirement that they "comply with all applicable ethics rules." See Presidential Appointee Initiative (2000). Bush emphasized at the outset that potential PAS appointees hired under either of the mechanisms just described would be considered federal government employees. It was also expected that the advisers or counselors hired per the Bush memo would qualify for treatment as special Government employees (SGEs) until they had been appointed to a Senate-confirmed position. As SGEs these individuals would be subject to somewhat less restrictive requirements under many of the ethics statutes and rules. See Office of Government Ethics, "Ethical Requirements Applicable to Potential PAS Appointees Employed as 'Advisors' or 'Counselors,'" March 15, 2001 (www.oge.gov/DisplayTemplates/ModelSub.aspx?id =2147483925).

49. Eric Lichtblau, "White House Revamps Ethics Team, without a Familiar Name," *New York Times,* August 6, 2010.

50. Obama for America, "Restore Trust in Government and Clean Up Washington," Obama '08 (http://obama.3cdn.net/2addfcb9c8a27ee8a5_v1eemv0s6 .pdf); Public Citizen, "Lobbying Disclosure Act: A Brief Synopsis of Key Components" (www.citizen.org/documents/Brief-Synopsis-of-LDA.pdf).

51. Barack Obama, "Executive Order 13490: Ethics Commitments by Executive Branch Personnel, January 21, 2009," APP; Barack Obama, "Remarks to White House Senior Staff, January 21, 2009," APP; Eli Saslow, "White House Ethics? 'Mr. No' Knows," *Washington Post,* March 13, 2009); U.S. Department of Justice, "Ethics Pledge, Executive Order 13490" (www.justice .gov/jmd/ethics-pledge-executive-order-13490); Dan Eggen and R. Jeffrey Smith, "Lobbying Rules Surpass Those of Previous Presidents, Experts Say," *Washington Post,* January 22, 2009; Thompson (2009); Thurber (2010); Juliet Eilperin, "Obama Promised to Curb the Influence of Lobbyists. Has He Succeeded?" *Washington Post,* March 22, 2015; Sheryl Gay Stolbergjan, "On

First Day, Obama Quickly Sets a New Tone," *New York Times*, January 21, 2009. In the letters, officials pledged to comply with specific federal government ethics laws and regulations and listed their conflicts of interest, past and present. See Olga Pierce and Christopher Weaver, "The Obama Team's Disclosure Documents," *ProPublica*, August 4, 2009 (http://projects.propublica.org /tables/the-obama-teams-disclosure-documents); Lichtblau, "White House Revamps Ethics Team."

52. Straus (2011b); Maskell (2014); Common Cause, Democracy 21, League of Women Voters, and USPIRG, "A Report Card on the Obama Administration's Executive Branch Lobbying, Ethics and Transparency Reforms in 2009," January 11, 2010 (www.democracy21.org/archives/whats-new/a -report-card-from-reform-groups-on-the-obama-administrations-executive -branch-lobbying-ethics-and-transparency-reforms-in-2009/).

53. Paul Blumenthal, "OGE Issues First Memo on Obama Ethics Order," Sunlight Foundation, February 17, 2009 (https://sunlightfoundation.com/blog /2009/02/17/oge-issues-first-memo-on-obama-ethics-order/).

54. Norm Eisen, "Lobbyists on Agency Boards and Commissions," September 23, 2009 (www.whitehouse.gov/blog/2009/09/23/lobbyists-agency-boards -and-commissions). Barack Obama, "Memorandum on Lobbyists on Agency Boards and Commissions, June 18, 2010," APP; General Service Administration, "Final Guidance on Appointment of Lobbyists to Federal Advisory Committees, Boards, and Commissions" (www.gsa.gov/portal/content/114307).

55. Rabkin (1993). "The Office of Counsel to the President was created in 1943, and is responsible for advising on all legal aspects of policy questions, legal issues arising in connection with the president's decision to sign or veto legislation, ethical questions, financial disclosures, and conflicts of interest during employment and post-employment" (https://en.wikipedia.org/wiki/White _House_Counsel).

56. Borrelli, Hult, and Kassop (2001).

57. Lichtblau, "White House Revamps Ethics Team."

58. Josh Gerstein, "How Obama Failed to Shut Washington's Revolving Door," *Politico*, December 31, 2015.

59. George H. W. Bush, "Executive Order 12731: Principles of Ethical Conduct for Government Officers and Employees, October 17, 1990," APP; Barack Obama, "Executive Order 13490: Ethics Commitments by Executive Branch Personnel, January 21, 2009," APP.

60. MacKenzie and Hafken (2002).

61. Revolving Door Working Group, "A Matter of Trust: How the Revolving Door Undermines Public Confidence in Government—and What to Do about It," October 2005 (www.cleanupwashington.org/documents/RevovDoor .pdf).

62. William J. Clinton, "Executive Order 13184: Revocation of Executive Order 12834, December 28, 2000," APP.

63. John Mintz, "Clinton Reverses 5-Year Ban on Lobbying by Appointees," *Washington Post,* December 29, 2000.

64. White House, "Memorandum for the Heads of Executive Departments and Agencies: Policy on Section 208(b)(1) Waivers with Respect to Negotiations for Post-Government Employment," January 6, 2004 (www.citizen.org /documents/WH_ethics_waiver_memo.pdf). Bush directed agencies "to examine existing delegations of the authority to grant such waivers to ensure that officials at an appropriate level of seniority and responsibility are involved in the decision making process."

65. Barack Obama, "Executive Order 13490"; Office of Government Ethics, "Memorandum to Agency Heads and Designated Agency Ethics Officials: Authorizations Pursuant to Section 3 of Executive Order 13490, 'Ethics Commitments by Executive Branch Personnel,'" February 23, 2009 (www.oge.gov /DisplayTemplates/ModelSub.aspx?id=244).

66. White House, "Ethics Pledges and Waivers" (www.whitehouse.gov /21stcenturygov/tools/ethics-waivers).

67. In a follow-up 2009 memo, Obama informed agencies that the director of the Office of Management and Budget had directed the designated federal agency ethics officials of each executive agency to exercise waiver authority in consultation with the Office of White House Counsel. See Office of Government Ethics, "Memorandum: Authorizations Pursuant to Section 3 of Executive Order 13490, 'Ethics Commitments by Executive Branch Personnel,'" February 23, 2009 (www.oge.gov/OGE-Advisories/Legal-Advisories/DO-09-008- -Authorizations-Pursuant-to-Section-3-of-Executive-Order-13490,-Ethics -Commitments-by-Executive-Branch-Personnel/).

68. "Ethics Waivers," *Judicial Watch,* March 14, 2012 (www.judicialwatch .org/bulletins/ethics-waivers/); Sam Stein, "William Lynn, Obama's First Ethics Exception, Causing Massive Headaches," *Huffington Post,* May 21, 2009 (www.huffingtonpost.com/2009/01/23/william-lynn-obamas-first_n_160512 .html).

69. Norman L. Eisen, "A Limited Waiver for Bob Bauer," May 7, 2010 (www .whitehouse.gov/blog/2010/05/07/a-limited-waiver-bob-bauer); Norman L. Eisen, "Limited Waiver Pursuant to Section 3 of Executive Order 13490," May 7, 2010 (www.whitehouse.gov/sites/default/files/rss_viewer/bauer_ltd _pledge_waiver.pdf); Kenneth P. Vogel, "W.H. Waives Ethics Rules for Counsel," *Politico,* May 7, 2010; "Ethics Waivers," *Judicial Watch,* March 14, 2012 (www.judicialwatch.org/bulletins/ethics-waivers/).

70. Office of Government Ethics, "Executive Branch Agency Ethics Pledge Waivers" (www.oge.gov/Open-Government/Executive-Branch-Agency-Ethics

-Pledge-Waivers/). Waivers issued by the White House and the Office of the Vice President are posted on the White House website. See White House, "Ethics Pledge Waivers Released by the White House" (www.whitehouse.gov/briefing -room/disclosures/ethics-pledge-waivers).

71. Kenneth P. Vogel, "Obama Administration's Revolving Door," *Politico,* January 18, 2011; Office of Government Ethics, "Executive Branch Agency Ethics Pledge Waivers." For an example of a waiver granted in 2014, see Neil Eggleston, "Memorandum: Limited Public Interest Waiver Pursuant to Section 3, Executive Order 13490," *Washington Post,* December 19, 2014.

72. Andy Sullivan, "Obama Lobbying Ban Faces Setback in Court," *Reuters,* January 17, 2014. The reversal occurred after several lobbyists filed a suit claiming that their constitutional rights had been violated by the ban, and a number of other trade association lobbyists challenged the rule after being kicked off of an industry trade advisory committee. The United States District Court for the District of Columbia ruled in 2012 that Obama was acting within his authority, and the case was dismissed. This ruling was subsequently overturned by the U.S. Court of Appeals for the District of Columbia, and the lower court was directed to take up the case again.

73. Byron Tau, "W.H. to Reverse Part of Lobbyist Ban," *Politico,* August 12, 2014. The White House clarified that the ban applies to persons serving on advisory committees, boards, and commissions in an individual capacity and does not apply if they are "specifically appointed to represent the interests of a nongovernmental entity, a recognizable group of persons, or nongovernmental entities (an industry sector, labor unions, environmental groups, and so forth), or state or local governments." See Julie Hirschfeld Davis, "Obama Administration Loosens Ban on Lobbyists in Government," *New York Times,* August 12, 2014.

74. Center for Responsive Politics, "Obama Officials Who Have Spun through the Revolving Door," *OpenSecrets.org* (www.opensecrets.org/obama /rev.php).

75. Gilman (1995).

76. Gerstein, "How Obama Failed to Shut Washington's Revolving Door."

77. Eilperin, "Obama Promised to Curb the Influence of Lobbyists."

78. "Text: Obama Transition Project Code of Ethical Conduct," *Huffington Post,* May 25, 2011 (www.huffingtonpost.com/2008/10/08/text-obama -transition-pro_n_133162.html).

79. Eilperin, "Obama Promised to Curb the Influence of Lobbyists."

CHAPTER EIGHT

1. Morone (2010).

2. Eugene Steuerle, "Health Costs, but Not Obamacare, Dominate the Future of Federal Spending," *Health Affairs Blog,* June 27, 2016 (http://health affairs.org/blog/2016/06/27/health-costs-but-not-obamacare-dominate-the -future-of-federal-spending/).

3. Lyndon B. Johnson assigned a senior-level aide to organize staff and develop domestic policy. See U.S. White House, "Domestic Policy Council" (www .whitehouse.gov/administration/eop/dpc).

4. White House, "Domestic Policy Council" (www.whitehouse.gov/admin istration/eop/dpc); White House, Office of the Press Secretary, "Fact Sheet: Economic Policy Council; Domestic Policy Council," April 11, 1985 (http:// digitalcollections.library.cmu.edu/awweb/awarchive?type=file&item=481859). Bill Clinton split the office, forming the current Domestic Policy Council and the National Economic Council. See Warshaw (1995); Ronald Reagan, "Statement on the Establishment of the Economic Policy Council and the Domestic Policy Council, April 11, 1985," (henceforth cited as APP); George H. W. Bush, "Statement on the Economic and Domestic Policy Councils, February 8, 1989," APP; William J. Clinton, "Executive Order 12859: Establishment of the Domestic Policy Council, August 16, 1993," APP; The White House— George W. Bush, "Domestic Policy Council" (https://georgewbush-whitehouse .archives.gov/dpc/).

5. Barack Obama, "Executive Order 13507: Establishment of the White House Office of Health Reform, April 8, 2009," APP; Nelson (1996).

6. Freedman (2009).

7. Tevi D. Troy, "How the Government as a Payer Shapes the Health Care Marketplace" (www.americanhealthpolicy.org/Content/documents/resources /Government_as_Payer_12012015.pdf).

8. Randolph Fillmore, "The Evolution of the U.S. Healthcare System," *Science Scribe,* 2001 (www.sciencescribe.net/articles/The_Evolution_of_the_U.S. _Healthcare_System.pdf). Aaron C. Catlin and Cathy A. Cowan, "History of Health Spending in the United States, 1960–2013," November 19, 2015 (www .cms.gov/Research-Statistics-Data-and-Systems/Statistics-Trends-and-Reports /NationalHealthExpendData/Downloads/HistoricalNHEPaper.pdf).

9. Congressional Budget Office, "Health Care" (www.cbo.gov/topics /health-care); Congressional Budget Office, "The Long-Term Outlook for Major Federal Health Care Programs," June 15, 2015 (www.cbo.gov/publication /50250).

10. Office of Management and Budget, Table 15.1, "Total Outlays for Health Programs: 1962–2021" (www.whitehouse.gov/omb/budget/Historicals).

11. Congressional Budget Office, "Federal Subsidies for Health Insurance Coverage for People Under Age 65: 2016 to 2026," March 24, 2016 (www.cbo .gov/publication/51385).

12. See Julie Topoleski, "Federal Spending on the Government's Major Health Care Programs Is Projected to Rise Substantially Relative to GDP," September 18, 2013 (www.cbo.gov/publication/44582).

13. Tricare, "About Us" (www.tricare.mil/about).

14. See U.S. Office of Personnel Management, "Healthcare Eligibility: Overview" (www.opm.gov/healthcare-insurance/healthcare/eligibility/).

15. U.S. Office of Personnel Management, "Healthcare Reference Materials: FEHB Program Handbook Introduction: General Overview" (www.opm .gov/healthcare-insurance/healthcare/reference-materials/fehb-handbook/).

16. Dallard (2004).

17. Centers for Medicare and Medicaid Services, "Fiscal Year 2016: Justification of Estimates for Appropriations Committees," *CMS.gov*, 2016 (www.cms .gov/About-CMS/Agency-Information/PerformanceBudget/Downloads/FY2016 -CJ-Final.pdf); Centers for Medicare and Medicaid Services, "National Health Expenditures 2014 Highlights" (www.cms.gov/Research-Statistics-Data-and -Systems/Statistics-Trends-and-Reports/NationalHealthExpendData /Downloads/highlights.pdf).

18. Nelson (1996). Congress, under the 1917 War Risk Insurance Act Amendments, established rehabilitation and vocational training for veterans with dismemberment, sight, hearing, and other permanent disabilities. By the 1920s, three federal agencies administered the benefits, including the Veterans Bureau, the Bureau of Pensions of the Interior Department, and the National Home for Disabled Volunteer Soldiers. See U.S. Department of Veterans Affairs, "History: Department of Veterans Affairs (VA)" (www.va.gov/about_va/vahistory.asp).

19. U.S. Congress, *An Act to Authorize the President to Consolidate and Coordinate Governmental Activities Affecting War Veterans*, 71st Cong., 2nd sess., 1930, 1016–1018. Hoover proposed consolidating agencies administering veterans' benefits. Congress created the Veterans Administration by uniting three bureaus: the Veterans Bureau, the Bureau of Pensions, and the National Home for Disabled Volunteer Soldiers.

20. Herbert Hoover, "Executive Order 5398: Establishing the Veterans' Administration, July 21, 1930," APP; Herbert Hoover, "Statement about the Establishment of the Veterans' Administration, July 8, 1930," APP; U.S. Department of Veterans Affairs, "History: Department of Veterans Affairs (VA)"; U.S. Department of Veterans Affairs, "VA History in Brief" (www.va.gov/opa /publications/archives/docs/history_in_brief.pdf); Oliver (2007).

21. U.S. Department of Veterans Affairs, "VA History in Brief"; Panangala (2015); U.S. House Committee on Veterans' Affairs, "History and Jurisdiction"

(https://veterans.house.gov/about/history-jurisdiction); Robert Pear, "History and Context of an Embattled Department of Veterans Affairs," *New York Times,* May 21, 2014.

22. U.S. Department of Veterans Affairs, "Veterans Health Administration" (www.va.gov/health/). The VHA is led by the undersecretary of veterans affairs for health, who implements the medical assistance program of the VA through the administration and operation of numerous VA medical centers, outpatient clinics, community-based outpatient clinics, and VA community living centers and VA nursing home programs.

23. "Dependents' Medical Care," *CQ Almanac 1956* (http://library.cqpress.com/cqalmanac/cqal56-1349374).

24. CHAMPUS was established as the military equivalent of a health insurance plan, administered by the Department of Defense, for dependents of active-duty servicemen, military retirees and the dependents of retirees, survivors of deceased members, and certain former spouses. CHAMPUS reimbursed beneficiaries for portions of the costs of health care received from civilian health-care providers. Under the old system, many aspects of military health care had been managed by the individual armed services—the Army, Navy, and Air Force). As a successor to CHAMPUS, TRICARE offers beneficiaries care through a DOD-managed health maintenance organization, a preferred-provider organization, or to continue to use regular CHAMPUS (now known as TRICARE Standard). Historically, health care for military personnel and dependents was provided in military medical facilities. Where military physicians were not available in a certain specialty or overcrowding of a military medical facility occurred, health care was also provided by civilian medical personnel through a referral system. TRICARE is a program for almost 9.5 million beneficiaries, including active-duty service members, National Guard and Reserve members, retirees, their families, survivors, certain former spouses, and others registered in the Defense Enrollment Eligibility Reporting System. See Best (2005); Potter (1990); Defense Health Agency, "Welcome" (www.tricare.mil/Welcome.aspx).

25. Best (2005); Military Health System, "MHS Home" (http://health.mil). As a chartered organization, TMA operated under the authority of the assistant secretary of defense for health affairs. The DOD established the Defense Health Agency as part of a larger effort meant to reorganize its health-care programs and services. Under the secretary of defense, the Military Health Services System is headed by the assistant secretary of defense for health affairs. Although the Military Health Services System is primarily designed to provide medical services to active-duty service members, it is a major source of medical care in both military and civilian facilities to the dependents of active-duty personnel, military retirees, and retirees' dependents.

26. Nancy Schlichting, "Joint VSO Letter to the Commission on Care," *Disabled American Veterans Charity,* April 1, 2016 (www.dav.org/learn-more /news/2016/joint-vso-letter-to-the-commission-on-care/).

27. George H. W. Bush, "Executive Order 12751: Health Care Services for Operation Desert Storm February 14, 1991," APP; "Furnishing of Health-Care Services to Members of the Armed Forces During a War or National Emergency," 38 U.S.C. §8111A; George Bush Presidential Library and Museum, "Persian Gulf Conflict" (https://bush41library.tamu.edu/files/persian-gulf/41-ND005-212539ss /41-nd005-212539ss.pdf); U.S. Department of Veterans Affairs, "Gulf War Era Veterans Report: Pre-9/11 (August 2, 1990 to September 10, 2001)," February 2011 (www.va.gov/vetdata/docs/specialreports/gw_pre911_report.pdf).

28. George H. W. Bush, "Executive Order 12722: Blocking Iraqi Government Property and Prohibiting Transactions with Iraq, August 2, 1990," APP; "Furnishing of Health-Care Services to Members of the Armed Forces During a War or National Emergency," 38 U.S.C. §8111A.

29. Prostate cancer and peripheral neuropathy, a nerve condition, were added to a list of seven other ailments linked to Agent Orange for which the VA already provided benefits. See William J. Clinton, "Remarks Announcing Agent Orange-Related Disability Benefits for Vietnam Veterans and an Exchange with Reporters, May 28, 1996," APP; Todd S. Purdum, "Clinton Orders Expanded Agent Orange Benefits for Veterans," *New York Times,* May 29, 1996; Paul Richter, "Clinton Expands U.S. Benefits for Veterans Exposed to Agent Orange," *Los Angeles Times,* May 29, 1996; Robert A. Rankin and Michael E. Ruane, "Agent Orange Victims Get Broadened Benefits; Vietnam Veterans with Prostate Cancer or a Nerve Disease Can Collect, President Clinton Announced," *Philly.com,* May 29, 1996 (http:// articles.philly.com/1996-05-29/news/25625894_1_vietnam-veterans-nerve -disease-first-time-veterans); John F. Harris and Bill McAllister, "President Adds VA Benefits After Agent Orange Study," *Washington Post,* May 29, 1996.

30. George W. Bush, "Executive Order 13214: Presidents Task Force to Improve Health Care Delivery for Our Nations Veterans May 28, 2001," APP; George W. Bush, "Executive Order 13426: Establishing a Commission on Care for America's Returning Wounded Warriors and a Task Force on Returning Global War on Terror Heroes, March 6, 2007," APP; The White House— George W. Bush, "The Bush Administration Has Provided Unprecedented Support for Our Veterans" (https://georgewbush-whitehouse.archives.gov/infocus /bushrecord/factsheets/veterans.html).

31. Thomas B. Edsall, "Funds for Health Care of Veterans $1 Billion Short," *Washington Post,* June 24, 2005.

32. Bush would later appoint the Commission on Care for America's Returning Wounded Warriors and a Task Force on Returning Global War on

Terror Heroes. Bush's charge for the commission was "to evaluate the coordi-
nation, management, and adequacy of the delivery of health care and other
benefits and services to returning wounded Global War on Terror service." See
Bush, "Executive Order 13426"; "The President's Commission on Care for
America's Returning Wounded Warriors, Final Report July 2007," July 24, 2007
(www.npr.org/documents/2007/jul/wounded_warriors_final.pdf); Hope Yen,
"Returning Troops Face Obstacles to Care," *Washington Post,* April 14, 2007;
Steve Vogel, "Overhaul Urged in Care for Soldiers," *Washington Post,* July 26,
2007; Dana Milbank, "Too Much, Too Late," *Washington Post,* March 8,
2007.

33. Bob Dole and Donna E. Shalala, "A Duty to the Wounded," *Washington Post,* October 16, 2007; Jim Rutenberg and David S. Cloud, "Bush Panel
Seeks Upgrade in Military Care," *New York Times,* July 26, 2007.

34. Barack Obama, "Executive Order 13625: Improving Access to Mental
Health Services for Veterans, Service Members, and Military Families, Au-
gust 31, 2012," APP; Barack Obama, "Remarks on Signing the Caregivers
and Veterans Omnibus Health Services Act of 2010, May 5, 2010," APP; Katie
Zezima, "Obama Pledges Better Mental Health Services, Other Initiatives
for Military, Vets," *Washington Post,* August 26, 2014; U.S. Department of
Veterans Affairs, "Interagency Task Force on Military and Veterans Mental
Health: 2013 Annual Report" (www.mentalhealth.va.gov/docs/2013_ITF
_Report-FINAL.pdf); White House, Office of the Press Secretary, "Fact Sheet:
President Obama Signs Executive Order to Improve Access to Mental Health
Services for Veterans, Service Members, and Military Families," August 31,
2012 (www.whitehouse.gov/the-press-office/2012/08/31/fact-sheet-president
-obama-signs-executive-order-improve-access-mental-h); U.S. Department of
Veterans Affairs, "VA Meets President's Mental Health Executive Order Hir-
ing Goal," November 5, 2013 (www.va.gov/opa/pressrel/pressrelease.cfm?id
=2487); American Legion, "Statement of Roscoe G. Butler, Deputy Director,
National Veterans Affairs and Rehabilitation Division, before the Committee
on Veterans' Affairs, United States Senate: 'VA Mental Health: Ensuring Access to Care,'" October 28, 2015 (www.veterans.senate.gov/imo/media/doc
/TAL%20Butler%20Testimony%2010.28.15.pdf); White House, Office of the
Press Secretary, "Fact Sheet: President Obama Announces New Executive Actions to Fulfill Our Promises to Service Members, Veterans, and Their Families," August 26, 2014 (www.whitehouse.gov/the-press-office/2014/08/26
/fact-sheet-president-obama-announces-new-executive-actions-fulfill-our-p);
U.S. Departments of Defense and Veterans Affairs, "Joint Fact Sheet: DOD
and VA Take New Steps to Support the Mental Health Needs of Service Members and Veterans," August 26, 2014 (www.va.gov/opa/docs/26-aug-joint-fact
-sheet-final.pdf).

35. U.S. Office of Personnel Management, "Healthcare Reference Materials: FEHB Program Handbook Introduction: General Overview" (www.opm.gov/healthcare-insurance/healthcare/reference-materials/fehb-handbook/).

36. "Government Employees Health Service," CQ Almanac, 1946. Harry S. Truman, "Executive Order 10317: Establishing the President's Commission of the Health Needs of the Nation, December 29, 1951," APP; Anderson and May (1971). U.S. private sector employer-sponsored health insurance became prevalent during World War II as one of the few ways in which the private sector could escape federal wage and price control limitations on employee wages. The relationship between employment and health insurance was strengthened during World War II when the War Labor Board ruled that controls over wages and prices imposed by the 1942 Stabilization Act did not apply to fringe benefits such as health insurance. In response, many private sector employers used insurance benefits to attract and retain scarce labor. By 1950 it was common for private sector employers to pay at least a portion of their employees' health insurance premiums. In 1948 and 1949, the National Labor Relations Board provided further impetus for employer-based coverage by ruling that health insurance and other employee welfare plans were subject to collective bargaining. Finally, in a landmark 1954 ruling, the Internal Revenue Service clarified an earlier administrative court ruling regarding the income tax status of employer-provided health insurance by exempting such benefits from income taxation. See Buchmueller and Monheit (2009).

37. Dwight D. Eisenhower, "Statement by the President on Proposed Improvements in the Federal Personnel Program, February 24, 1954," APP.

38. Although Eisenhower proposed a health insurance program for federal employees, he opposed the congressionally proposed Federal Employees Health Benefits Act. See Dwight D. Eisenhower, "Special Message to the Congress on Federal Personnel Management, January 11, 1955," APP.

39. "Federal Health Program," CQ Almanac, 1960. Prior to the FEHBP, federal employees were not able to secure health insurance coverage through the federal government; instead, employees who wanted health insurance could voluntarily purchase coverage on their own or through a few union and employee association plans that were offered to federal employees. See Ruddock (1966). Congress considered a system that would revolve around one dominant government-directed plan, but unions and employee associations, which had sponsored their own health plans, opposed such a reform. In response to these demands, Congress ensured that these existing plans were "grandfathered" into the FEHBP. See U.S. General Accounting Office (2002). The final plan allowed federal employees an unrestricted choice of enrollment in one of several health plans covering basic services and extended illness: service benefit (such as Blue Cross-Blue Shield), indemnity benefit (provided by insurance firms),

employee organization plans (such as carried by the National Association of Letter Carriers), and comprehensive prepayment plans (such as Group Health Associate of Washington). Congress also passed the Retired Federal Employees Health Benefits Act in 1960, which created a health benefits program for federal employees and their family members who had retired or become disabled. See Mach and Cornell (2014). Like most federal agencies, the U.S. Postal Service offers health benefits to its employees through FEHBP. However, collective bargaining rights and prefunding obligations for retiree health costs make the USPS unique among federal agencies with regard to health benefits. Some federal employees, including postal workers, have a higher portion of their premiums paid as the result of collective bargaining agreements. See Blom and Cornell (2015a).

40. Although Congress did not require a standard benefit package for FEHBP, all health plans must cover basic hospital, surgical, physician, and emergency care. The FEHBP does not have the authority to contract with health plans that offer limited services, such as dental or vision plans, prescription drug plans, and supplemental insurance and disability insurance. Each health insurance plan contracts with the OPM to offer medical services, such as doctor's office visits, hospitalization, emergency care, prescription drug coverage, and treatment of mental conditions and substance abuse. See U.S. Office of Personnel Management, "Healthcare Carriers: Overview" (www.opm.gov/healthcare-insurance /healthcare/carriers/).

41. The Civil Service Commission was given authority to implement rules, contract with plans, establish benefits, and administer the program. See U.S. Office of Personnel Management, "FEHB Program Handbook Introduction" (www.opm.gov/healthcare-insurance/healthcare/reference-materials/fehb -handbook/). Initially, Congress delegated authority the CSC to contract for a federal-government-wide service benefit plan and a government-wide indemnity plan. The FEHBP began operation in 1960, offering twenty-eight plans, with fifteen available in the Washington, D.C., area. See Karl Polzer, "The Federal Employees Health Benefits Program: What Lessons Can It Offer Policymakers?" *National Health Policy Forum: Issue Brief,* March 12, 1998 (www.nhpf.org /library/issue-briefs/IB715_FEHBP_3-12-98.pdf).

42. See Blom and Cornell (2015a); U.S. General Accounting Office (2002).

43. John F. Kennedy, "Letter to Secretary Ribicoff Concerning the Role of the Federal Government in the Field of Mental Health, December 1, 1961," APP; John F. Kennedy, "Special Message to the Congress on Mental Illness and Mental Retardation, February 5, 1963," APP.

44. Kennedy, "Special Message to the Congress."

45. Hustead and others (1985).

46. See U.S. Department of Health and Human Services (2004); Barry, Huskamp, and Goldman (2010); Regier and others (2008); U.S. Office of

Personnel Management, "EHB Program Carrier Letter, Letter No. 1999-027," June 7, 1999 (www.opm.gov/healthcare-insurance/healthcare/carriers/1999/99 -27.pdf).

47. Ronald Reagan, "Executive Order 12564: Drug-Free Federal Workplace, September 15, 1986," APP.

48. See Kruger (1987); Reagan, "Executive Order 12564"; Ronald Reagan, "Memorandum on Federal Initiatives for a Drug-Free America, October 4, 1986," APP.

49. See U.S. Office of Personnel Management, "Work-Life Employee Assistance Programs: Substance Abuse" (www.opm.gov/policy-data-oversight /worklife/employee-assistance-programs/#url=Substance-Abuse); U.S. Office of Personnel Management, "Work-Life Employee Assistance Programs: Guidance & Legislation" (www.opm.gov/policy-data-oversight/worklife/employee -assistance-programs/#url=EAP); Substance Abuse and Mental Health Services Administration, "Drug-Free Workplace Programs" (www.samhsa.gov /workplace).

50. William J. Clinton, "Remarks at the White House Conference on Mental Health, June 7, 1999," APP.

51. Janice R. Lachance, "Mental Health and Substance Abuse Parity Implementation in the Federal Employees Health Benefits (FEHB) Program," Chief Human Capital Officers Council, July 13, 2000 (www.chcoc.gov /content/mental-health-and-substance-abuse-parity-implementation-federal -employees-health-benefits); Apgar (2000). Clinton directed the OPM to notify all 285 participating health plans that, "as a condition of participation and as a desired outcome as an employer, . . . FEHBP will be offering both mental health and chemical and substance abuse parity." See William J. Clinton, "Press Briefing on 6/7/99 Mental Health Conference by Chris Jennings, Deputy Assistant to the President for Health Policy, June 6, 1999," APP; William J. Clinton, "Remarks at the White House Conference on Mental Health June 7, 1999," APP; U.S. Department of Health and Human Services (2004); U.S. Office of Personnel Management, "FEHB Program Carrier Letter: Call Letter for Contract Year 2001—Policy Guidance," Letter 2000-17, April 11, 2000 (www.opm.gov/healthcare-insurance/healthcare/carriers/2000/2000-17 .pdf).

52. Bush established the President's New Freedom Commission on Mental Health in 2003 "to conduct a comprehensive study of the United States mental health service delivery system, including public and private sector providers, and to advise the president on methods of improving the system." See George W. Bush, "Executive Order 13263, President's New Freedom Commission on Mental Health, April 29, 2002," APP; The White House—George W. Bush, "Freedom Initiative" (http://georgewbush-whitehouse.archives.gov/news/freedominitiative /text/freedominitiative.html).

53. President's New Freedom Commission on Mental Health (2003); Barry, Huskamp, and Goldman (2010); Goldman (2005); George W. Bush, "Remarks at the University of New Mexico in Albuquerque, New Mexico, April 29, 2002," APP.

54. National Cancer Institute (1997); William J. Clinton, "Remarks on National Cancer Institute Recommendations on Mammography and an Exchange With Reporters, March 27, 1997," APP; William J. Clinton, "Press Briefing by Mike McCurry, March 27, 1997," APP. The NCI guidelines recommend screening mammograms every one to two years for women ages forty to forty-nine if they are at average risk of breast cancer. See National Cancer Institute (1997); Clinton, "Remarks on National Cancer Institute Recommendations."

55. See William J. Clinton, "Memorandum on Preventive Health Services at the Federal Workplace, January 4, 2001," APP; Bob Arguero, "Federal Workers to Get Time Off for Health Screening," *GovCon.com*, January 8, 2001 (www.govcon.com/doc/federal-workers-to-get-time-off-for-health-sc -0001).

56. FEHBP plans must provide all preventive services recommended with an A or B rating by the United States Preventive Services Task Force with no member cost sharing. Nine items were added to the list or updated in 2014, including screening for gestational diabetes, screening for a variety of infections, and intensive behavioral counseling for adults who are overweight or obese and have cardiovascular risk factors. See Blom and Cornell (2015a); U.S. Office of Personnel Management, "FEHB Program Carrier Letter: Updated FEHB Guidance on Preventive Care," Letter 2015-14, July 28, 2015 (www.opm.gov/healthcare-insurance/healthcare/carriers/2015/2015-14 .pdf).

57. In 1990, the OPM required all plans to include coverage of prescription drugs. See Blom and Cornell (2015b). Subsequently, the OPM has expanded and modified prescription drug coverage requirements. Following an agreement between Clinton and Congress in the 1998 Treasury and General Government Appropriations Act, FEHBP health plans were required to offer contraception coverage as part of their prescription drug coverage. Congress included an exemption for five religious-based health plans (certain plans that object to such coverage on the basis of religious beliefs)—Providence Health Plan, Personal Care's HMO, Personal Choices, OSF Health Plans, Yellowstone Community Health Plan—and for any existing or future plans that objected to such coverage on the basis of religious belief. See William J. Clinton, "Statement on Signing the Omnibus Consolidated and Emergency Supplemental Appropriations Act, 1999, October 23, 1998," APP; U.S. House of Representatives (1999).

58. U.S. Office of Personnel Management, "Benefits Administration Letter: Federal Employees Health Benefits (FEHB) Program: Expanded Coverage of Contraceptives for 1999," November 6, 1998 (www.opm.gov/retirement -services/publications-forms/benefits-administration-letters/1998/98-418.pdf). In George W. Bush's first budget request to Congress, he was unsuccessful in removing the past expansion of contraception coverage. See Dallard (2004).

59. U.S. Office of Personnel Management, "Benefits Administration Letter: Federal Employees Health Benefits (FEHB) Program: Expanded Coverage of Contraceptives for 1999," November 6, 1998 (www.opm.gov/retirement -services/publications-forms/benefits-administration-letters/1998/98-418.pdf). In George W. Bush's first budget request to Congress, he was unsuccessful in removing the past expansion of contraception coverage. See Dallard (2004); Blom and Cornell (2015b).

60. For example, in 1983, Congress prohibited use of appropriated federal funds to cover abortions in all cases except those in which the life of the woman was in danger. This provision was renewed with few changes every year except 1994 and 1995, when the 103rd Congress—with Democrats in political control—excluded the provision. See Blom and Cornell (2015b). Congress subsequently reinstated the provision and prohibited the use of federal funds for abortion except for when the life of the woman was in danger or in cases of rape or incest; this provision has been included in subsequent appropriations bills each year. See Mach and Cornell (2014).

61. U.S. Office of Personnel Management, "FEHB Program Carrier Letter: Gender Identity Disorder/Gender Dysphoria," No. 2014-17, June 13, 2014 (www.opm.gov/healthcare-insurance/healthcare/carriers/2015/2015-14.pdf).

62. U.S. Office of Personnel Management, "FEHB Program Carrier Letter: Federal Employees Health Benefits Program Call Letter," Letter No. 2015-02, March 13, 2015 (www.opm.gov/healthcare-insurance/healthcare/carriers /2015/2015-02.pdf). For the 2016 plan year, the OPM "encouraged" health plans to propose services for members with gender dysphoria as they do for all other medical conditions. A White House spokesperson said that Obama "supported the change." See U.S. Office of Personnel Management, "FEHB Program Carrier Letter: Covered Benefits for Gender Transition Services," Letter No. 2015-12, June 23, 2015 (www.opm.gov/healthcare-insurance/healthcare /carriers/2015/2015-12.pdf); Joe Davidson, "State Allows Employee Health Insurance to Cover Transgender Services," *Washington Post*, October 12, 2014; "Issue Briefs: OPM Outlines 2016 FEHB Features," *FEDweek.com*, March 25, 2015 (www.fedweek.com/issue-briefs/opm-outlines-2016-fehb -features-2/); National Partnership for Women and Families, "Some Health Plans for Federal Employees to Cover Transgender Care; Largest Carrier Will Not Include Coverage," *Women's Health Policy Report*, November 12, 2014

(http://go.nationalpartnership.org/site/News2?abbr=daily2_&page =NewsArticle&id=46061); Chris Johnson, "OPM Bans Trans Exclusion in Federal Health Plans," *Washington Blade,* June 23, 2015 (www.washingtonblade .com/2015/06/23/opm-to-ban-trans-exclusion-in-federal-health-plans/#sthash .TzhWqxij.JNZO4WCh.dpuf). The American Foreign Service Protective Association's (AFSPA) Foreign Service Benefit Plan was the first to comply. Transgender exclusion essentially "denies coverage to transgender people for the same treatments available to non-transgender policy holders, without regard to medical necessity." See Davidson, "State Allows Employee Health Insurance."

63. See Blom and Cornell (2015b).

64. For a full account of statutory changes to FEHPB eligibility, see Blom and Cornell (2015b).

65. U.S. Office of Personnel Management, "OPM Announces Rule Change to Allow Federal Firefighters Access to Health Insurance," July 17, 2012 (www .opm.gov/news/releases/2012/07/opm-announces-rule-change-to-allow -federal-firefighters-access-to-health-insurance/); White House, Office of the Press Secretary, "Statement by the President on Extending Health Coverage to Federal Firefighters," July 17, 2012 (www.whitehouse.gov/the-press-office /2012/07/17/statement-president-extending-health-coverage-federal-firefighters). The OPM, in collaboration with the Department of Agriculture and the Department of the Interior, provided thousands of temporary federal firefighters and their families with an expedited process to gain access to health coverage. See U.S. Office of Personnel Management, "Healthcare Eligibility: Temp Firefighters" (www.opm.gov/healthcare-insurance/healthcare/eligibility/#url =Temp-Firefighters); Joe Davidson, "Obama Says Part-Time Firefighters Can Buy Employee Health Insurance," *Washington Post,* July 10, 2012.

66. U.S. Office of Personnel Management, "Federal Employees Health Benefits Program Modification of Eligibility to Certain Employees on Temporary Appointments and Certain Employees on Seasonal and Intermittent Schedules," *Federal Register,* October 17, 2014 (www.gpo.gov/fdsys/pkg/FR-2014 -10-17/pdf/2014-24652.pdf).

67. U.S. Office of Personnel Management, "Healthcare Eligibility: Temp Firefighters."

68. U.S. Office of Personnel Management, "Life Events, Me/My Family: I Have a Same Sex Marriage" (www.opm.gov/healthcare-insurance/life-events /memy-family/i-have-a-same-sex-marriage/); U.S. Office of Personnel Management, "Healthcare Reference Materials: Family Members" (www.opm.gov /healthcare-insurance/healthcare/reference-materials/reference/family -members/); U.S. Office of Personnel Management, "FEHB Program Carrier Letter: Coverage of Same-Sex Spouses," Letter No. 2013-20, July 3, 2013 (www.opm.gov/healthcare-insurance/healthcare/carriers/2013/2013-20.pdf); U.S. Office of Personnel Management, "Benefits Administration Letter: Cover-

age of Same-Sex Spouses," Letter No. 13-203, July 17, 2013 (www.opm.gov
/retirement-services/publications-forms/benefits-administration-letters/2013
/13-203.pdf).

69. See U.S. Office of Personnel Management, "Benefits Administration
Letter: Coverage of Children of Same-Sex Domestic Partners," Number: 13-211,
OPM.gov, December 11, 2013 (www.opm.gov/retirement-services/publications
-forms/benefits-administration-letters/2013/13-211.pdf); Emma Green, "The
Federal Government Quietly Expands Transgender Rights," *The Atlantic,*
May 16, 2016 (www.theatlantic.com/politics/archive/2016/05/department-of
-health-and-human-services-transgender-rights/482934/); Roger Severino and
Ryan T. Anderson, "Proposed Obamacare Gender Identity Mandate Threatens
Freedom of Conscience and the Independence of Physicians," The Heritage
Foundation, 2016 (www.heritage.org/research/reports/2016/01/proposed
-obamacare-gender-identity-mandate-threatens-freedom-of-conscience-and
-the-independence-of-physicians).

70. Centers for Medicare and Medicaid Services, "History: CMS' Program History" (www.cms.gov/About-CMS/Agency-Information/History/index
.html).

71. Centers for Medicare and Medicaid Services, "Brief Summaries of
Medicare & Medicaid" (www.cms.gov/Research-Statistics-Data-and-Systems
/Statistics-Trends-and-Reports/MedicareProgramRatesStats/SummaryMedi
careMedicaid.html).

72. Centers for Medicare and Medicaid Services, "Medicare" (www.cms
.gov/Medicare/Medicare.html). Since Medicare's inception, private health-care
insurers have processed medical claims for Medicare beneficiaries. See Swendiman (2012).

73. Jost (2004); Centers for Medicare and Medicaid Services, "Regulations & Guidance" (www.cms.gov/regulations-and-guidance/regulations-and
-guidance.html). The CMS issues regulations to codify policies based on
statutory provisions of the Social Security Act. See Medicaid, "Federal Policy
Guidance" (www.medicaid.gov/federal-policy-guidance/federal-policy-guidance
.html).

74. CHIP was established as part of the 1997 Balanced Budget Act (BBA97;
P.L. 105-33) under a new Title XXI of the Social Security Act. See Baum-
rucker and Mitchell (2015); Social Security Administration, "Compilation
of the Social Security Laws: Title XXI—State Children's Health Insurance
Program" (www.ssa.gov/OP_Home/ssact/title21/2100.htm); Centers for Medi-
care and Medicaid Services, "Fiscal Year 2016: Justification of Estimates for
Appropriations Committees" (www.cms.gov/About-CMS/Agency-Information
/PerformanceBudget/Downloads/FY2016-CJ-Final.pdf).

75. U.S. Department of Health and Human Services, "Read the Law"
(www.hhs.gov/healthcare/about-the-law/read-the-law/index.html). The CMS

also became responsible for the implementation of the ACA's consumer protections and private health insurance market rules. See Regulatory Information Service Center, "Introduction to the Unified Agenda of Federal Regulatory and Deregulatory Actions," *Federal Register,* December 15, 2015 (www .federalregister.gov/articles/2015/12/15/2015-30690/introduction-to-the -unified-agenda-of-federal-regulatory-and-deregulatory-actions).

76. U.S. Department of Health and Human Services, "Nondiscrimination in Health Programs and Activities Proposed Rule: Section 1557 of the Affordable Care Act" (www.hhs.gov/civil-rights/for-individuals/section-1557/nondis crimination-health-programs-and-activities-proposed-rule/index.html).

77. Lyndon B. Johnson, "Executive Order 11279: Establishing the President's Committee on Health Manpower and the National Advisory Commission on Health Manpower, May 7, 1966," APP; Stewart (1969); Lyndon B. Johnson, "Statement by the President Upon Establishing the National Advisory Commission on Health Manpower, May 7, 1966," APP; Leuchtenburg (2015); Centers for Medicare and Medicaid Services, "CMS History Project President's Speeches" (www.cms.gov/About-CMS/Agency-Information/History /downloads/CMSPresidentsSpeeches.pdf). Johnson charged a National Advisory Commission on Health Manpower with "develop[ing] recommendations for action by the federal government . . . for improving the availability and utilization of health manpower." See U.S. National Advisory Commission on Health Manpower (1967).

78. "Congress Extends Major Health Manpower Legislation," *CQ Almanac 1968* (http://library.cqpress.com.libproxy.lib.unc.edu/cqalmanac/cqal68 -1283910); National Institutes of Health Office of History, "Legislative Chronology" (https://history.nih.gov/research/sources_legislative_chronology .html); "Message to Congress: Johnson on Education and Health," *CQ Almanac 1967* (https://library.cqpress.com/cqalmanac/document.php?id=cqal67 -1312057).

79. Kenneth T. Walsh, "The Politics of Medicare and Medicaid, 50 Years Later," *U.S. News and World Report,* July 30, 2015.

80. Julie Rovner, "Medicare: Where Presidential Politics and Policy Collide," *Shots: Health News from NPR,* October 16, 2012 (www.npr.org/sections /health-shots/2012/10/16/163025327/medicare-where-preisdential-politics -and-policy-collide).

81. Robert Pear, "Clinton to Order Medicare to Pay New Costs," *New York Times,* June 7, 2000; Barnes and Korn (2005). Clinton directed the CMS to inform beneficiaries of the new coverage, track Medicare payments, and report back on other means to promote medical research important to Medicare participants. Clinton required the CMS to notify all claims-processing contractors to reimburse for the routine patient care costs as well as costs due to

medical complications associated with participation in a clinical trial, removing this barrier to participation. The CMS was directed to implement a system to track clinical trial spending to which Medicare contributes financial support. See William J. Clinton, "Memorandum on Increasing Participation of Medicare Beneficiaries in Clinical Trials, June 7, 2000," APP; U.S. Department of Health and Human Services, "President Clinton Takes New Action to Encourage Participation in Clinical Trials," June 7, 2000 (http://archive.hhs .gov/news/press/2000pres/20000607.html).

82. Centers for Medicare and Medicaid Services, "Medicare Clinical Trial Policies" (www.cms.gov/Medicare/Coverage/ClinicalTrialPolicies/index .html). The Clinton memo followed an agreement between the National Cancer Institute and TRICARE, which allowed beneficiaries to participate in NCI's prevention, early detection, and treatment trials. See Arnold and Vastag (2000).

83. Robert Pear, "President Moves to Protect Half of Uninsured Children," *New York Times,* February 7, 1997; White House, Office of the Press Secretary, "The Clinton-Gore Administration Takes New Steps to Increase Enrollment of Uninsured Children," October 12, 1999 (http://clinton6.nara.gov/1999/10 /1999-10-12-fact-sheet-on-increasing-enrollment-of-uninsured-children-a .html); Government Printing Office, "Remarks at a Reception for Representative James P. Moran," February 18, 1998 (www.gpo.gov/fdsys/pkg/WCPD -1998-02-23/pdf/WCPD-1998-02-23-Pg276.pdf); U.S Department of Health and Human Services, "The Clinton-Gore Administration Takes New Steps to Increase Enrollment of Uninsured Children"; Government Printing Office, "Memorandum on School-Based Health Insurance Outreach for Children," October 12, 1999 (www.gpo.gov/fdsys/pkg/PPP-1999-book2/html/PPP-1999 -book2-doc-pg1755.htm); Centers for Medicare and Medicaid Services, "Memorandum: School-Based Health Insurance Outreach for Children," October 12, 1999 (https://downloads.cms.gov/cmsgov/archived-downloads/SMDL /downloads/sho090800attA.pdf).

84. Centers for Medicare and Medicaid Services, "Letter to State Health Officials," August 17, 2007 (https://downloads.cms.gov/cmsgov/archived -downloads/SMDL/downloads/SHO081707.pdf); Oberlander and Lyons (2009).

85. Cindy Mann and Jocelyn Guyer, "SCHIP: The Administration's New Directive," *Health Affairs Blog,* September 7, 2007 (http://healthaffairs.org /blog/2007/09/07/schip-the-administrations-new-directive/); Nina Owcharenko, "The Administration's SCHIP Regulations: A Sound Prescription," Heritage Foundation, August 27, 2007 (www.heritage.org/research/reports /2007/08/the-administrations-schip-regulations-a-sound-prescription); Robert Pear, "President is Rebuffed on Program for Children," *New York Times,* April 19, 2008; Jacob Goldstein, "Is Bush Softening in Fight over Children's

Health Insurance?," *Wall Street Journal Health Blog,* May 8, 2008 (http://blogs.wsj.com/health/2008/05/08/is-bush-softening-in-fight-over-childrens-health-insurance/); Center for Medicare and Medicaid Services, "Letter to State Health Officials," May 7, 2008 (www.medicaid.gov/Federal-Policy-Guidance/downloads/SHO050708.pdf).

86. White House, Office of the Press Secretary, "Presidential Memorandum: State Children's Health Insurance Program," February 04, 2009 (www.whitehouse.gov/the-press-office/presidential-memorandum-state-childrens-health-insurance-program); Jacob Goldstein, "Obama Lifts Bush's SCHIP Eligibility Restrictions," *Wall Street Journal Health Blog,* February 6, 2009 (http://blogs.wsj.com/health/2009/02/06/obama-lifts-bushs-schip-eligibility-restrictions/).

87. "Clinton's Health Care Plan Laid to Rest," in *CQ Almanac 1994,* 50th ed., 319–55. Washington, D.C.: Congressional Quarterly, 1995; "Lawmakers Agree on Need for Changes in Managed Care—But Only in Principle," in *CQ Almanac 1998,* 54th ed., 14-3–14-15. Washington, D.C.: Congressional Quarterly, 1999.

88. William J. Clinton, "Executive Order 13017: Advisory Commission on Consumer Protection and Quality in the Health Care Industry, September 5, 1996," APP. For the entire interim report, see President's Advisory Commission on Consumer Protection and Quality in the Health Care Industry, "Consumer Bill of Rights and Responsibilities, 1997," Agency for Healthcare Research and Quality (http://archive.ahrq.gov/hcqual/final/append_a.html).

89. William J. Clinton, "Memorandum on the Health Care 'Consumer Bill of Rights and Responsibilities,' November 20, 1997," APP; William J. Clinton, "Memorandum on Federal Agency Compliance With the Patient Bill of Rights, February 20, 1998," APP; U.S. Office of Personnel Management, "Healthcare Consumer Protections: What Is the Patients' Bill of Rights?" (www.opm.gov/healthcare-insurance/healthcare/consumer-protections/#url=Bill-of-Rights); Government Accountability Office, "Consumer Health Care Information: Many Quality Commission Disclosure Recommendations Are Not Current Practice," April 30, 1998 (www.gao.gov/assets/230/225798.pdf); U.S. Department of Defense, "Directive: Patient Bill of Rights and Responsibilities in the Military Health System (MHS)," July 30, 1998 (http://biotech.law.lsu.edu/blaw/dodd/corres/html2/d600014x.htm); U.S. Department of Health and Human Services, "Progress Report in Implementing the Patient's Bill of Rights at the Department of Health & Human Services," November 2, 1998 (https://aspe.hhs.gov/basic-report/report-vice-president-united-states); Misocky (1998); U.S. Department of Health and Human Services, "The Patients' Bill of Rights in Medicare and Medicaid," April 12, 1999 (http://archive.hhs.gov/news/press/1999pres/990412.html); U.S. Department of Health and Human Services, "Medicare and Medicaid Programs; Hospital Conditions of Participation: Pa-

tients' Rights," *Federal Register,* July 2, 1999 (www.gpo.gov/fdsys/pkg/FR -1999-07-02/pdf/99-16543.pdf); U.S. Department of Health and Human Services, "Medicare and Medicaid Programs; Programs of All-Inclusive Care for the Elderly (PACE)," *Federal Register,* November 24, 1999 (www.gpo.gov/fdsys /pkg/FR-1999-11-24/pdf/99-29706.pdf).

90. Amy Goldstein and Terry M. Neal, "Clinton Tackles Health Care Incrementally," *Washington Post,* August 11, 1998. Some large corporations and other private organizations such as the National Committee of Quality Assurance, the Joint Commission of the Accreditation of Health Care, and the Utilization Review Accreditation Commission adopted aspects of the CBRR. See Gitterman (2000).

91. William J. Clinton, "Memorandum on Establishment of the Quality Interagency Coordination Task Force, March 13, 1998," APP. Specifically, the commission also recommended the creation of a broadly represented, publicly administered Advisory Council for Health Care Quality and a privately administered Forum for Health Care Quality Measurement and Reporting. See Schulman and Kim (2000). Clinton directed the Quality Interagency Coordination Task Force to develop strategies to improve health-care quality and protect patient safety. See William J. Clinton, "Memorandum on Improving Health Care Quality and Ensuring Patient Safety, December 7, 1999," APP.

92. Robert Pear, "A Clinton Order Seeks to Reduce Medical Errors," *New York Times,* December 7, 1999. Clinton directed the Quality Interagency Coordination Task Force to evaluate the recommendations in the Institute of Medicine report, "To Err Is Human: Building a Safer Health System" (https:// iom.nationalacademies.org/~/media/Files/Report%20Files/1999/To-Err-is -Human/To%20Err%20is%20Human%201999%20%20report%20brief.pdf), and propose a strategy to identify prevalent threats to patient safety and reduce medical errors. He directed federal agencies to evaluate and implement the latest error reduction techniques. See Clinton, "Memorandum on Improving Health Care Quality"; U.S. Department of Human and Health Services, "Doing What Counts for Patient Safety: Federal Actions to Reduce Medical Errors and Their Impact" (http://archive.ahrq.gov/quic/report/mederr2.htm); White House, Office of the Press Secretary, "Fact Sheet: Clinton-Gore Administration Takes Strong New Steps to Improve Health Care Quality and Ensure Patient Safety," December 7, 1999 (http://clinton6.nara.gov/1999/12/1999-12-07-fact-sheet-on-health -care-quality-and-patient-safety.html); Marc Kaufman, "Clinton Proposes Medical Error-Reporting Plan," *Washington Post,* February 22, 2000; William J. Clinton, "Remarks on Efforts to Improve Patient Safety, February 22, 2000," APP; Robert Pear, "Clinton to Order Steps to Reduce Medical Mistakes," *New York Times,* February 22, 2000.

93. White House, Office of the Press Secretary, "Clinton-Gore Administration Announces New Actions to Improve Patient Safety and Assure Health

Care Quality," February 22, 2000 (http://clinton5.nara.gov/WH/New/html /20000222_1.html); Schulman and Kim (2000).

94. William J. Clinton, "Executive Order 13181: To Protect the Privacy of Protected Health Information in Oversight Investigations, December 20, 2000," APP; Robert Pear, "Clinton Will Issue New Privacy Rules to Shield Patients," *New York Times,* December 20, 2000; Laurie McGinley, "Clinton Will Issue New Rules for Medical-Records Privacy," *Wall Street Journal,* December 20, 2000.

95. See Clinton, "Executive Order 13181"; Larry D. Thompson, "Memorandum: Impact of HHS Privacy Rules on Department Operations," U.S. Department of Justice, July 30, 2003 (www.justice.gov/usam/criminal-resource -manual-979-impact-hhs-privacy-rules-department-operations).

96. George W. Bush, "Executive Order 13335: Incentives for the Use of Health Information Technology and Establishing the Position of the National Health Information Technology Coordinator, April 27, 2004," APP; U.S. White House, "Transforming Health Care: The President's Health Information Technology Plan," *WhiteHouse.gov,* 2004 (http://georgewbush-whitehouse .archives.gov/infocus/technology/economic_policy200404/chap3.html); McLaughlin (2007).

97. George W. Bush, "Executive Order 13410: Promoting Quality and Efficient Health Care in Federal Government Administered or Sponsored Health Care Programs, August 22, 2006," APP; Michael A. Fletcher, "Bush Signs Order on Health Care," *Washington Post,* August 23, 2006; Bailit Health Purchasing, LLC, "The Purchaser Guide to Value-Driven Health Care," December 7, 2007 (www.leapfroggroup.org/media/file/Purchaser_Guide_Final2 -07-07.pdf); Carlos (2008); "Executive Order Is Helping 'Change the Culture' in Health Care to Achieve Better Quality, Value, and Affordability, HHS Secretary Leavitt Reports," *PR Newswire,* August 23, 2007 (www.prnewswire .com/news-releases/executive-order-is-helping-change-the-culture-in-health -care-to-achieve-better-quality-value-and-affordability-hhs-secretary-leavitt -reports-58540752.html). For more about the implementation of Bush's executive order, see U.S. Department of Health and Human Services, "Progress Report on Implementation of the Executive Order 13410" (http://archive.hhs.gov /valuedriven/federal/eoreport.html); Claiborne, Hesse, and Roble (2009).

98. Kaiser Health News, "Obama Executive Order Establishes White House Office of Health Reform," April 9, 2009 (http://khn.org/morning-breakout /dr00057946/).

99. Barack Obama, "Executive Order 13507: Establishment of the White House Office of Health Reform, April 8, 2009," APP.

100. Carrie Budoff Brown, "Obama Taps DeParle as Health Czar," *Politico,* March 2, 2009; Stuart Whatley, "Nancy Ann-DeParle, White House Of-

fice of Health Reform," *Huffington Post,* April 2, 2009 (www.huffingtonpost .com/2009/03/02/nancy-ann-deparle-white-h_n_171131.html).

101. Saiger (2011).

102. See Barack Obama, "Executive Order 13535: Ensuring Enforcement and Implementation of Abortion Restrictions in the Patient Protection and Affordable Care Act, March 24, 2010," APP. Congress had banned the use of federal funds for abortion services except in cases of rape or incest, or when the life of the woman would be endangered.

103. Lori Montgomery and Shailagh Murray, "In Deal with Stupak, White House Announces Executive Order on Abortion," *Washington Post,* March 21, 2010; Fox News, "Choice, Life Groups Slam Obama Order on Abortion Funding," March 21, 2010 (www.foxnews.com/politics/2010/03/21/stupak-says -health-care-deal-looming-abortion-funding.html); Michael D. Shear, "Obama Signs Executive Order on Abortion out of Sight of Media Glare," *Washington Post,* March 24, 2010.

104. Barack Obama, "Memorandum on Respecting the Rights of Hospital Patients to Receive Visitors and to Designate Surrogate Decision Makers for Medical Emergencies, April 15, 2010," APP.

105. Ed O'Keefe, "Hospital Visitation Rights for Same-Sex Partners Now Required by Federal Rules," *Washington Post,* January 19, 2011.

106. Michael D. Shear, "Obama Extends Hospital Visitation Rights to Same-Sex Partners of Gays," *Washington Post,* April 16, 2010.

107. Brian Bond, "New Rules Require Equal Visitation Rights for All Patients," November 17, 2010 (www.whitehouse.gov/blog/2010/11/17/new-rules -require-equal-visitation-rights-all-patients); Michael Shear, "Obama Extends Hospital Visitation Rights to Same-Sex Partners of Gays," *Washington Post,* April 16, 2010; Human Rights Campaign, "Healthcare Equality Index: Sample Visitation Policies," *HRC.org,* 2016 (www.hrc.org/hei/sample-visitation -policies).

108. Copeland (2011); Carey (2014).

109. National Women's Law Center, "Nondiscrimination Protection in the Affordable Care Act: Section 1557" (http://nwlc.org/resources/nondiscrimination -protection-affordable-care-act-section-1557/); U.S. Department of Health and Human Services, "Section 1557 of the Patient Protection and Affordable Care Act" (www.hhs.gov/civil-rights/for-individuals/section-1557/index.html); U.S. Department of Health and Human Services, "Discrimination on the Basis of Religion" (www.hhs.gov/civil-rights/for-individuals/religion/index.html). Section 1557 is the nondiscrimination provision of the Affordable Care Act. The law prohibits discrimination on the basis of race, color, national origin, sex, age, or disability in certain health programs or activities. Section 1557 builds on long-standing and familiar federal civil rights laws: Title VI of the Civil Rights Act of

1964, Title IX of the Education Amendments of 1972, Section 504 of the Rehabilitation Act of 1973 and the Age Discrimination Act of 1975. See U.S. Department of Health and Human Services, "Section 1557 of the Patient Protection and Affordable Care Act" (www.hhs.gov/civil-rights/for-individuals/section-1557/); U.S. Department of Health and Human Services, "Nondiscrimination in Health Programs and Activities: Final Rule," *Federal Register,* May 18, 2016 (www .federalregister.gov/articles/2016/05/18/2016-11458/nondiscrimination-in-health -programs-and-activities).

110. Juliet Eilperin, "Obama Administration: Insurers Must Provide Services Regardless of Gender Identity," *Washington Post,* May 13, 2016; Kaiser Health News, "Administration Unveils Protections for Transgender Patients' Health Services," September 4, 2015 (http://khn.org/morning-breakout/administration -unveils-protections-for-transgender-patients-health-services/).

111. U.S. Department of Veterans Affairs, "VHA Directive 2013-003: Providing Health Care for Transgender and Intersex Veterans," February 8, 2013 (www.va.gov/vhapublications/ViewPublication.asp?pub_ID=2863).

112. U.S. Department of Defense, "Transgender Service Member Policy Implementation Fact Sheet" (www.defense.gov/Portals/1/features/2016/0616 _policy/Transgender-Implementation-Fact-Sheet.pdf).

113. Green, "Federal Government Quietly Expands Transgender Rights"; Severino and Anderson, "Proposed Obamacare Gender Identity Mandate Threatens Freedom of Conscience and the Independence of Physicians."

114. Cameron Brenchley, "President Obama Signs Bill to Give the VA the Resources It Needs," August 7, 2014 (www.whitehouse.gov/blog/2014/08/07 /president-obama-signs-bill-give-va-resources-it-needs); Josh Hicks, "The New VA-Reform Deal, and How the Costs Shrank over Time," *Washington Post,* July 28, 2014.

115. U.S. Department of Health and Human Services, "The ONC-Coordinated Federal Health Information Technology Strategic Plan: 2008–2012" (www.healthit.gov/sites/default/files/hit-strategic-plan-summary-508-2.pdf); "ARRA Stimulus Package," *Sandlot Solutions,* 2016 (www.sandlotsolutions.com /resources/stimulus-package).

116. Julian Pecquet, "President Obama Unveils Patient's Bill of Rights," *The Hill,* June 22, 2010 (http://thehill.com/policy/healthcare/104767-president -obama-unveils-patients-bill-of-rights); Timothy Jost, "Implementing Health Reform: A Patient Bill Of Rights," *Health Affairs,* June 23, 2010 (http:// healthaffairs.org/blog/2010/06/23/implementing-health-reform-a-patient-bill -of-rights/).

117. Troy (2015).

CHAPTER NINE

1. Newland (2015).

2. Ann O'Leary, "The Power to Act," *American Prospect,* September 1, 2010 (http://prospect.org/article/power-act-0); Ian Urbina, "The Shopping List as Policy Tool," *New York Times,* January 25, 2014; Gregory Korte, "Through Executive Orders, Obama Tests Power as Purchaser-in-Chief," *USA Today,* October 11, 2015.

3. 40 U.S. Code § 101; 40 U.S. Code § 121.

4. Chu and Garvey (2014).

5. Ibid.

6. Newland (2015).

7. Burrows and Manuel (2011).

8. Ibid.

9. For a full review, see Burrows and Manuel (2011).

10. *Chamber of Commerce v. Napolitano,* 648 F. Supp. 2d 726 (D. Md. 2009); *Building & Construction Trades Department v. Allbaugh,* 295 F.3d 28 (D.C. Cir. 2002); *UAW-Labor Employment & Training Corp. v. Chao,* 325 F.3d 360, 364 (D.C. Cir. 2003).

11. Burrows and Manuel (2011).

12. Scott Shane and Ron Nixon, "U.S. Contractors Becoming a Fourth Branch of Government," *New York Times,* February 4, 2007.

13. Charles S. Clark, "Obama Officials Defend Fair Pay Rule against 'Blacklist' Charges," *Government Executive,* September 29, 2015 (www.govexec.com/management/2015/09/obama-officials-defend-fair-pay-rule-against-blacklist-charges/122357/); Lydia Wheeler, "Businesses Blast Obama's 'Blacklisting' Regulations," *The Hill,* June 4, 2015 (http://thehill.com/regulation/243987-businesses-blast-obamas-blacklisting-regulations).

14. "Government Contracting Associations' Letter to Mr. McDonough and Ms. Jarrett, August 3, 2015," National Defense Industrial Association (www.ndia.org/Documents/Associations_letter_on_EOs_Aug_3_2015.pdf); Karla Walter, "Opponents of the Fair Pay and Safe Workplaces Executive Order Claim Cost Concerns in a Last Ditch Effort to Delay Final Implementation," Center for American Progress Action Fund, February 9, 2016 (www.americanprogressaction.org/issues/economy/news/2016/02/09/130767/).

15. Dean Baker, "Federal Government as Employer: High Road or Bottom Feeder?," *Huffington Post,* November 2, 2015 (www.huffingtonpost.com/dean-baker/federal-government-as-employer_b_8457094.html); David Madland and Karla Walter, "High-Road Government: A Contracting Policy That Helps Workers, Taxpayers and Businesses," Center for American Progress Fund, August 20, 2010 (www.americanprogressaction.org/issues/labor/report/2010/08/20/8192/high-road-government/).

16. U.S. Office of Personnel Management, "Accountability: Legal Authorities" (www.opm.gov/policy-data-oversight/oversight-activities/accountability/#url=Legal-Authorities); U.S. Merit Systems Protection Board, "The U.S. Office of Personnel Management in Retrospect: Achievements and Challenges after Two Decades," December 2001 (www.mspb.gov/netsearch/viewdocs.aspx?docnumber=253640&version=253927).

17. "Regulatory Agenda" (http://resources.regulations.gov/public/custom/jsp/navigation/main.jsp).

18. Federal Labor Relations Authority, "The Federal Service Labor-Management Relations Statute" (www.flra.gov/statute). Congress established the Federal Labor Relations Authority (FLRA) as the primary agency to administer and enforce the statute.

19. Naff and Riccucci (2007). However, a lawsuit filed by major public employee unions resulted in federal courts upholding employees' right to collective bargaining, thereby nullifying that section of the DHS Act.

20. U.S. Department of Labor, "Office of Workers' Compensation Programs (OWCP)" (www.dol.gov/owcp/owcpabot.htm). Currently, the Energy Employees Occupational Illness Compensation Program and the Federal Employees' Compensation Program is administered by the Department of Labor's Office of Workers' Compensation Programs.

21. Federal Labor Relations Authority, "Federal Employees Flexible and Compressed Work Schedules Act" (www.flra.gov/fsip_flexact).

22. Georgetown University Law Center, Workplace Flexibility 2010, "The Federal Employees Flexible and Compressed Work Schedules Act (FEFCWA), Spring 2006" (http://workplaceflexibility2010.org/images/uploads/C_LegalMemo_FEFCWA.pdf).

23. U.S. Office of Personnel Management, "Report to Congress on the 'Federal Employees Family Friendly Leave Act' (Public Law 103-388)" (www.opm.gov/policy-data-oversight/pay-leave/reference-materials/reports/federal-employees-family-friendly-leave-act/).

24. U.S. Department of Labor, "Need Time?: The Employee's Guide to Military Family Leave Under the Family and Medical Leave Act" (www.dol.gov/whd/fmla/2013rule/FMLA_Military_Guide_ENGLISH.pdf); U.S. Department of Labor, "Forms: Final Rule to Implement Statutory Amendments to the Family and Medical Leave Act" (www.dol.gov/whd/fmla/2013rule/militaryForms.htm).

25. U.S. Office of Personnel Management, "Our Mission, Role & History: What We Do" (www.opm.gov/about-us/our-mission-role-history/what-we-do/); U.S. Merit Systems Protection Board, "The Federal Government: A Model Employer or a Work In Progress? Perspectives from 25 Years of the Merit Principles Survey," September 2008 (www.mspb.gov/netsearch/viewdocs.aspx?docnumber=384592&version=385338).

26. Bernie Sanders and others, "Letter to President Barack Obama, May 15, 2015," *Huffington Post* (http://big.assets.huffingtonpost.com /modelemployerletter.pdf); Amanda Sakuma, "Senators Urge Obama to Give Preference to 'Model Employers,'" *MSNBC,* May 15, 2015 (www.msnbc.com /msnbc/senators-urge-obama-give-preference-model-employers).

27. U.S. Department of Labor, Office of Federal Contract Compliance Programs, "Executive Order 11246—Equal Employment Opportunity" (www .dol.gov/ofccp/regs/compliance/ca_11246.htm).

28. Richard Nixon, "Executive Order 11478: Equal Employment Opportunity in the Federal Government, August 8, 1969," American Presidency Project (henceforth cited as APP).

29. Equal Employment Opportunity Commission, "EEOC Coordination of Federal Government Equal Employment Opportunity" (www.eeoc.gov/federal /coordination.cfm); Equal Employment Opportunity Commission, "How EEOC Leads and Coordinates" (www.eeoc.gov/federal/coordination/eeocleads .cfm).

30. The Office of Special Counsel and the U.S. Merit Systems Protection Board enforce the prohibitions against federal employment discrimination codified in the CSRA. See U.S. Office of Personnel Management, "§ 2302. Prohibited Personnel Practices" (https://archive.opm.gov/ovrsight/proidx.asp); Office of Special Counsel, "Prohibited Personnel Practices; How to File a Complaint" (https://osc.gov/Pages/ppp-fileacomplaint.aspx).

31. This policy of equal opportunity applies to and must be an integral part of every aspect of personnel policy and practice in the employment, development, advancement, and treatment of civilian employees of the federal government. See Equal Employment Opportunity Commission, "Facts about Discrimination in Federal Government Employment Based on Marital Status, Political Affiliation, Status as a Parent, Sexual Orientation, and Gender Identity" (www.eeoc.gov /federal/otherprotections.cfm); Barack Obama, "Executive Order 13672: Further Amendments to Executive Order 11478, Equal Employment Opportunity in the Federal Government, and Executive Order 11246, Equal Employment Opportunity, July 21, 2014," APP.

32. Equal Employment Opportunity Commission, "Pregnancy Discrimination" (www.eeoc.gov/laws/types/pregnancy.cfm); Equal Employment Opportunity Commission, "Laws Enforced by EEOC" (www.eeoc.gov/laws/statutes/); Equal Employment Opportunity Commission, "Discrimination by Type" (www .eeoc.gov/laws/types/index.cfm).

33. Kennedy, "Special Message to the Congress on Conflict-of-Interest Legislation."

34. Office of Government Ethics, "The Ethics in Government Act" (https:// oge.gov/web/oge.nsf/Civil+Statutes).

35. George H. W. Bush, "Executive Order 12674: Principles of Ethical Conduct for Government Officers and Employees, April 12, 1989," APP. Bush's orders replace Johnson's Executive Order 11222 of May 8, 1965, and Reagan's Executive Order 12565 of September 25, 1986.

36. William J. Clinton, "Executive Order 12834: Ethics Commitments by Executive Branch Appointees, January 20, 1993," APP.

37. Brian Knowlton, "Obama Transition Team Adopts Ethics Rules," *New York Times,* November 11, 2008; Jeanne Cummings, "Obama's Ethics Rules for Lobbyists," *Politico,* November 11, 2008 (www.politico.com/story/2008 /11/obamas-ethics-rules-for-lobbyists-015515#ixzz3wclusNHj).

38. Ibid.; Dan Eggen and R. Jeffrey Smith, "Lobbying Rules Surpass Those of Previous Presidents, Experts Say," *Washington Post,* January 22, 2009.

39. Office of Government Ethics, "Executive Branch Agency Ethics Pledge" (www.oge.gov/Open-Government/Executive-Branch-Agency-Ethics-Pledge -Waivers/); Office of Government Ethics, "Annual Report on Executive Order 13490 (2014)" (www2.oge.gov/Web/OGE.nsf/All%20Documents/876E1CFD E699F4C285257EBC00669563/).

40. Office of Government Ethics, "Annual Report Pursuant to Executive Order 13490: Ethics Commitments by Executive Branch Personnel, January 1, 2014-December 31, 2014" (www.oge.gov/Open-Government/Annual-Report -on-Executive-Order-13490-(Ethics-Pledge)-(2014)/).

41. Copeland (2011); Carey (2014).

42. U.S. Department of Health and Human Services, "Nondiscrimination in Health Programs and Activities: Final Rule," *Federal Register,* May 18, 2016 (www.federalregister.gov/articles/2016/05/18/2016-11458/nondiscrimination -in-health-programs-and-activities); Juliet Eilperin, "Obama Administration: Insurers Must Provide Services Regardless of Gender Identity," *Washington Post,* May 13, 2016 (www.washingtonpost.com/politics/obama-administration -insurers-must-provide-services-regardless-of-gender-identity/2016/05/13 /a223f7ec-1913-11e6-924d-838753295f9a_story.html); "Administration Unveils Protections For Transgender Patients' Health Services," *Kaiser Health News,* September 4, 2015 (http://khn.org/morning-breakout/administration-unveils -protections-for-transgender-patients-health-services/).

43. Kagan (2001).

44. Todd F. Gaziano, "The Use and Abuse of Executive Orders and Other Presidential Directives," Heritage Foundation, February 21, 2001 (www.heritage .org/research/reports/2001/02/the-use-and-abuse-of-executive-orders-and-other -presidential-directives). Elizabeth Slattery and Andrew Kloster, "An Executive Unbound: The Obama Administration's Unilateral Actions," Heritage Foundation, February 12, 2014 (www.heritage.org/research/reports/2014/02/an -executive-unbound-the-obama-administrations-unilateral-actions).

45. Eric A. Posner, "The Presidency Comes with Executive Power. Deal with It," *New Republic,* February 3, 2014 (https://newrepublic.com/article/116450/obama-use-executive-power-unexceptional).

46. Howell and Mayer (2005).

47. Howell (2005).

References

Aaron, Benjamin, Joyce M. Najita, and James L. Stern, eds. 1988. *Public-Sector Bargaining*. Industrial Relations Research Association. Washington: Bureau of National Affairs.

Abarca, Maria Graciela. 2001. "'Discontented but Not Inevitably Reactionary': Organized Labor in the Nixon Years." Ph.D. diss., University of Massachusetts–Amherst.

Al-Hibri, Azizah, Jean Bethke Elshtain, and Charles C. Haynes. 2001. *Religion in American Public Life: Living with Our Deepest Differences*. New York: W. W. Norton.

Anderson, Odin W., and J. Joel May. 1971. *The Federal Employees Health Benefits Program, 1961–1968: A Model for National Health Insurance?* University of Chicago, Center for Health Administration Studies.

Apgar, Kristen Reasoner. 2000. "Large Employer Experiences and Best Practices in Design, Administration, and Evaluation of Mental Health and Substance Abuse Benefits: A Look at Parity in Employer-Sponsored Health Benefit Programs." Report prepared for the Office of Personnel Management. Washington: Washington Business Group on Health (www.csam-asam.org/sites/default/files/pdf/misc/WBGH_Report_on_Parity.pdf).

Arnold, Katherine, and Brian Vastag. 2000. "Medicare to Cover Routine Care Costs in Clinical Trials." *Journal of the National Cancer Institute* 92, no. 13: 1032.

Ashford, Nicholas A. 1976. *Crisis in the Workplace: Occupational Disease and Injury.* MIT Press.

Bailey, Christopher J. 2008. "Clearing the Air: The New Politics of Public Smoking." In *The Federal Nation: Perspectives on American Federalism*, edited by Iwan W. Morgan and Philip Davies, pp. 207–22. New York: Palgrave Macmillan.

Barnes, Mark, and Jerald Korn. 2005. "Medicare Reimbursement for Clinical Trial Services: Understanding Medicare Coverage in Establishing a Clinical Trial Budget." *Journal of Health Law* 38, no. 4 (Fall): 611–33.

Barry, Colleen L., Haiden A. Huskamp, and Howard H. Goldman. 2010. "A Political History of Federal Mental Health and Addiction Insurance Parity." *Milbank Quarterly* 88, no. 3: 404–33.

Bartrip, Peter W. J. 2006. *Beyond the Factory Gates: Asbestos and Health in Twentieth Century America.* London: Continuum.

Baruch, Susannah, and Kathy Hudson. 2008. "Civilian and Military Genetics: Nondiscrimination Policy in a Post-GINA World." *American Journal of Human Genetics* 83, no. 4: 435–44.

Baumrucker, Evelyne P., and Alison Mitchell. 2015. "State Children's Health Insurance Program: An Overview Analyst in Health Care Financing." Report R43627. Library of Congress, Congressional Research Service.

Berman, William C. 1970. *The Politics of Civil Rights in the Truman Administration.* Ohio State University Press.

Best, Richard A. 2005. "Military Medical Care Services: Questions and Answers." Congressional Research Service Issue Brief for Congress, Order Code IB93103. Library of Congress, Congressional Research Service.

Black, Conrad. 2007. *Richard M. Nixon: A Life in Full.* New York: PublicAffairs.

Blais, André, Donald E. Blake, and Stéphane Dion. 1997. *Governments, Parties, and Public Sector Employees: Canada, United States, Britain, and France.* University of Pittsburgh Press.

Blom, Kirstin B., and Ada S. Cornell. 2015a. "Federal Employees Health Benefits (FEHB) Program: An Overview." Report R43922. Library of Congress, Congressional Research Service.

———. 2015b. "Laws Affecting the Federal Employees Health Benefits (FEHB) Program." Report R42741. Library of Congress, Congressional Research Service.

Blumenauer, Earl, Zoe Lofgren, and Charlers Schumer. 1998. "Firearm Safety Locks: Federal Agency Implementation of the Presidential Directive." Report B-280647. General Accounting Office (September).

Blumenthal, Sidney. 2003. *The Clinton Wars.* New York: Farrar, Straus & Giroux.

Boden, Martha A. 2006. "Compassion Inaction: Why President Bush's Faith-Based Initiatives Violate the Establishment Clause." *Seattle University Law Review* 29, no. 29: 991–1030.

Borrelli, Maryanne, Karen Hult, and Nancy Kassop. 2001. "The White House Counsel's Office." *Presidential Studies Quarterly* 31, no. 4: 561–84.

Buchmueller, Thomas C., and Alan C. Monheit. 2009. "Employer-Sponsored Health Insurance and the Promise of Health Insurance Reform." NBER Working Paper 14839. Cambridge, Mass.: National Bureau of Economic Research (April).

Burrows, Vanessa K., and Kate M. Manuel. 2011. "Presidential Authority to Impose Requirements on Federal Contractors." Report R41866. Library of Congress, Congressional Research Service.

Carey, Maeve P. 2014. "Upcoming Rules Pursuant to the Patient Protection and Affordable Care Act: The Spring 2014 Unified Agenda." Report No. R43622. Library of Congress, Congressional Research Service.

Carlos, Ruth C. 2008. "Value-Driven Health Care: The Purchasers' Perspective." *Journal of the American College of Radiology* 5, no. 6: 719–26.

Carlson-Thies, Stanley W. 2009. "Faith-Based Initiative 2.0: The Bush Faith-Based and Community Initiative." *Harvard Journal of Law and Public Policy* 32, no. 3: 931–47.

Cashman, John W., Pearl Bierman, and Beverlee A. Myers. 1968. "The 'Why' of Conditions of Participation in the Medicare Program." *Public Health Reports* 83, no. 9: 714–18.

Chase, J. D. Catherine. 2014. "U.S. State and Federal Laws Targeting Distracted Driving." *Annals of Advances in Automotive Medicine* 58 (March): 84–98.

Christopherson, Gary A. 1998. "Policy Memorandum: Improving Patient Participation in Treatment Decisions in the Military Health System (MHS)." U.S. Department of Defense (April 27) (www.health.mil/Policies/1998/04/27/Policy-Memorandum--Improving-Patient-Participation-in-Treatment-Decisions-in-the-Military-Health-Sys).

Chu, Vivian S., and Todd Garvey. 2014. "Executive Orders: Issuance, Modification, and Revocation." Report RS20846. Library of Congress, Congressional Research Service.

Claiborne, Anne B., Julia R. Hesse, and Daniel T. Roble. 2009. "Legal Impediments to Implementing Value-Based Purchasing in Health Care." *American Journal of Law and Medicine* 35, no. 4: 442–504.

Clark, Major, Chad Moutray, and Radwan Saade. 2006. *The Government's Role in Aiding Small Business Federal Subcontracting Programs in the United States.* Working Paper 281. Washington: Small Business Administration, Office of Advocacy (September).

Coglianese, Cary. 2009. *The Transparency President? The Obama Administration and Open Government.* University of Pennsylvania Law School, Legal Scholarship Repository.

Cohen, Jeffrey, and George Krause. 1997. "Presidential Epochs and the Issuance of Executive Orders, 1901–1994." *Proceedings of the Fifty-Fifth Annual Meeting of the Midwest Political Science Association.* Chicago, April 10–12.

Collins, William J. 2001. "The Labor-Market Impact of State-Level Anti-Discrimination Laws, 1940–60." Working Paper No. 01-W08. Nashville: Vanderbilt University Department of Economics (http://as.vanderbilt.edu /econ/wparchive/workpaper/vu01-w08.pdf).

Condrey, Stephen E., ed. 2010. *Handbook of Human Resource Management in Government.* 3rd ed. San Francisco: Jossey-Bass.

Contrubis, John. 1999. "Executive Orders and Proclamations." Report 95-722 A. Library of Congress, Congressional Research Service.

Cook, Daniel M., and Lisa A. Bero. 2009. "The Politics of Smoking in Federal Buildings: An Executive Order Case Study." *American Journal of Public Health* 99, no. 9 (September): 1588–95.

Cooper, Phillip. 1986. "By Order of the President: Administration by Executive Order and Proclamation." *Administration and Society* 18, no. 2: 233–62.

———. 1997. "Power Tools for an Effective and Responsible Presidency." *Administration and Society* 29, no. 5: 529–56.

———. 2001. "Presidential Memoranda and Executive Orders: Of Patchwork Quilts, Trump Cards, and Shell Games." *Presidential Studies Quarterly* 31, no. 1: 126–41.

———. 2002. *By Order of the President: The Use and Abuse of Executive Direct Action.* University Press of Kansas.

Cooper, Terry L. 2012. *The Responsible Administrator: An Approach to Ethics for the Administrative Role.* 6th ed. San Francisco: Jossey-Bass.

Copeland, Curtis W. 2011. "Rulemaking Requirements and Authorities in the Patient Protection and Affordable Care Act (PPACA)." Report No. R41180. Library of Congress, Congressional Research Service.

Dallard, Cynthia. 2004. "Contraceptive Coverage: A 10-Year Retrospective." *Guttmacher Report* 7, no. 2 (June): 6–9.

Dark, Taylor E. 1999. *The Unions and the Democrats: An Enduring Alliance.* Cornell University, ILR Press.

Deering, Christopher J., and Forrest Maltzman. 1999. "The Politics of Executive Orders: Legislative Constraints on Presidential Power." *Political Research Quarterly* 52, no. 4: 767–83.

Dodds, Graham G. 2013. *Take up Your Pen: Unilateral Presidential Directives in American Politics.* University of Pennsylvania Press.

Dolan, Julie, and David H. Rosenbloom, eds. 2003. *Representative Bureaucracy: Classic Readings and Continuing Controversies.* Armonk, N.Y.: M. E. Sharpe.

Douglas, Paul H. 1952. "Improvement of Ethical Standards in the Federal Government: Problems and Proposals." *Annals of the American Academy of Political and Social Science* 280, no. 1 (March): 149–57.

Edwards, George C. 2005. *Readings in Presidential Politics.* Boston: Cengage.

Egerton, Kimberly A. 1980. "Presidential Power over Federal Contracts under the Federal Property and Administrative Services Act: The Close Nexus Test of *AFL-CIO v. Kahn.*" *Duke Law Journal* 29, no. 1: 205–33.

Elsbernd, Samson R. 2010. "Labor and Employment Law: The Future of Work Status Legislation and E-Verify." *Engage* 11, no. 1: 104–08.

Elwood, William N. 1994. *Rhetoric in the War on Drugs: The Triumphs and Tragedies of Public Relations.* Westport, Conn.: Praeger.

Esbeck, Carl H. 2015. "Federal Contractors, Title VII, and LGBT Employment Discrimination: Can Religious Organizations Continue to Staff on a Religious Basis?" *Oxford Journal of Law and Religion* 4, no. 3: 368–97.

Fishback, Price V. 2007. *Government and the American Economy: A New History.* University of Chicago Press.

Fleishman, Joel L., and Arthur H. Aufes. 1976. "Law and Orders: The Problem of Presidential Legislation." Pt. 2. *Law and Contemporary Problems* 40, no. 3: 1–45.

Freedman, Tom. 2009. "Domestic Policy Council." In *Change for America: A Progressive Blueprint for the 44th President,* edited by Mark J. Green and Michele Jolin, pp. 28–32. New York: Basic Books.

Freund, David M. P. 2004. *"Democracy's Unfinished Business": Federal Policy and the Search for Fair Housing, 1961–1968.* Washington: Poverty and Race Research Action Council (June).

Gilman, Michele Estrin. 2007. "If at First You Don't Succeed, Sign an Executive Order: President Bush and the Expansion of Charitable Choice." *William and Mary Bill of Rights Journal* 15, no. 4: 1103–72.

Gilman, Stuart C. 1995. "Presidential Ethics and the Ethics of the Presidency." *Annals of the American Academy of Political and Social Science* 537, no. 1 (January): 58–75.

Ginsberg, Wendy, and John J. Topoleski. 2013. "Federal Benefits and the Same-Sex Partners of Federal Employees." Report R42873. Library of Congress, Congressional Research Service.

Gitterman, Daniel P. 2000. "The President and the Power of the Purchaser: Consumer Protection and Managed Care in the United States." *California Management Review* 43, no. 1: 103–20.

———. 2013. "The American Presidency and the Power of the Purchaser." *Presidential Studies Quarterly* 43, no. 2: 225–51.

Goldenziel, Jill. 2005. "Administratively Quirky, Constitutionally Murky: The Bush Faith-Based Initiative." *Legislation and Public Policy* 8, no. 2: 359–88.

Goldfield, Michael. 1989. "Public Sector Union Growth and Public Policy." *Policy Studies Journal* 18, no. 2 (Winter): 404–20.

Goldman, Howard H. 2005. "Making Progress in Mental Health Policy in Conservative Times: One Step at a Time." *Schizophrenia Bulletin* 32, no. 3: 424–27.

Goldstein, Robert Justin. 2006. "Prelude to McCarthyism: The Making of a Blacklist." *Prologue* 28, no. 3 (www.archives.gov/publications/prologue /2006/fall/agloso.html).

Gomez, Brad, and Steven Shull. 1995. "Presidential Decision Making: Explaining the Use of Executive Orders." Paper presented at the Annual Meeting of the Southern Political Science Association, Tampa, Fla., November 2–4.

Gooding, Frederick W., and Michael Kazin. 2013. "American Dream Deferred: Black Federal Workers in Washington, D.C., 1941–1981." Ph.D. diss., Georgetown University.

Goodwin, Doris Kearns. 1976. *Lyndon Johnson and the American Dream*. New York: Harper & Row.

Graham, Hugh D. 1992. *Civil Rights and the Presidency: Race and Gender in American Politics 1960–1972*. Oxford University Press.

Gregory, Raymond F. 2001. *Age Discrimination in the American Workplace: Old at a Young Age*. Rutgers University Press.

Griffin, Leslie C. 2013. "Divining the Scope of the Ministerial Exception." *Human Rights Magazine* 39, no. 2: 19–20.

Grossman, Jonathan. 1975. "The Coal Strike of 1902—Turning Point in U.S. Policy." *Monthly Labor Review* 98 (October): 21–28.

Hampton, Robert E. 1972. "Federal Labor-Management Relations: A Program in Evolution." *Catholic University Law Review* 21, no. 3 (Spring): 493–511.

Handlin, Amy H., ed. 2014. *Dirty Deals?: An Encyclopedia of Lobbying, Political Influence, and Corruption*. Santa Barbara, Calif.: ABC-CLIO.

Hansen, Drew D. 1999. "The American Invention of Child Support: Dependency and Punishment in Early American Child Support Law." *Yale Law Journal* 108, no. 5 (March): 1123–53.

Harrison, Cynthia Ellen. 1980. "A New Frontier for Women: The Public Policy of the Kennedy Administration." *Journal of American History* 67, no. 3: 630–46.

———. 1989. *On Account of Sex: The Politics of Women's Issues, 1945–1968*. University of California Press.

Hegji, Alexandra. 2012. "Federal Labor Relations Statutes: An Overview." Report R42526. Library of Congress, Congressional Research Service.

Heifetz, Kimberly R. 1998. "Striking a Balance between Government Efficiency and Fairness to Contractors: Past Performance Evaluations in Government Contracts." *Administrative Law Review* 50, no. 1: 235–54.

Hoover, Dennis R. 2002. "Faith Based Administration." *Religion in the News* 5, no. 3 (Fall): 12–13.

Howell, William G. 2005. "Unilateral Powers: A Brief Overview." *Presidential Studies Quarterly* 35, no. 3 (September): 417–39.

Howell, William, and David Lewis. 2002. "Agencies by Presidential Design." *Journal of Politics* 64, no. 4: 1095–1114.

Howell, William, and Kenneth R. Mayer. 2005. "The Last One Hundred Days." *Presidential Studies Quarterly* 35, no. 3 (September): 533–53.

Hustead, Edwin, Steven Sharfstein, Samuel Muszynski, Jo Brady, and Judith Cahill. 1985. "Reductions in Coverage for Mental and Nervous Illness in the Federal Employees Health Benefits Program, 1980–1984." *American Journal of Psychiatry* 142, no. 2: 181–86.

Ingraham, Patricia W., and Carolyn Ban, eds. 1984. *Legislating Bureaucratic Change: The Civil Service Reform Act of 1978.* State University of New York Press.

Ingraham, Patricia W., and David H. Rosenbloom, eds. 1992. *The Promise and Paradox of Civil Service Reform.* University of Pittsburgh Press.

Interagency Task Force on Veterans Small Business Development. 2011. "Report to the President: Empowering Veterans through Entrepreneurship." Small Business Administration (November 1) (www.sba.gov/sites/default /files/FY2012-Final%20Veterans%20TF%20Report%20to%20President .pdf).

Johnson, David K. 2004. *The Lavender Scare: The Cold War Persecution of Gays and Lesbians in the Federal Government.* University of Chicago Press.

Johnson, Ronald N., and Gary D. Libecap. 1994. *The Federal Civil Service System and the Problem of Bureaucracy: The Economics and Politics of Institutional Change.* University of Chicago Press.

Jost, Timothy Stoltzfus. 2004. "Health Law and Administrative Law: A Marriage Most Convenient." Report 49. Washington and Lee University School of Law.

Kagan, Elena. 2001. "Presidential Administration." *Harvard Law Review* 114, no. 8: 2245–385.

Kaufman, Bruce E., ed. 1997. *Government Regulation of the Employment Relationship.* Cornell University Press.

Kearney, Richard C., and Patrice M. Mareschal. 2008. *Labor Relations in the Public Sector.* 4th ed. Boca Raton, Fla.: CRC Press.

Kellough, J. Edward. 1992. "Affirmative Action in Government Employment." *Annals of the American Academy of Political and Social Science* 523, no. 1 (September): 117–30.

Kellough, J. Edward, Lloyd G. Nigro, and Gene A. Brewer. 2010. "Civil Service Reform under George W. Bush: Ideology, Politics, and Public Personnel Administration." *Review of Public Personnel Administration* 20, no. 10: 1–19.

Kelman, Steven. 2002. "Remaking Federal Procurement." *Public Contract Law Journal* 31, no. 4 (July): 581–622.

Kessler-Harris, Alice. 2001. *In Pursuit of Equity: Women, Men, and the Quest for Economic Citizenship in 20th Century America.* Oxford University Press.

Kimmett, Thomas. 1996. "Permanent Replacements, Presidential Power, and Politics: Judicial Overreaching." *Yale Law Journal* 106, no. 3: 811–44.

Krause, George, and David B. Cohen. 1997. "Presidential Use of Executive Orders, 1953–1994." *American Politics Research* 25, no. 4: 458–81.

———. 2000. "Opportunity, Constraints, and the Evolution of the Institutional Presidency: The Issuance of Executive Orders." *Journal of Politics* 62, no. 1 (February): 88–114.

Kruger, Robert M. 1987. "Executive Order 12,564: Toward a Drug-Free Federal Workplace." *Journal of Law and Health* 2, no. 15: 15–26.

Leuchtenburg, William E. 2015. *The American President: From Teddy Roosevelt to Bill Clinton.* Oxford University Press.

Lewis, David E. 2009a. "Revisiting the Administrative Presidency: Policy, Patronage, and Agency Competence." *Presidential Studies Quarterly* 39, no. 1: 60–73.

———. 2009b. "Where Do Presidents Politicize? Evidence from the George W. Bush Administration." Vanderbilt University, Department of Political Science (www.vanderbilt.edu/csdi/archived/working%20papers/Politicization .pdf).

Lewis, Gregory B. 2013. "The Impact of Veterans' Preference on the Composition and Quality of the Federal Civil Service." Paper 9. Georgia State University, Public Management and Policy Faculty Publications (http://scholarworks .gsu.edu/pmap_facpubs/9).

Liechty, Janet M., and Elaine A. Anderson. 2007. "Flexible Workplace Policies: Lessons from the Federal Alternative Work Schedules Act." *Family Relations* 56, no. 3 (September): 304–17.

Lin, Tom C. W. 2014. "CEOs and Presidents." *UC Davis Law Review* 47, no. 4: 1351–416.

Lowande, Kenneth S. 2014. "The Contemporary Presidency after the Orders: Presidential Memoranda and Unilateral Action." *Presidential Studies Quarterly* 44, no. 4: 724–41.

Mach, Annie L., and Ada S. Cornell. 2014. "Laws Affecting the Federal Employees Health Benefits Program (FEHBP)." Report R42741. Library of Congress, Congressional Research Service.

MacKenzie, G. Calvin, and Michael Hafken. 2002. *Scandal Proof: Do Ethics Laws Make Government Ethical?* Brookings Institution Press.

MacLaury, Judson. 1981. "The Job Safety Law of 1970: Its Passage Was Perilous." *Monthly Labor Review* 104, no. 3 (March): 18–24.

———. 2008. *To Advance Their Opportunities: Federal Policies toward African American Workers from World War I to the Civil Rights Act of 1964.* Knoxville, Tenn.: Newfound Press.

Maskell, Jack. 2014. "Post-Employment, 'Revolving Door,' Laws for Federal Personnel." Report R42728. Library of Congress, Congressional Research Service.

Mason, Robert. 2004. *Richard Nixon and the Quest for a New Majority.* University of North Carolina Press.

Masters, Marick F. 2004. "Federal Sector Unions: Current Status and Future Directions." *Journal of Labor Research* 25 (Winter): 55–82.

Masters, Marick F., and Robert R. Albright. 1999. "The Federal Sector Labor Relations Climate under Executive Order 12871." *Journal of Collective Negotiations in the Public Sector* 28, no. 1: 69–82.

Masters, Marick F., Robert R. Albright, and David Eplion. 2003. "From PATCO to Partnership: Transforming Federal Sector Labor Relations?" Unpublished paper. University of Pittsburgh (www.researchgate.net/publication /228893279).

Maxwell, Jewerl Thomas. 2008. "Presidential Affirmative Action: The Role of Presidential Executive Orders in the Establishment, Institutionalization, and Expansion of Federal Equal Employment Opportunity Policies." Ph.D. diss., Miami University.

Maxwell, Nan, Albert Liu, Nathan Wozny, and Caroline Massad Francis. 2013. "Addressing Return-to-Work Issues in the Federal Employees' Compensation Act with Administrative Data." Report. Mathematica Policy Research (www.dol.gov/asp/evaluation/completed-studies/Addressing_Return_to _Work_Issues/FINAL_REPORT_addressing_return_to_work_issues.pdf).

Mayer, Kenneth R. 1996. "The Importance of Moving First: Executive Orders and Presidential Initiative." Proceedings of the 92nd Annual Meeting of the American Political Science Association, San Francisco.

———. 1997. "Executive Orders and Presidential Power." Unpublished paper. University of Wisconsin–Madison (http://users.polisci.wisc.edu /kmayer/Professional/Executive%20Orders%20and%20Presidential%20 Power.pdf).

———. 1999. "Executive Orders and Presidential Power." *Journal of Politics* 61, no. 2 (May): 445–66.

———. 2001. *With the Stroke of a Pen: Executive Orders and Presidential Power.* Princeton University Press.

Mayer, Kenneth R., and Kevin Price. 2002. "Unilateral Presidential Powers: Significant Executive Orders, 1949–99." *Presidential Studies Quarterly* 32, no. 2: 367–86.

McCaffrey, David P. 1982. *OSHA and the Politics of Health Regulation*. New York: Plenum Press.

McCartin, Joseph A. 2011. *Collision Course: Ronald Reagan, the Air Traffic Controllers, and the Strike That Changed America*. Oxford University Press.

McGann, Kelly. 2014. "Benign Neglect: Veteran Owned Small Business in Federal Procurement Today." *Veterans Law Review* 6, no. 1: 187–212.

McGuire, John Thomas. 2008. "'The Most Unjust Piece of Legislation': Section 213 of the Economy Act of 1932 and Feminism during the New Deal." *Journal of Policy History* 20, no. 4: 516–41.

McLaughlin, Sean T. 2007. "Pandora's Box: Can HIPAA Still Protect Patient Privacy under a National Health Care Information Network?" *Gonzaga Law Review* 42, no. 1: 29–60.

Medina, Meggan. 2013. "A Nightmare Trifecta for Small Business Contractors: False Claims Act, Implied Certification and Presumed Loss Rule." *Journal of Contract Management* 11 (Summer): 41–59.

Menzel, Donald C., and Harvey L. White, eds. 2011. *The State of Public Administration: Issues, Challenges, and Opportunities*. Armonk, N.Y.: M. E. Sharpe.

Mikusko, M. Brady, and F. John Miller. 2014. *Carriers in a Common Cause: A History of Letter Carriers and the NALC*. Washington: National Association of Letter Carriers (www.nalc.org/about/facts-and-history/body/Carriers-in-a-Common-Cause.pdf).

Milkman, Ruth, and Joseph A. McCartin. 2013. "The Legacy and Lessons of the PATCO Strike Thirty Years Later: A Dialogue." *Labor History* 54, no. 2: 123–37.

Millenson, Debra A. 1999. "Whither Affirmative Action: The Future of Executive Order 11,246." *University of Memphis Law Review* 29, nos. 3–4 (Spring/Summer): 679–737.

Miller, Neil. 2008. *Out of the Past: Gay and Lesbian History from 1869 to the Present*. Los Angeles: Advocate Books.

Misocky, Michael. 1998. "The Patients' Bill of Rights: Managed Care under Siege." *Journal of Contemporary Health Law and Policy* 15, no. 1: 57–100.

Moberly, Robert B. 2006. "Labor Management Relations during the Clinton Administration." *Hofstra Labor and Employment Law Journal* 24, no. 1 (Fall): 31–61.

Moe, Terry M. 1985. "The Politicized Presidency." In *The New Direction in American Politics*, edited by John E. Chubb and Paul E. Peterson, pp. 235–71. Brookings Institution Press.

———. 1993. "Presidents, Institutions, and Theory." In *Researching the Presidency: Vital Questions, New Approaches*, edited by George C. Edwards,

John H. Kessel, and Bert A. Rockman, pp. 337–85. University of Pittsburgh Press.

Moe, Terry M., and William G. Howell. 1999a. "The Presidential Power of Unilateral Action." *Journal of Law, Economics, and Organization* 15, no. 1: 132–79.

———. 1999b. "Unilateral Action and Presidential Power: A Theory." *Presidential Studies Quarterly* 29, no. 4: 850–73.

Moe, Terry M., and Scott A. Wilson. 1994. "Presidents and the Politics of Structure." *Law and Contemporary Problems* 57, no. 2: 1–44.

Moffit, Robert E., George Nesterczuk, and Donald J. Devine. 2001. *Taking Charge of Federal Personnel.* Heritage Foundation Backgrounder #1404, January 10. Washington: Heritage Foundation.

Morgan, Thomas D. 1980. "Appropriate Limits on Participation by a Former Agency Official in Matters before an Agency." *Duke Law Journal* 1980, no. 1 (February): 1–63.

Morone, James A. 2010. "Presidents and Health Reform: From Franklin D. Roosevelt to Barack Obama." *Health Affairs* 29, no. 6: 1096–1100.

Moskow, Michael H., J. Joseph Loewenberg, and Edward Clifford Koziara, eds. 1970. *Collective Bargaining in Public Employment.* New York: Random House.

Moynihan, Donald P. 2004. "Protection versus Flexibility: The Civil Service Reform Act, Competing Administrative Doctrines, and the Roots of Contemporary Public Management Debate." *Journal of Policy History* 16, no. 1: 1–33.

Naff, Katherine C., and Norma M. Riccucci. 2007. *Personnel Management in Government: Politics and Process.* 6th ed. Boca Raton, Fla.: CRC Press.

National Cancer Institute. 1997. "NCI Adopts New Mammography Screening Guidelines for Women." *Journal of the National Cancer Institute* 89, no. 8: 538–40.

National Research Council. 2005. *Analyzing Information on Women-Owned Small Businesses in Federal Contracting.* Washington: National Academies Press.

Nelson, Michael. 1996. *Guide to the Presidency.* Washington: Congressional Quarterly.

Nesbitt, Murray B. 1976. *Labor Relations in the Federal Government Service.* Washington: Bureau of National Affairs.

Neumark, David. 2001. "Age Discrimination Legislation in the United States." NBER Working Paper 8152. Cambridge, Mass.: National Bureau of Economic Research (March).

Newland, Erica. 2015. "Executive Orders in Court." *Yale Law Journal* 124, no. 6 (April) (www.yalelawjournal.org/note/executive-orders-in-court).

Nordlund, Willis J. 1991. "The Federal Employees' Compensation Act." *Monthly Labor Review* 114, no. 9 (September): 3–13.

Normand, Jacques, Richard O. Lempert, and Charles P. O'Brien, eds. 1994. *Under the Influence? Drugs and the American Work Force*. Washington: National Academy Press.

Oberlander, Jonathan B., and Barbara Lyons. 2009. "Beyond Incrementalism? SCHIP and the Politics of Health Reform." *Health Affairs* 28, no. 3: w399–w410.

Oliver, Adam. 2007. "The Veterans Health Administration: An American Success Story?" *Milbank Quarterly* 85, no. 1: 5–35.

Panangala, Sidath Viranga. 2015. "Health Care for Veterans: Answers to Frequently Asked Questions." Report R42747. Library of Congress, Congressional Research Service.

Pelka, Fred. 2012. *What We Have Done: An Oral History of the Disability Rights Movement*. University of Massachusetts Press.

Pennsylvania, Department of Mines. 1903. *Report of the Department of Mines*. Harrisburg, Pa.: Wm. Stanley Ray, State Printer of Pennsylvania (https://babel.hathitrust.org/cgi/pt?id=nyp.33433090920863;view=1up;seq =8).

Pohlmann, Marcus D., and Linda Vallar Whisenhunt. 2002. *Student's Guide to Landmark Congressional Laws*. Santa Barbara, Calif.: Greenwood.

Porter, Robert. 2006. "Contract Claims against the Federal Government: Sovereign Immunity and Contractual Remedies." Harvard Law School Federal Budget Policy Seminar, Briefing Paper No. 22 (www.law.harvard.edu/faculty /hjackson/ContractClaims_22.pdf).

Potter, M. 1990. "Military Dependent Medical Care during World War II." *Military Medicine* 155, no. 2: 45–47.

Presidential Appointee Initiative. 2000. "Staffing a New Administration: A Guide to Personnel Appointments in a Presidential Transition." Brookings Institution Press (www.brookings.edu/wp-content/uploads/2016/06/20000711 staffing.pdf).

President's Committee on Civil Rights. 1947. *To Secure These Rights: The Report of the President's Committee on Civil Rights*. New York: Simon & Schuster.

President's New Freedom Commission on Mental Health. 2003. "Achieving the Promise: Transforming Mental Health Care in America." President's New Freedom Commission on Mental Health (July 22) (http://govinfo .library.unt.edu/mentalhealthcommission/reports/FinalReport/downloads /FinalReport.pdf).

Quinn, Gerard, Aisling de Paor, and Peter Blanck, eds. 2014. *Genetic Discrimination: Transatlantic Perspectives on the Case for a European-Level Legal Response*. New York: Routledge.

Quint, Peter E. 1984. "The Separation of Powers under Carter." *Texas Law Review* 62, no. 5: 785–94.

Rabkin, Jeremy. 1993. "At the President's Side: The Role of the White House Counsel in Constitutional Policy." *Law and Contemporary Problems* 56, no. 4: 63–98.

Raza, M. Ali., A. Janell Anderson, and Harry Glynn Custred Jr. 1999. *The Ups and Downs of Affirmative Action Preferences.* Westport, Conn.: Praeger.

Reeves, Stephen V. 1996. "The Ghosts of Acquisition Reform: Past, Present and Future." Executive Research Project. Washington: National Defense University, Industrial College of the Armed Forces.

Regier, Darrel A., Lynn F. Bufka, Tracy Whitaker, Farifteh F. Duffy, William E. Narrow, Donald S. Rae, Geoffrey M. Reed, et al. 2008. "Parity and the Use of Out-of-Network Mental Health Benefits in the FEHB Program." *Health Affairs* 27, no. 1: w70–w83.

Reider-Gordon, Mikhail, and Marcus T. Funk. 2012. "Switching to Offense in Government Contracting: Contractors Conscripted to Join the Fight against Human Trafficking." *White-Collar Crime* 27, no. 3: 3–5.

Relyea, Harold C. 2008. "Presidential Directives: Background and Overview." Order Code 98-611 GOV. Library of Congress, Congressional Research Service.

Roberts, Robert North. 1988. *White House Ethics: The History of the Politics of Conflict of Interest Regulation.* New York: Greenwood Press.

Roberts, Robert North, and Marion T. Doss. 1997. *From Watergate to Whitewater: The Public Integrity War.* Westport, Conn.: Praeger.

Rockman, Bert A., and Richard W. Waterman. 2007. *Presidential Leadership: The Vortex of Power.* Oxford University Press.

Rockoff, Hugh. 1984. *Drastic Measures: A History of Wage and Price Controls in the United States.* Cambridge University Press.

Rose, Winfield H., and Tiang Ping Chia. 1978. "The Impact of the Equal Employment Opportunity Act of 1972 on Black Employment in the Federal Service: A Preliminary Analysis." *Public Administration Review* 38, no. 3 (May–June): 245–51.

Rosner, David, and Gerald E. Markowitz, eds. 1989. *Dying for Work: Workers' Safety and Health in Twentieth-Century America.* Indiana University Press.

Ruddock, Andrew E. 1966. "Federal Employees Health Benefits Program." *American Journal of Public Health and the Nation's Health* 56, no. 1: 50–53.

Rung, Margaret C. 1997. "Gender and Public Personnel Administration in the New Deal Civil Service. *American Review of Public Administration* 27, no. 4 (December): 307–23

Saiger, Aaron J. 2011. "Obama's 'Czars' for Domestic Policy and the Law of the White House Staff." *Fordham Law Review* 79, no. 6: 2577–615.

Sargeant, Malcolm. 2011. *Age Discrimination: Ageism in Employment and Service Provision*. Farnham, U.K.: Gower.

Schulman, Kevin A., and John J. Kim. 2000. "Medical Errors: How the US Government Is Addressing the Problem." *Current Controlled Trials in Cardiovascular Medicine* 1, no. 1: 35–37.

Shane, Bonnie. 1981. "The White House Conference on Families: Recommendations and Conclusions." *Law Forum* 11, no. 1: 15–17.

Shanley, Robert. 1983. "Presidential Executive Orders and Environmental Policy." *Presidential Studies Quarterly* 13, no. 3: 405–16.

Sipos, Charles C. 2002. "The Disappearing Settlement: The Contractual Regulation of Smith & Wesson Firearms." *Vanderbilt Law Review* 55, no. 4: 1297–340.

Siskin, Alison, and Liana Sun Wyler. 2012. "Trafficking in Persons: U.S. Policy and Issues for Congress." Report RL34317. Library of Congress, Congressional Research Service.

Skrentny, John David. 1996. *The Ironies of Affirmative Action: Politics, Culture, and Justice in America*. University of Chicago Press.

Sky, Theodore. 1969. "Defense Procurement Preferences as a Remedy for Subemployment: A Comment." *Harvard Law Review* 82, no. 6: 1266–81.

Spitzer, Eliot, and Peter Pope. 2009. "Gun Control without Gun Laws: How Obama Can Use Government Procurement Regulations to Limit Gun Violence." *Slate,* April 29, 2009.

Stack, Kevin M. 2005. "The Statutory President." *Iowa Law Review* 90, no. 539: 539–600.

Stathis, Stephen W. 2003. *Landmark Legislation 1774–2002: Major U.S. Acts and Treaties*. Washington: CQ Press.

Stewart, William H. 1969. "Implementing the Report of the National Advisory Commission on Health Manpower." *Journal of the American Medical Association* 210, no. 10 (December 8): 1911–913.

Stimson, John P. 2004. "Veterans' Preference Act of 1944." In *Major Acts of Congress*, edited by Brian K. Landsberg. New York: Macmillan Reference U.S.A.

Straus, Jacob R. 2011a. "Enforcement of Congressional Rules of Conduct: An Historical Overview." Report RL30764. Library of Congress, Congressional Research Service.

———. 2011b. "Lobbying the Executive Branch: Current Practices and Options for Change." Report R40947. Library of Congress, Congressional Research Service.

———. 2013. "House Office of Congressional Ethics: History, Authority, and Procedures." Report R40760. Library of Congress, Congressional Research Service.

Strober, Gerald S., and Deborah H. Strober. 1994. *Nixon: An Oral History of His Presidency.* New York: HarperCollins.

Swendiman, Kathleen S. 2012. "Health Care: Constitutional Rights and Legislative Powers." Report R40846. Library of Congress, Congressional Research Service.

Szymendera, Scott. 2011. "Reviewing Workers' Compensation for Federal Employees." Statement for U.S. House of Representatives Committee on Education and the Workforce. Library of Congress, Congressional Research Service.

———. 2013. "The Federal Employees' Compensation Act (FECA): Workers' Compensation for Federal Employees." Report R42107. Library of Congress, Congressional Research Service.

Tenpas, Kathryn Dunn. 2002. "Can an Office Change a Country? The White House Office of Faith-Based and Community Initiatives: A Year in Review." Report prepared for the Pew Forum on Religion and Public Life. University of Pennsylvania (www.pewforum.org/files/2002/02/022002-tenpas .pdf).

Thompson, Dennis F. 2009. "Obama's Ethics Agenda: The Challenge of Coordinated Change." *The Forum* 7, no. 1: 1–22.

Thurber, James A. 2010. "Changing the Way Washington Works? President Obama's Battle with Lobbyists." Paper presented at the Conference on the Early Obama Presidency, Centre for the Study of Democracy, Westminster University, London, May 14 (www.american.edu/spa/ccps/upload/Thurber -Paper-Obama-and-Lobbyists.pdf).

Troy, Tevi D. 2015. "How the Government as a Payer Shapes the Health Care Marketplace." Report prepared for the American Health Policy Institute. Washington: American Health Policy Institute (www.americanhealthpolicy .org/Content/documents/resources/Government_as_Payer_12012015 .pdf).

U.S. Civil Service Commission. 1889. *Fifth Annual Report of the United States Civil Service Commission.* Government Printing Office.

———. 1895. *Eleventh Annual Report of the United States Civil Service Commission.* Government Printing Office.

———. 1914. *Thirtieth Annual Report of the United States Civil Service Commission.* Government Printing Office.

———. 1921. *Thirty-Seventh Annual Report of the United States Civil Service Commission.* Government Printing Office.

———. 1977. *Financial Disclosure for High-Level Executive Officials: The Current System and the New Commitment.* Publication FPDC-77-59. Government Printing Office (www.gao.gov/assets/120/119369.pdf).

U.S. Commission on Civil Rights. 1961. *Justice: 1961 Commission on Civil Rights Report.* Government Printing Office.

U.S. Department of Health and Human Services. 2004. "Evaluation of Parity in the Federal Employees Health Benefits (FEHB) Program: Final Report." Office of the Assistant Secretary for Planning and Evaluation (December 31) (https://aspe.hhs.gov/report/evaluation-parity-federal-employees-health -benefits-fehb-program-final-report).

U.S. General Accounting Office. 1992. *The Changing Workforce: Comparison of Federal and Nonfederal Work/Family Programs and Approaches.* Government Printing Office.

———. 2002. "Federal Employees' Health Plans: Premium Growth and OPM's Role in Negotiating Benefits." Report GAO-03-236 (www.gao.gov/assets /240/236777.pdf).

U.S. General Services Administration. 2000. *The Evolution of Telework in the Federal Government.* Government Printing Office (www.gsa.gov/graphics /ogp/Evolutiontelework.doc).

———. 2005. "Federal Acquisition Regulation." (www.acquisition.gov/sites /default/files/current/far/pdf/FAR.pdf).

U.S. House of Representatives. 1915. *To Increase the Efficiency of the Military Establishment of the United States: Hearings before the Committee on Military Affairs.* Government Printing Office.

———. 1999. "Treasury and General Government Appropriations Act, 2000." C-SPAN, July 15, transcript of hearing (www.c-span.org/congress/bills /billAction/?1145285).

———. 2014a. *Sexual Orientation and the Federal Workplace: Policy and Perception.* Government Printing Office.

———. 2014b. *Veterans' Employment Redress Laws in the Federal Civil Service.* Government Printing Office.

U.S. Merit Systems Protection Board. 2010. *Prohibited Personnel Practices: A Study Retrospective.* Government Printing Office.

———. 2014a. *Sexual Orientation and the Federal Workplace: Policy and Perception.* Government Printing Office.

———. 2014b. *Veterans' Employment Redress Laws in the Federal Civil Service.* Government Printing Office.

U.S. National Advisory Commission on Health Manpower. 1967. "Report of the National Advisory Commission on Health Manpower," volume 1. Government Printing Office.

U.S. Office of Personnel Management. 1981. *Alternative Work Schedules Experimental Program: Interim Report to the President and the Congress.* Government Printing Office.

———. 1991. *The Federal Flexible Workplace Project Flexiplace: General Questions and Answers.* Government Printing Office.

———. 1993. *HRM07: Enhance Programs to Provide Family-Friendly Workplaces.* Government Printing Office.

———. 1997. *Balancing Work and Family Demands through Telecommuting.* Government Printing Office.

———. 2003. *Biography of an Ideal: A History of the Federal Civil Service.* Government Printing Office.

U.S. President's Advisory Council on Faith-Based and Neighborhood Partnerships. 2010. *A New Era of Partnerships: Report of Recommendations to the President.* (March) (www.whitehouse.gov/sites/default/files/docs/ofbnp-council-final-report.pdf).

U.S. Senate Committee on Veterans' Affairs. 1970. *Readjustment and Job Assistance for Vietnam Veterans: Hearings before the Subcommittee on Readjustment Education, and Employment of the Committee on Veterans' Affairs*, 92nd Cong., 1st sess., April 28, May 10. Government Printing Office.

Walker, Samuel. 2012. *Presidents and Civil Liberties from Wilson to Obama.* Cambridge University Press.

Walsh, John, and Garth L. Mangum. 1992. *Labor Struggle in the Post Office: From Selective Lobbying to Collective Bargaining.* Armonk, N.Y.: M. E. Sharpe.

Warshaw, Shirley Anne. 1995. "White House Control of Domestic Policy Making: The Reagan Years." *Public Administration Review* 55, no. 3: 247–53.

———. 2004. *The Clinton Years.* New York: Facts On File.

Waterman, Richard W. 2009. "The Administrative Presidency, Unilateral Power, and the Unitary Executive Theory." *Presidential Studies Quarterly* 39, no. 1: 5–9.

Weiner, Daniel I., Lawrence Norden, and Brent Ferguson. 2015. "Requiring Government Contractors to Disclose Political Spending." New York University School of Law, Brennan Center for Justice.

Weissman, Robert. 1999. "Controlling Corporate Scofflaws or Blacklisting? The Clinton Administration's Proposed 'Responsible Contractor' Legislation." *Multinational Monitor* 20, no. 7 (July–August): 30–32.

Wigton, John. 1991. "Recent Presidential Experience with Executive Orders." *Presidential Studies Quarterly* 26, no. 2: 473–84.

Wisensale, Steven K. 2001. *Family Leave Policy: The Political Economy of Work and Family in America.* Armonk, N.Y.: M. E. Sharpe.

Wright, David J. 2009. "Taking Stock: The Bush Faith-Based Initiative and What Lies Ahead." Report prepared for the Roundtable on Religion and Social Welfare Policy. New York: Nelson A. Rockefeller Institute of Government.

Yarbrough, Jean M. 2012. *Theodore Roosevelt: Progressive Crusader.* Heritage Foundation Makers of American Political Thought Series 3. Washington: Heritage Foundation.

Zank, Neal S. 1996. *Measuring the Employment Effects of Regulation: Where Did the Jobs Go?* Westport, Conn.: Quorum Books.

Zucker, Kiren Dosanjh, and Bruce Zucker. 2009. "The Spring of Hope: Labor and Employment Rights in the Early Days of the Obama Era." *Labor Law Journal* 60, no. 4 (Winter): 210–21.

Index